ETHICAL DILEMMAS IN FERTILITY COUNSELING

ETHICAL DILEMMAS IN FERTILITY COUNSELING

Judith E. Horowitz
Joann Paley Galst
Nanette Elster

American Psychological Association • Washington, DC

Published by
American Psychological Association
750 First Street, NE
Washington, DC 20002
www.apa.org

To order
APA Order Department
P.O. Box 92984
Washington, DC 20090-2984
Tel: (800) 374-2721; Direct: (202) 336-5510
Fax: (202) 336-5502; TDD/TTY: (202) 336-6123
Online: www.apa.org/books/
E-mail: order@apa.org

In the U.K., Europe, Africa, and the Middle East, copies may be ordered from
American Psychological Association
3 Henrietta Street
Covent Garden, London
WC2E 8LU England

Typeset in Goudy by Circle Graphics, Inc., Columbia, MD

Printer: United Book Press, Inc., Baltimore, MD
Cover Designer: Mercury Publishing Services, Rockville, MD

The opinions and statements published are the responsibility of the authors, and such opinions and statements do not necessarily represent the policies of the American Psychological Association.

Library of Congress Cataloging-in-Publication Data

Horowitz, Judith E.
  Ethical dilemmas in fertility counseling / Judith E. Horowitz, Joann Paley Galst, and Nanette Elster. — 1st ed.
      p. ; cm.
  Includes bibliographical references and index.
  ISBN-13: 978-1-4338-0760-2
  ISBN-10: 1-4338-0760-2
1. Infertility—Patients—Counseling of—Moral and ethical aspects. 2. Counseling psychologists—Professional ethics. I. Galst, Joann Paley. II. Elster, Nanette. III. American Psychological Association. IV. Title.
  [DNLM: 1. Infertility—psychology. 2. Reproductive Medicine—ethics. 3. Counseling—methods. 4. Reproductive Techniques, Assisted—ethics. WQ 200 H816e 2010]

  RC889.H57 2010
  616.6'920651—dc22
                                  2009040990

British Library Cataloguing-in-Publication Data

A CIP record is available from the British Library.

Printed in the United States of America
First Edition

This book is dedicated to our children.

CONTENTS

ACKNOWLEDGMENTS

This book was inspired by postings on the Mental Health Professional Group listserv, where brave psychotherapists grappling with issues regarding reproductive medicine have reached out to their peers for answers and guidance.

Judith E. Horowitz wishes to acknowledge the editors and the supportive staff of the American Psychological Association Books Program for recognizing the importance of the message contained in this book and supporting its publication.

She thanks her unwavering writing partner, Dr. Joann Paley Galst, whose dedication, grace, kindness, and unflagging encouragement helped make this book become a reality; the physicians, nurses, and the other psychologists who entrusted her with their patients' care; as well as those in the field who educated and guided her professional development. She remains humbled by the many patients who have shared with her their varied journeys of pain, sorrow, hope, despair, and elation on the roller coaster ride that is infertility.

Judith is grateful to her family, who encouraged her, especially her son, who never fails to put a smile on her face. She would not have dared to embark on this venture if her parents had not showered her with their confidence in her abilities. Regrettably and with deep sorrow, she must posthumously acknowledge them. She thanks her family and friends who said "good-bye and so long" to her and encouraged her to disappear into her work for the past 4 years with only minor objections. Last, and with love, she thanks her "person," her editor, her friend, lover, and husband, Jeffrey Sarrow, for a wonderful life and their exceptional children Michael and Tova.

Joann Paley Galst wishes to extend thanks to her colleague, Dr. Judith Horowitz, for inviting her to take this long journey to authorship with her and for remaining a steadfast friend through all of its convolutions and complexity.

Joann dedicates her contributions to this book to her husband, Jay, who through his unending love, support, and patience gave her the courage and perspective to complete this project; to her son, David, whose eternal high expectations of her have pushed her to be her best and to laugh whenever possible; to her father, whose unconditional love during his too brief life lit up her life; to her mother, who, although unable to see the completion of this book, provided the model of strength, independence, and persistence in the face of adversity that inspired her as a woman; to her patients, who demonstrate the strength and beauty of human resilience on a daily basis; to her colleagues, who provide the ongoing intellectual challenge that allows continual growth; and to her friends, whom she looks forward to rejoining in fun at the completion of this project.

Nanette Elster would like to acknowledge and thank her students, who are always challenging her to think about new ethical dilemmas; Lori Andrews for introducing her to this field and mentoring her; her mother, who is always willing to read and reread every draft and who has an immense heart and endless patience and who provides unconditional encouragement and support in every facet of her life; her father, who during his lifetime was her biggest champion and whose love and confidence in her continues to motivate her each and every day; her husband, the bioethicist she aspires to be, for whose love she has waited her whole life and whose devotion envelops and strengthens her; and finally, her daughter, her inspiration, her heart, her joy and her treasure.

ETHICAL DILEMMAS IN FERTILITY COUNSELING

INTRODUCTION: DEFINING THE ROLE OF MENTAL HEALTH PROFESSIONALS IN REPRODUCTIVE MEDICINE

The most important questions don't seem to have ready answers, but the questions themselves have healing power when they are shared. An answer is an invitation to stop thinking about something, to stop wondering. An unanswered question is a fine traveling companion. It sharpens your eye for the road.

—Rachel Naomi Remen, *Kitchen Table Wisdom*

Advances in reproductive medicine are being made at dizzying speeds. Keeping up with developments within the field of reproductive medicine is in and of itself a daunting task without also considering the constellation of laws, policies, professional practice guidelines, and codes of ethics that are developing. The ethics of assisted reproductive technology (ART) have been debated since the advent of in vitro fertilization (IVF). Even before the historic birth of Louise Brown in 1978, assisted reproduction has been steeped in controversy and dissension. Although the ethical principles espoused by the American Psychological Association provide the ideal to which psychologists aspire, they do not always provide specific answers as to what to do in a particular clinical situation. The American Society for Reproductive Medicine has enacted many ethical guidelines for its Mental Health Professional Group members, but unique situations do arise that are challenging and can fall into murky, gray areas. As with most ethical dilemmas, no black-and-white solutions exist.

An increasing number of people are expected to seek treatment for fertility problems. Accordingly, there is a need for more psychologists to develop the expertise to practice in this dynamic specialty. Currently, there are over 400 members of the Mental Health Professional Group of the American Society for Reproductive Medicine. This reflects an increase of approximately

25% over the past 5 years, barely keeping up with the demand from not only the patients seeking fertility treatment but also the burgeoning numbers of physicians and clinics entering the field of reproductive medicine.

This book is for practicing psychologists in the field of fertility counseling and those considering entering this relatively new and evolving field. The goal is for these professionals to have a resource to help them resolve ethical dilemmas they encounter in their work. Using this book as a knowledge base will assist psychologists who are working with individuals and couples using the various ARTs and those needing to fulfill, according to American Society of Reproductive Medicine guidelines, the psychological component of their assessment prior to being admitted into ART protocols. Our goal in this book is to provide guidance to mental health professionals and help them to avoid inadvertently crossing ethical boundaries.

This book is meant to be thought provoking. We have undertaken to frame the issues and set forth the factors that should be considered when confronting a novel ethical problem fraught with conflicting social and personal values. We provide a framework within which mental health professionals can attempt to balance the full range of perspectives and work toward a resolution of complex, ever-changing questions. The information contained in this book is concentrated on the relevant psychological, moral, ethical, and legal aspects of reproductive medicine as well as the various roles psychologists may play in fertility counseling.

COMMON AREAS OF ETHICAL CONCERN IN FERTILITY COUNSELING

Advances in the field of the ARTs permit mental health professionals to separate parenthood into distinguishable components composed of the intended parents who will nurture the child, the genetic contributor(s), and the gestational carrier. The separation of genetics and gestation has spawned innumerable ethical concerns and questions, not to mention legal challenges. Motivated by a desire to become parents, fertility patients are making very difficult choices that often pit their personal desire to have a child against their cultural or religious views of how and when life begins. The mental health professional practicing within the area of fertility counseling will be called on to help clients consider a variety of psychosocial issues posed by the range of alternative treatment possibilities and their cost both to individuals and to society at large.

A variety of professional organizations have published ethics codes and other documents that offer guidance to mental health professionals working in the reproductive health field. Table I.1 gives a list of the specific professional

TABLE I.1

Ethical Standards, Practice Guidelines, and Other Policy Statements
Pertinent to Assisted Reproductive Technologies

Professional group	Type of policy statement	Topic
American Academy of Pediatrics	Practice guidelines (2003)	Types of parenting that put children at risk those that help them flourish
	Ethical standards (2004)	Surrogate motherhood
American College of Obstetrics and Gynecology	Practice guidelines (1994)	Conducting preembryo research
	Ethical standards (2002)	Surrogate motherhood
American Psychological Association	Ethical principles and code of conduct (2002)	Comprehensive ethical principles and standards for professional practice
	Practice guidelines (2005)	Privacy rights for minors
American Society for Reproductive Medicine	Practice guidelines (2002)	Sperm donation and oocyte donation
	Ethical standards (2004)	Childrearing ability of recipients of fertility treatment, disposition of abandoned embryos, family members as gamete donors or surrogates, financial incentives in oocyte donor recruitment, informing offspring of method of conception, and sex selection and preimplantation
	Practice guidelines (2006)	Informed consent, repetitive oocyte donation
	Ethical standards (2007)	Financial compensation of oocyte donors
	Practice guidelines (2008)	Gamete and embryo donation, number of embryos transferred
	Ethical standards (2009)	Rights of oocyte donors donating embryos for research
Asia & Oceana Federation of Obstetrics and Gynaecology	Ethical standards (2002)	Assisted reproductive technology and surrogacy
European Society of Human Reproduction and Embryology	Ethical and legal standards (2002)	Gamete and embryo donation
	Ethical and legal standards (2003)	Multiple pregnancies
	Ethical and legal standards (2005)	Surrogacy
Food and Drug Administration	Regulations (1999)	Cellular and tissue-based products
National Academy of Sciences	Practice guidelines (2005)	Human embryo and stem cell research

(*continues*)

TABLE I.1
Ethical Standards, Practice Guidelines, and Other Policy Statements Pertinent to Assisted Reproductive Technologies *(Continued)*

Professional group	Type of policy statement	Topic
National Advisory Board on Ethics in Reproduction	Ethical opinions (1996)	Oocyte donation and oocyte donors
New York State Task Force	Legal opinions (1998)	Treatment of infertility
Presidents Council on Bioethics, Reproduction, and Responsibility	Ethical standards (2003)	Assisted reproductive technology
U.S. Department of Health and Human Services	Legal standards (2003)	Protection of patients' health information

guideline documents we reference in this book as well as others that may be applicable.

In this book, we deal with a variety of ethical issues, some of which are more cut-and-dried than others. Some may be resolved with reference to the broadest principles of professional ethics, whereas others are more circumscribed, leading professionals on a circuitous journey looking for answers. Many of the ethical issues we discuss in this book fall into the categories described in the sections that follow: access, religious beliefs, informed consent, and disclosure. Additionally, we address the knowledge and skills necessary for competent psychological practice in reproductive health and medicine. We have also found it important for practitioners to be able to articulate their philosophical stance when it comes to helping others make decisions about procreation.

Access

One ethical quandary is posed by the accessibility of ART, which is unaffordable to most people. Psychologists should consider from an ethical perspective whether fertility treatment should be accessible to all people without economic consideration or remain available only to those who can afford it. Consequently, professionals must then analyze the popular assumption of one's incontrovertible right to reproduce versus one's entitlement to have a reproductive condition medically examined and treated.

Parenting licenses are not required for people reproducing without assistance, so one must wonder whether it is ethical to restrict access to fertility treatment on the basis of presumptions about one's potential skills or ability to parent.

Different standards have been applied to natural conception as compared with adoption or assisted conception. Physicians and mental health professionals have been required to assess patients' appropriateness for fertility treatment. Some ethicists believe these judgment calls may not be warranted or justified.

Religious Beliefs

Mental health professionals will likely need to examine their own moral and religious feelings about ART as well as those of their clients. Some religious critics argue the use of all ARTs is unethical because it bypasses the natural method of conception by creating life in a laboratory. These religious opponents assert the embryos are devalued because they are "manufactured" and sustained in an unnatural environment. Furthermore, some religions view life as beginning at conception and argue that embryos are, in fact, living human beings. Others view the use of ART as one means of fulfilling the biblical directive to be "fruitful and multiply."

Some critics insist it is unethical to create embryos, freeze them, and keep them "in limbo." Ethical criticism has been aimed at the embryologists who are fertilizing more embryos than some believe are necessary. Discarding embryos because they are unwanted or destroying them during the process of scientific research has also been scrutinized by ethicists. On the other hand, there are those who argue it would be unethical to limit the number of embryos created because it might mean greater financial expense for the couple as well as more medical risks to the woman, who, if an attempt is unsuccessful, would have to take more medications and undergo additional surgical procedure(s) to stimulate her ovaries and extract mature oocytes.

Justification for choosing select embryos for transfer and discarding others, which have been examined by preimplantation genetic diagnosis, has been quite controversial. Questions of commodification of children, creation of "designer babies," and the possible development of a genetic underclass abound. In addition, the modification of embryos has also been challenged.

Informed Consent

Psychologists entering the field of reproductive health are likely to deal with issues of informed consent. Some medical experts consider infertility a disease. Others disagree, stating that infertility does not threaten one's life or health. Ethical issues are present regarding the use of untested technologies and their potential long-term effects. Given that much of ART occurs in the private sector, which may or may not use a formal institutional review process, the same protection of human subjects that applies to federally funded research does not exist in this context.

Disclosure

Treatment concerns can also involve disclosure issues. To whom should the patients disclose? Family? Friends? The children born as a result of ART? As genetic research has evolved, health professionals are increasingly aware of the push and pull of nature versus nurture. Therefore, when a child is brought into the world with unknown origins, health professionals must recognize the ethical considerations that permeate the issue of identity disclosure as has been evident in the adoption context and also in the donor context in different countries.

A child who wishes to obtain knowledge of his or her genetic background and medical history will not necessarily have his or her genetic contributor's identity revealed. However, this issue forces a balancing of the welfare of one who would not have existed at all but for the actions of the genetic contributor(s) against those who usually participate with an expectation of anonymity. Some patients proceeding through ART have no intention of disclosing to their children the origins of their conception; meanwhile, anonymity of gamete donors has been opposed by those who contend that children have a right to know who genetically contributed to their existence. One must wonder whether the intended parents can be expected to objectively evaluate the implications of disclosure versus the ramifications of withholding information, and the psychological welfare of their yet-to-be-born child or other children who may already be in the household.

Competent Practice: Knowledge of Medical and Legal Issues

Competency is the cornerstone of ethical practice, and mental health professionals should be careful not to practice outside of their area(s) of expertise. As Principle A, Beneficence and Nonmaleficence, in the American Psychological Association's (2002) "Ethical Principles for Psychologists and Code of Conduct" states, psychologists must endeavor to benefit their clients and do them no harm, a goal quite synonymous with the Hippocratic oath taken by all physicians, including those who practice in reproductive medicine. Familiarizing oneself with the fundamentals of human reproduction and the elementary aspects of treatment is essential for those considering a specialization in the area of infertility.

Many of those patients who have initiated psychotherapy with us had previously met with mental health professionals not specializing in the treatment of fertility problems. Fertility patients are generally extremely well versed in the nature of their physical problems, the treatments they will be receiving from their reproductive endocrinologists, and the medical protocols on which they will be placed. Counseling is frequently prematurely terminated by exasperated and frustrated patients who needed to educate their therapists regarding the names and side effects of their fertility medications and the specifics of the medical procedures they will be undergoing as they proceed through fertility treatment. We strongly suggest that before attempting to practice in the area of fertility counseling, psychologists familiarize themselves with the treatment options that have been discussed extensively in other books.

Framing the ethical issues is also essential to defining the legal issues. Often ethical dilemmas are the impetus for legal action. To date, the law has been piecemeal with respect to ART. In the United States, those powers not specifically granted to the federal government in the Constitution are reserved for the states. Laws about reproduction have largely been left to the states to regulate, meaning it is possible to have as many different laws as there are states. Unlike the over 20 countries that regulate ART at the international level, the United States to date has taken a rather laissez faire approach resulting in no uniformity, no consistency, and at times, completely incongruous legislation among the states. The legal issues that continue to confront professionals and consumers in this field include quality of care, licensing of professionals, reporting of success rates, parentage of children created through collaborative arrangements, rights and obligations of donors and surrogates, anonymity of donors, inheritance rights of children conceived after the death of a genetic parent, the status of the human embryo, and insurance coverage, to name but a few. These issues are addressed throughout the chapters in this book, revealing how important it is to consider a multidisciplinary approach to treatment and counseling that includes legal and ethical considerations.

Divergent Philosophies: Procreative Liberty Versus Gatekeeping

Most psychologists within the field of fertility counseling wrestle with the matters debated in this book from two different points of view. One perspective asserts that in society people enjoy the right to procreate. Therefore, as the same social and psychological drives are applicable for infertile people, they, too, should also have the right to parent, unless there is the possibility that the potential child(ren) would be at serious risk. Procreative libertarians, as they are called, believe the role of the medical provider is to offer the technology as appropriate, rather than to decide who deserves to become a parent and how children ought to be created. Reproductive libertarians champion patient autonomy, and contend it is an individual's prerogative to choose whether, when, and how to create children and families.

The contrasting point of view is that mental health professionals should assume the role of *gatekeeper*. Gatekeepers believe that when individuals or couples ask for assistance in procreating, the medical and psychological teams are obligated to consider the risks to the patient(s) as well as to the unborn and yet to be conceived children. Gatekeepers believe to ignore the best interests of the children would be an abdication of responsibility and might potentially violate the ethical principle of beneficence if harm could befall the potential child. Furthermore, gatekeepers claim those individuals whom they view as inappropriate candidates should be prohibited from proceeding through fertility protocols, and consequently the prospective gamete donors, recipients, and others seeking fertility treatment would be prevented from harming themselves or others. We frequently vacillate between both positions.

ORGANIZATION OF THIS BOOK

Psychologists who work in the area of reproductive medicine come from all theoretical backgrounds, including behavioral, developmental, psychoanalytic, and others. In Chapter 1, we cover the ways in which various theories of psychological distress have been applied as treatment strategies in fertility counseling. Issues regarding infertile patients who also have physical disabilities and/or psychological and social problems are presented in Chapter 2 so that mental health professionals are better able to determine who should and should not be treated for infertility. The embryos created through the ARTs are the subject matter of Chapter 3, and Chapter 4 concentrates on the challenges of multiple gestation. In Chapter 5, we address oocyte recipiency and donation, and Chapter 6 concerns sperm donation and recipiency. Chapter 7 focuses on both traditional surrogacy and gestational carriers. In Chapter 8, we discuss the children whose existence was made possible through the use of the ARTs. Frontiers in infertility counseling are presented in Chapter 9.

Chapters 2 through 8 follow an identical structure. We provide a problem-solving format that can guide mental health professionals attempting to resolve the ethical dilemmas they are likely to be confronted with in this field. The beginning of each chapter includes reviews of the medical, psychosocial, and bioethical literature, followed by applicable policies and legislation. The remainder of the chapter emanates from a clinical vignette and the identification of the ethical conundrums contained within the scenario. The relevant professional societies' practice and ethical guidelines are discussed, followed by possible conflicts as well as the multiple perspectives held by society, IVF centers and physicians, the prospective parent(s), the donors and/or surrogates, and the potential and existing children. Practical considerations are addressed, and finally, our conclusions and recommendations as mental health professionals are presented.

Readers may refer to Appendices A and B for quick reference guides to religious perspectives and international laws dealing with each aspect of ART that is mentioned in this book. Because there is likely some diversity among practitioners of each faith regarding how closely they abide by their religious teachings on reproduction, readers should use Appendix A not as a definitive guide but as a starting point for discussion with clients about how their beliefs may influence their choices about reproductive technology.

We believe this book is an invaluable resource for mental health professionals, IVF clinic practice managers, and physicians practicing in the field of reproductive medicine and reproductive health. We hope that readers will join us in the multifaceted analysis of the ethical issues intrinsic in the treatment of infertility and do not become intolerably frustrated because we do not and, in fact, cannot offer a definitive answer to each of the ethical questions we raise. We do believe, though, as a result of examining the topics within this book, in addition to becoming increasingly insightful about their own biases, readers will be in a better position to make sound clinical decisions and help those patients who seek their assistance during fertility treatment. Our goal is to frame the questions, as ethical solutions often emerge through consideration of the many controversial matters that are raised, while trying to balance the interests of all who may be impacted.

1

PSYCHOLOGICAL THEORIES
OF DISTRESS AND MODELS
OF TREATMENT FOR INFERTILITY

Although the world is full of suffering, it is full also of the overcoming of it.
—Helen Keller, *Optimism*

As mentioned in the Introduction to this volume, mental health professionals with a variety of theoretical orientations are entering the field of reproductive medicine. There are many sound theoretical approaches that can be used to gain insight into infertility, including grief, attachment, developmental, family systems, stigma, social exchange, and crisis theories. Likewise, each of these approaches can offer helpful treatments. In this chapter, we review theories and related therapy strategies that apply to the scenarios depicted throughout the book.

GRIEF THEORY

People's reactions to grief and loss vary in duration and degree of turmoil. Whereas grief is not necessarily pathological, it permeates one's physical, emotional, spiritual, sexual, cognitive, and behavioral being. Our clients often state that after repeated and unsuccessful medical interventions to achieve a pregnancy, each menstrual cycle feels like the death of their dreamed for child. Miscarriages present yet another potentially devastating blow to the subfertile patient.

Historically, the maintenance of an emotional bond with the dead was accepted as the norm (Klass, Silverman, & Nickman, 1996). Within the past 100 years there has been a shift in psychological theory that has encouraged people to look at death and their resulting grief from an entirely different perspective. Freud (as cited in Strachey, 1974) believed people ought to disengage themselves from the deceased. Once people accomplished detachment, he believed they would be healthy and free to move on, putting their past behind them. Concurrent with Freud's theorizing, the popularity of believing in the supernatural and the existence of an afterlife diminished.

An individual's initial reaction to loss may be met with physical symptoms that include shortness of breath, tightness of the chest, insomnia, and the loss of appetite (Parkes, 1972). Additionally, Parkes (1972) thought the bereaved often have difficulty concentrating, feel isolated and lonely, and experience restlessness; should anger, guilt, and fear remain unexpressed, disruptive panic attacks may follow. Other commonly experienced physical symptoms are heavy and repeated sighing, overeating, fatigue, or weakness of the muscles (Fitzgerald, 1994). Cognitive changes can include confusion, a preoccupation with, or a sense of presence of the departed, and infrequently, auditory or visual hallucinations (Fitzgerald, 1994). Behavioral changes may include searching and calling out for the dead, absent-mindedness, and visiting places or carrying objects that remind the survivor of the deceased (Fitzgerald, 1994). Many, if not all, of these symptoms are reported by fertility patients.

Viewing grief as a process can help psychologists understand infertility. Worden (1983, 1991) thought grief consisted of four nonlinear tasks, necessitating the bereaved to attend to their emotional loss while also adjusting to the accompanying changes to their identity, roles, and circumstances.

Conceptualizing grief as consisting of five stages (Kübler-Ross, 1970), that is, (a) denial (this cannot be), (b) anger (why is this happening to me?), (c) bargaining (I'll do X, Y, or Z so this will no longer exist), (d) depression (there is nothing I can do to change this), and finally (e) acceptance (OK, this is real, and I must cope with it and whatever comes next), can help mental health professionals understand the reactions of fertility patients. These stages by no means progress in a linear fashion, as grief usually comes in waves.

Infertility patients report that without warning or any external cues they abruptly feel intense pining, yearning, and sadness. Although patients may experience intermittent periods of happiness and optimism as they proceed through fertility treatment, they also cry and often feel unhappy.

More recently, the dual process model of grief work has been proposed (Stroebe & Schut, 1999). This model theorizes that grief is a dynamic process and both expression and control of one's feelings are important, so while individuals heal, they necessarily oscillate between the two. The mourner needs to both focus on and avoid focusing on the loss, a loss orientation versus a restoration orientation. According to this theory, adjustment can be achieved when the individual focuses on both revitalization and grief (Stroebe & Schut, 1999). Educating patients about the grief process will help normalize it for them.

DEVELOPMENTAL THEORY

The theory of personality development proposed by Erikson (1963) is extremely inclusive, taking into account historical, biological, cultural, and cognitive factors. Erikson's generativity stage of development addresses the adult's need to create or nurture those things that will continue past his or her own demise as well as to transmit the values of his or her culture. Should individuals be unable to become parents, Erikson concluded, they may stagnate, unable to achieve the appropriate developmental tasks and meet society's expectations. According to Erikson, having children is a positive event that enables one to feel useful and accomplished. From Erikson's theory psychologists can extrapolate that infertile couples will necessarily experience despair, although he also believed individuals could fulfill the need for generativity through the creation of ideas or products (Erikson, 1963).

Women's psychological development theory is also relevant to infertility and its treatment During the past 35 years, many women have placed a greater emphasis on higher education and their careers (Chodorow, 1978). However, despite their advances in other areas, girls continue to be expected to grow into young women and bear children. Some of the original developmental theorists believed it is through conception and childbirth that gender identification and female development are achieved (Chesler, 1972). These developmental theorists equated motherhood with creativity, and giving birth was seen as the continuation of personal growth. It was thought that only when a woman conceived was she able to identify with her own parents, and should she be unable to conceive, she would fail to develop and likely be viewed as deviant (Etaugh & Bridges, 2005).

Within the past 50 years, feminist developmental theorists have departed from those beliefs. Presently, feminists are scrutinizing society's values and the pressure exerted on women to bear children (P. C. Broderick & Blewitt, 2005). Thus, from an ethical standpoint, they question whether a woman is really free to choose not to have children in our society. Furthermore, some feminists believe the availability of reproductive medicine unduly influences women to pursue the role of motherhood (Gilligan, 1993).

ATTACHMENT THEORY

Attachment theory, as proposed by Mary Ainsworth (1985) and John Bowlby (1982), suggests that grief and mourning occur when the attachment figure is no longer available to an individual. Although a baby does not yet exist, individuals report suffering when their dreamed of, fully genetically related child will be impossible to conceive. Bowlby (1961) discussed the numbing that occurs, the yearning and searching that is prevalent, and the disorganization and despair that transpire after loss. Fertility patients report all of these feelings and behaviors. Expounding on Bowlby's attachment theory, Parkes (1972) proposed that grief is a process toward forming a new identity.

CRISIS THEORY

Crisis theory focuses on the personality disintegration that occurs in response to the loss of an emotionally significant person (Lindemann, 1963). Coping methods, crisis theorists contend, may be both realistic and unrealistic. As psychologists observe in therapy, the crisis of infertility, like other crises, is characterized by feelings of failure, loss, guilt, anger, anxiety, depression, self-blame, and self-pity (Boisen, 1936). The couple's future plans, marital satisfaction, mental and physical health, and well-being are affected by the crisis of infertility (Switzer, 1974). It is thought that after one passes through a crisis, one will reach a higher level of development and a reintegration of one's personality, providing new insights, perspectives, and strength (Valentine, 1986).

Crisis theory addresses the anxiety that is manifested in the breakdown of an individual's old pattern of thinking and relating (Switzer, 1974). Patients experiencing infertility, as do others facing crises, begin to lose their identity as physically and emotionally healthy people (Caplan, 1964). Objectively, alternatives to family building can be viewed as positive and hopeful, but as crisis theory suggests, these alternatives will still require patients to depart from their former level of psychological stability (Caplan, 1964). Furthermore, crisis theory proposes the objective difficulty of any specific situation is not the factor determining the situation's impact (Morley, 1965). Rather it is the importance the situation holds for the individual experiencing the crisis, the extent of ego involvement, the amount of threat felt, the expected duration of the crisis, the person's perception of available resources, and the appraisal of the person's ability to cope with the crisis that are the factors needing to be assessed (Lazarus & Folkman, 1984; Lewis & Roberts, 2001; Morley, 1965).

Caplan (1964) described four distinct phases of a crisis. The first phase is the experience of anxiety due to the perceived threat, which draws on the person's habitual problem-solving responses and can cause a decrease in memory. The second phase of a crisis is caused by the novelty of the situation and its meaningfulness and relevance to the individuals. The third phase, Caplan explained, involves trial-and-error behavior. The individual will experience a decrease in the ability to plan for the future. Simultaneously, the affected person must modify his or her behavior and consequently his or her identity. According to Caplan, this will result in either active resignation or additional strength as new methods are incorporated into the individual's coping repertoire. The final stage occurs if the problem remains unresolved to the individual's standards, and thus the unresolved anxiety may cause personality decompensation, eventually creating an identity distortion and ineffective, socially unacceptable, rigid, and compulsive behavior or extreme isolation. Mental health professionals have an opportunity to make a profound impact on patients' lives by helping them advance through the crisis, teaching new methods of coping, and assisting them to become more effective problem solvers.

Understanding the diagnosis of infertility as a crisis, mental health professionals can help clients explore their sense of shock at the unexpectedness of the loss. Although many individuals presenting in therapy appear disorganized and out of control, they can be helped to make sense of their loss partly through normalizing their feelings so they do not feel crazy.

FAMILY SYSTEMS THEORY

Family systems theory addresses the impact infertility will have on the couple's marriage, on the individuals within the marriage, and on each other in relation to their families of origin (Ackerman, 1958). Mental health professionals using the family systems approach to counseling pay close attention to additional dynamics typically observed in couples (Diamond, Kezur, Meyers, Scharf, & Weinshel, 1999).

Having taken their fertility for granted, most individuals are surprised to learn they cannot conceive. Anxiety occurs as the couple worries about the impact of this diagnosis on their relationship. Anger is expressed at this cruel twist of fate and is often directed toward each other. Frequently the husband feels upset if his wife has fallen apart and is not fully functioning, as if his love is not "enough." With fertility treatment looming, the wife often is angry at her husband for nonchalantly accepting oocyte recipiency and for not feeling the loss to the same extent as she does. The wife may think her husband is fine with the alternative because, after all, the procedure will be using his sperm. Rather, he may appear to calmly accept oocyte recipiency as a show of support for his wife's decision to carry a child. Should a couple need to use donated sperm, the dynamics are reversed, with the husband hurt that his wife may seem less upset than he is. Opportunities for misunderstanding one another can and do arise.

The infertile patient's identity dramatically suffers (Cooper-Hilbert, 1998). The individual may no longer feel feminine or masculine, sexually attractive, or worthy. Women may feel incredibly sad at the prospect of being unable to experience pregnancy and childbirth. The infertile patient's loss of genetic continuity will be twofold. He or she will be unable to provide the genealogical continuity of his or her bloodline, but just as devastating, he or she will be unable to transmit his or her genetics, to ever see in the child the similar traits or aptitudes that would be a reflection of him- or herself (Titelman, 1998).

One member of the couple may think his or her partner does not understand his or her feelings because of gender differences; that the partner is not as determined to have a child, stay the course; or that the partner is not as involved or invested in the process (Cooper-Hilbert, 1998). Problems can occur with family members, friends, or colleagues (Diamond et al., 1999) who may give insensitive suggestions such as "relax and it will happen," "have a glass of wine," "what you need is a vacation," "there's always adoption," "buck up," or "there are worse things out there, you should count your blessings."

As they become more involved in fertility treatment, the couple may become isolated and alienated from others (Lalos, Lalos, Jacobsson, & von Schoultz, 1986). Some patients cannot go to church (too many young children), the mall (too many strollers), family functions (too many questions), or even ride in traffic (too many infant car seats), which may impact their relationship with their spouse or their nuclear and/or extended families.

The clients' sex lives are almost always compromised as a result of regimentation (Zolbrod, 1993). Their sexual activities are microscopically and endlessly examined, which can be emotionally debilitating. Both men and women begin to think they are baby-making machines who have or whose partner has faulty equipment. The joy of sex often becomes the job of sex.

STIGMA THEORY

Regrettably, psychologists observe that the new identity formed by fertility patients is often of their being defective, damaged pariahs who are unable to accomplish what everyone around them is doing with such apparent ease. Stigma theory, also pertinent to this population, contends that both diseases and disorders are stigmatized and cause blame, exclusion, devaluation, and rejection (Weiss & Ramakrishna, 2001). According to Goffman (1963), stigma can be derived from a physical infirmity and is often associated with "blemishes of individual character," which result in an "undesired differentness," shame, blame, and damage to one's identity.

Charlene Miall (1985), who conducted research with childless women, stated that unstigmatized individuals, that is, those not experiencing infertility, believe the causes of childlessness originate from psychological problems or sexual dysfunction. She found women married to infertile men self-label infertility as a stigmatizing problem without necessarily receiving external cues from others (Miall, 1986). Childless women's impressions have been supported by research that also suggests men are more stigmatized by infertility than women (Miall, 1994). Miall (1989) believed women who are in heterosexual relationships participate in insemination with donor sperm in part to avoid the stigma of involuntary childlessness.

Stigmatized individuals learn through firsthand experiences that the potential for bias and injury regularly occurs in various social interactions, for example, at church, with family, and at friendly gatherings (Goffman, 1963). Additionally, infertile individuals or couples suffer from the uncertainty of not knowing whether those with whom they are interacting are prejudiced or unbiased. Because the physical aspects of infertility render it a concealed stigma, infertile individuals are believed to be hypervigilant when they interact with nonstigmatized people and look for signs to determine whether others know they are infertile (Blascovich, Mendes, Hunter, & Lickel, 2000). Moreover, infertile individuals or couples may be involved in numerous strategies to keep their stigma concealed (Kleck, 1968). Therefore, support groups composed exclusively of individuals or couples diagnosed with infertility may help decrease their anxiety, depression, and social isolation (Frable, Platt, & Hoey, 1998).

Both cognitive and affective processes appear to play a role in the stigma involved in social interactions (Blascovich et al., 2000). Infertile individuals frequently experience fight–flight responses. Patients recount numerous situations from which they wished to depart hastily, for example, shopping at a mall where smiling children perched on Santa's lap while their parents took pictures or attending religious ceremonies such as christenings, baby showers, or friends' children's birthday parties. However, infertile individuals may choose to fight, for example, by telling people who ask them why they remain childless to mind their own business; they can be rude or worse. Some fantasize about verbally attacking their inquisitive relatives by explaining they are childless because they are selfish, narcissistic, egocentric people who could not possibly share the spotlight with a child.

Blascovich et al. (2000) researched how stigmatized individuals evaluated threat. Infertile individuals or couples feel quite vulnerable while proceeding through various medical protocols and are constantly reevaluating the likelihood they will conceive. Fertility patients who lack funds for treatment may feel especially jeopardized.

Furthermore, clients will need help coping with social expectations whereby childless couples are viewed as hedonistic or selfish. For those previously married individuals, children may signal a new beginning, a true commitment to their new partner. Those unable to conceive often feel punished and wonder what they ever did to deserve infertility, sometimes questioning whether God thinks they are unworthy of being parents. Clients express feelings of failure, inadequacy, and persecution. People begin to see themselves as exclusively defined by their infertility.

SOCIAL EXCHANGE THEORY

The theory of social exchange has been advanced by the work of economists, anthropologists, political scientists, and social and behavioral psychologists. The premise is profit centered and theorizes that social interactions are designed to maximize gain for both parties through the evaluation of alternatives and the use of cost–benefit analysis. Social exchange theory assumes people who interact attempt to maximize tangible or intangible gains in a rational and calculated fashion (Homans, 1961).

It is thought that people help only those who currently are assisting them or who are expected to be useful to them in the future and that they refuse to accommodate those who they perceive are of no benefit (Blau, 1994; K. Cook, 1990). Human behavior, according to this theory, is motivated by benefit versus avoidance of cost, reward versus punishment, as well as pleasure versus pain. Tantamount to this theory is one's rational pursuit of self-interest.

Whereas some proponents of social exchange theory contend the ultimate goal of a relationship is intimacy (Trivers, 1971), such is not the case in assisted reproductive technology, especially when the donors and recipients are anonymous (K. Miller, 2005). The theory may account for the compensation provided to sperm and oocyte donors by their recipients (Applegarth, 2006). Although some social exchange theorists refute the concept of altruism (Moore, 1984), researchers have found altruism to be an important motivating factor in gamete donation (Braverman, 2001; Daniels, 2007; Lalos, Daniels, Gottlieb, & Lalos, 2003).

Although psychologists cannot reverse their patients' physical limitations or control the medical treatments, they can help them master their feelings about the events. Mental health professionals can teach patients how to protect their privacy during their fertility treatments. Learning how to better communicate the need for their partner's support may decrease marital conflict. Assertiveness training is especially effective, so individuals can meet their own needs. This technique furthers personal responsibility through honest and open communication, which then reduces the acrimony and hostility that often emerge during this emotional crisis.

CONCLUSION

Psychologists can help clients learn multiple coping methods and come to accept that all people must grieve at their own pace. Fertility counselors often suggest relaxation exercises, meditation, and support groups. Introducing writing and art techniques to grieving patients as well as helping them create memorializing rituals can promote healing.

Typically, as individuals and couples more fully understand the physical, emotional, and financial issues, they can begin the process of reorganization and use effective coping skills. Those who possess behavioral and cognitive flexibility and resilience in addition to intact social support systems will likely weather the crisis and may actually grow stronger. Couples with a high degree of marital and sexual satisfaction and who have feelings of deep, abiding affection for each other and their respective families can become a more cohesive unit.

As with any population, no one theoretical approach applies to all fertility patients. We suggest psychologists choosing to work with fertility patients integrate and combine the theories contained in this chapter. The various theoretical as well as practical approaches that may be best suited for this patient population are discussed in the remaining chapters.

2

ISSUES OF ACCESS TO TREATMENT

Procreation involves one of the basic civil rights of men . . . fundamental
to the very existence and survival of the race.
—Supreme Court Justice William O. Douglas, *Skinner v. Oklahoma*

No doubt those health care providers working in the field of reproductive medicine have all felt concern, at times, as to whether the couple or individual sitting before them has the capacity to create a nurturing, loving family
environment for the child the health care providers are helping them create.
Health care providers have been directed by professional guidelines and feel
an ethical responsibility to take into consideration the welfare of the children
they help to create. Yet, few rights are as fundamental in American society as
the right to the care, control, and upbringing of children.

Procreative libertarians argue that because the United States Constitution,
as interpreted by the Supreme Court, affords people the right to procreate
coitally, it also gives individuals the right to procreate noncoitally (Robertson,
1994). If this right does, in fact, exist, it amounts to a negative right rather
than a positive right. However, limitations are set such that not everyone who
wishes to become a parent through adoption is deemed to be eligible. One difference may be that in adoption, the state, acting in loco parentis, bears responsibility for the welfare of the existing child. Yet, of all parental perpetrators
of child maltreatment reported in the United States in 2005, 90.6% were
biological parents, and only 7% were adoptive parents (U.S. Department of
Health and Human Services, 2003).

Certainly all health care providers care about the children they help to create and would never wish any of them to face abuse. So, do these professionals working in the field of assisted reproductive technology (ART) have an ethical obligation to protect prospective children from potential harm at the hands of their parents? Can fitness to parent be determined on the basis of age, marital status, sexual orientation, physical abilities, religion, HIV status? Are individuals with physical, intellectual, or psychological limitations or social differences from a two-parent heterosexual family fit to parent? What qualities, traits, and/or behaviors would providers discourage or encourage? What happens to eccentrics?

Remarkably little is known about the long-term consequences of various styles of child rearing, such as authoritative or laissez-faire styles. Research has failed to produce anything like an empirically supported consensus about what works and what does not. Lacking specific and uniform criteria, there is tremendous potential for arbitrariness and prejudice in trying to assess who will make a fit parent. Mental health professionals also aspire to treat the individuals with whom they work in a just and fair manner. Because naturally conceiving individuals are not assessed for parental fitness in any manner in advance of becoming parents, does justice prevail by only assessing the infertile?

Other access issues are also of ethical concern in the field of reproductive medicine, reflecting, as they do, on the ethical principle of distributive justice: high cost; differential treatment availability throughout the country and the world (Ombelet & Campo, 2007); racial, ethnic, and socioeconomic disparities as minorities use reproductive medicine less often yet are more likely to experience infertility (Abma, Chandra, Mosher, Peterson, & Piccino, 1997; Bitler & Schmidt, 2006; Stephen & Chandra, 2000); fair allocation of donor oocytes (Pennings, 2001, 2005); marital status issues (e.g., Gurmankin, Caplan, & Braverman, 2005); and discrimination on the basis of the sexual orientation of potential patients, even between men and women (e.g., Gurmankin et al., 2005). Many of these issues reflect health care policy issues that are important to address on a national level, although some may reflect continued discriminatory attitudes about who deserves parenthood. The issues mental health professionals in reproductive medicine most frequently confront, however, involve whether individuals seeking reproductive assistance are fit to undergo treatment, fit to be parents, and whether a child conceived by them will be adequately parented. These are the primary issues addressed in this chapter.

MEDICAL BACKGROUND

In their ethical obligation to do no harm, physicians may refuse treatment for infertility to a patient for several medical reasons, for example: The health risks are too great; there is a high risk of transmitting a serious genetically based disorder to the offspring; the likelihood of success is too small to subject the patient to the risks entailed. Yet, as demonstrated in the following review, other reasons may come into play as well.

Physician and Clinic Approach to Access to Treatment Issues

Research has found considerable variability between clinicians and programs in terms of access to treatment. Although an early study found that mental health professional members of the American Society of Reproductive Medicine (ASRM), an organization of physicians and allied health professionals working in the field of reproductive medicine, followed no formal policy, red flags such as substance abuse, physical abuse, severe marital discord, and coercion of one partner by another were used as criteria for treatment rejection, and more stringent criteria were used for clients seeking gamete donation than those using their own gametes (Leiblum & Williams, 1993). When ART clinic directors were surveyed, 40% reported having written policies, but no universal agreement was found on treating single women (79% treat), patients with a history of schizophrenia (27% treat), patients who use alcohol excessively (10% treat), women with HIV (7% treat), and even those previously convicted of child abuse (2% treat; Stern, Cramer, Garrod, & Green, 2001). Many ART clinic directors voiced more restrictive opinions regarding access to treatment than was suggested by their clinic's formal policy on all categories of patients measured (e.g., marital status, age, sexual orientation, substance abuse, psychiatric history, convicted or suspected of abuse, possibility of transmitting a genetic disorder; Stern, Cramer, Garrod, & Green, 2002). Because of the diversity in opinions of clinic directors, these researchers suggested the importance of written policies and the use of a multidisciplinary ethics committee to make access decisions.

Substantial variation in actual screening policies has also been found across U.S. ART programs (Gurmankin et al., 2005). On average, programs reported turning away 4% of prospective patients each year (3% for medical reasons and 1% for psychological or social reasons). The moral complexity posed by this issue and the resulting inconsistencies are demonstrated by the following finding: Whereas 59% of Society for Assisted Reproductive Technology clinics agreed that they do not have the right to stop anyone from attempting to conceive, 70% felt it was acceptable to consider a prospective parent's fitness before helping him or her conceive a child.

Age of Prospective Parents

Debate as to whether it is ethical to extend ART to overcome natural aging, whether scarce resources available for ART should be used on older women and men, and whether an upper age limit should be imposed for medical assistance, particularly for women, to conceive has been vigorous in the literature (Hope, Lockwood, & Lockwood, 1995; Porter, Peddie, & Bhattacharya, 2007), bringing with it questions about who would make these decisions and who would enforce them. When using ovum donation with careful medical monitoring, "there does not appear to be any definitive medical reason for excluding these women [in their 6th decade of life] from attempting pregnancy on the basis of age alone" (Paulson et al., 2002, p. 2323), although some in vitro fertilization (IVF) programs may set upper age limits between 45 and 55 years of age for women, require that at least one member of the couple be under age 50 or that the combined ages of the couple be under 110 (M. Bustillo, personal communication, November 11, 2008; M. Davidson, personal communication, November 4, 2008).

Assisted Reproductive Technology for Patients With Cancer or HIV

Individuals diagnosed with cancer or HIV are the two groups of medical patients most likely to request the services of ART clinics, the former because of the possibility of being rendered infertile as a result of treatment for the illness and the latter because of the possibility of horizontal and vertical transmission of the virus to unaffected partners or a baby through unprotected intercourse and natural conception.

Although modern cancer treatment can offer lifelong cures, permanent damage to organ systems can occur. Loss of fertility after treatment can affect the psychological equilibrium and quality of life for cancer survivors and has been found to be a major concern to them (Bahadur et al., 2002; Langeveld, Grootenhuis, Voute, de Haan, & van den Bos, 2004; Partridge et al., 2004; Schover, 1999). It is currently possible to preserve the fertility potential of cancer patients through techniques such as cryopreservation of embryos, oocytes, or ovarian tissue with subsequent thawing and transplantation for women (Kim, 2006; Oktay & Sonmezer, 2007) and sperm cryopreservation with subsequent insemination or intracytoplasmic sperm injection for men (Meseguer et al., 2006; Revel et al., 2005). Many patients have been found to lack information, however, and counseling to help facilitate decision making around fertility preservation is far from universally offered (Tschudin & Bitzer, 2009). We believe it is important that oncologists and others treating children, adolescents, and young adults in their reproductive years be aware of the availability of these procedures and discuss them with patients in advance of treatment (Schover, Brey, Lichtin, Lipschultz, & Jeha, 2002) because giving patients some present and future choices is preferable to eliminating their options and ultimately respects autonomy. However, it may not be deemed safe for some patients to delay cancer treatment or be exposed to the medications used for ovarian stimulation.

Treatment with retroviral medications has transformed HIV from a terminal illness to a chronic disease for many receiving this diagnosis. With appropriate antenatal and postnatal care, the risk of vertical transmission has been reduced to less than 1% (Lyall et al., 2001), and with this, the demand for ART by both HIV-concordant and HIV-discordant couples has increased significantly (J. L. Chen, Phillips, Kanouse, Collins, & Miu, 2001; Politch & Anderson, 2002; Sauer, 2005; Semprini et al., 1992). Sperm washing significantly reduces the risk of HIV transmission from HIV-discordant men to their uninfected partners or future offspring (Bujard et al., 2007). Maternal vertical transmission risks to the baby can be reduced to less than 1% with the use of antiretroviral medications in the second and third trimesters of pregnancy, elective cesarean section (if any viral load continues to be detected), and avoidance of breast feeding (Lyall et al., 2001). Use of these procedures safeguards the couple and the potential child, whereas unprotected intercourse and natural conception protects neither an uninfected partner nor the child (Mandelbrot, Heard, Henrion-Geant, & Henrion, 1997).

It would appear that physicians, to fulfill their ethical obligation to social justice and nondiscrimination on the basis of sexual orientation, may be ethically obligated to provide treatment for patients infected with HIV (Ethics Committee of the American Society for Reproductive Medicine, 2004e; Phelps, 2007) because offering ART to HIV-discordant couples appears to produce more benefit and less harm than withholding treatment. In addition, the Americans With Disabilities Act of 1990 (ADA, 2008) might prohibit a physician from refusing to treat a patient on the basis of his or her HIV status. However, it has been reported that the majority of U.S. ART clinic directors are reluctant to offer care to these couples because only approximately 7% of directors believed they should treat HIV-infected women, whereas 82% disfavored such treatment (Stern et al., 2001).

PSYCHOSOCIAL LITERATURE

Some psychiatric disorders tend to run in families. The disorders most likely to have a strong genetic component include autism, major depressive disorder, bipolar disorder, schizophrenia, attention-deficit/hyperactivity disorder, and substance use disorders (Cardno et al., 1999; Faraone et al., 2005; Kendler, Karkowski, Corey, Prescott, & Neale, 1999; Kendler, Pedersen, Neale, & Mathé, 1995; Kendler & Prescott, 1999; National Institute of Mental Health, 1998; Prescott & Kendler, 1999). Studies comparing twins reared apart versus together clearly demonstrate, however, that both nature and nurture play important roles in the genesis of psychopathology and substance use disorders (Tsuang, Bar, Stone, & Faraone, 2004), with genes and environment often interacting. Well-functioning adoptive parents, for example, can buffer children at genetic risk even for schizophrenia (Tienari et al., 1994; Wahlberg et al., 1997). The growing interest in the genetic inheritability of all sorts of traits and characteristics ignores the potential for malleability, even in characteristics that are heavily influenced by heredity, and no psychological disorder, trait, or characteristic has been found to be 100% heritable. Nevertheless, patients presenting with a history of psychiatric illness themselves or within their families should be informed of the possibility of inheritability of the condition. When mental illness is present, collaboration with genetic counselors is essential as accurate information can benefit patients.

Fitness to Parent

Does a body of knowledge exist that objectively defines what constitutes fit parenting? Most people seem to have an opinion on what constitutes bad parenting. Serious physical or sexual abuse of a child is viewed as unacceptable by the majority of people (Browne & Finkelhor, 1986; Conaway & Hansen, 1989; Malinosky-Rummel & Hansen, 1993; McCord, 1983). Research consistently suggests that families characterized by overt family conflict, manifested in recurrent episodes of anger and aggression, and deficient in nurturing, especially cold, unsupportive, and neglectful family relationships, are associated with poor mental and physical health outcomes in their children (Repetti, Taylor, & Seeman, 2002).

Disparities in the assessment of potential parents definitely exist, for example, between those adopting a child and those having a child through embryo donation, both of which result in parents with no genetic relationship to the child they will raise. Yet, significant differences exist between these two means of family building; in adoption, a child will already exist at the time the adoption occurs. Thus, parenting criteria for adoption have focused on social and emotional factors needed by the child, whereas for embryo donation the focus has been on medical and psychological criteria (Widdows & MacCallum, 2002). This is also, in part, reflected by the fact that every state has laws regarding adoption and only a handful of states have laws that address embryo donation.

There are so many variants of good parenting, however, that it is difficult to determine what is good enough parenting without running the risk of introducing arbitrariness or being discriminatory. Mental health professionals, too, may have their own biases, possibly toward advocating optimally nurturing and supportive family environments for children (Crawford, McLeod, Zamboni, & Jordan, 1999).

The notion that a consensus could be reached on good parenting is difficult enough to believe. However, the possibility that health care providers can predict future fitness to parent in individuals who are not yet parents, that is, the majority of their infertile patients, is even less likely, especially because professionals know that a child's temperament and behavior have an effect on parents and vice versa (Collins, Maccoby, Steinberg, Hetherington, & Bornstein, 2000). Because it is difficult, if not impossible, to observe parenting skills in advance of someone becoming a parent, are there any other specific risk factors for child abuse or neglect?

Risk Factors for Child Abuse, Neglect, or Problematic Behavioral Outcomes

Individuals' own history of physical, sexual, and substance abuse, including alcoholism (Dubowitz et al., 2001; Duke et al., 2001; Kaufman & Zigler, 1987; Peddle & Wang, 2001; Widom, 1989); low intellectual functioning (Dowdney & Skuse, 1993); and mental illness, including psychotic, personality, and mood disorders (Anderson & Hammen, 1993; Chaffin, Kelleher, & Hollenberg, 1996; Downey & Coyne, 1990; Minkovitz et al., 2005; Wolfe, 1985), increases the likelihood that parents will abuse and/or neglect their children. However, the relationship with abuse is neither simple nor direct, and no psychiatric illness, basic character disorder, or underlying personality trait has been found to predict the risk of becoming a child abuser (Wolfe, 1985). If a parent has been diagnosed as mentally ill, however, those with insight into their illness, who adhere to psychopharmacological and treatment recommendations, and who have social support from others are less likely to abuse their children. Those who have more difficulty with impulse control, are impaired in their capacity for empathy, or have poor self-esteem are more likely, although not certain, to be abusive toward their children (Mullick, Miller, & Jacobsen, 2001). Poor adaptive and social functioning, being a spousal abuser, having limited parenting knowledge, having unrealistic expectations of children, experiencing greater emotional reactivity to aversive child behavior, or being stressed or unhappy about one's parenting role are also risk factors for child abusive behavior (Azar & Rohrbeck, 1986; Haskett, Smith Scott, Grant, Ward, & Robinson, 2003; Jouriles, Barling, & O'Leary, 1987; Perez-Albeniz & de Paul, 2003; Rohrback & Twentyman, 1986).

No research has found that children being raised by disabled, gay or lesbian, older, or single parents through ART, either mothers or fathers, are in greater danger of abuse or neglect or suffer, in general, more than children raised by nondisabled, heterosexual married couples (Kirshbaum & Olkin, 2002). In addition, the behavioral and emotional well-being of children created through ART has not been found to be adversely affected by older maternal age (Boivin et al., 2009) or the marital status or sexual orientation of the parents (see Chapter 8, this volume).

Poverty, low economic level, neighborhood violence, chronic unemployment, homelessness, and low educational level tend to add stress to a family and are associated with child maltreatment but are not sufficient to cause abuse (Melton & Flood, 1994; National Research Council, 1993).

Child abuse appears to be determined and is often the product of an interactive process between parental competence, situational demand, and characteristics of the child (Belsky, 1993). No specific psychological patterns have been found to be present in all or even most abusive or neglectful parents (Wolfe, 1985). Researchers have no universal criteria and no well-validated assessment techniques for determining parenting competence, either (Benjet, Azar, & Kuersten-Hogan, 2003). Thus, it must be concluded that researchers' ability to predict the likelihood of a potential parent to maltreat his or her future, as yet unconceived, child is extremely limited. However, if a potential parent is unable to care for him- or herself, even with available assistance, one could justifiably question his or her potential ability to care for a child.

Ability to Provide Informed Consent

If it is determined that a prospective patient is unable to provide informed consent, access to treatment should be postponed until this can be remediated. Informed consent has three essential components: The patient gives consent voluntarily (in the absence of coercion, undue influence, or duress), has been fully informed (given relevant information in language that is understandable to him or her), and has adequate ability to make the decision (the potential patient has a level of decision-making capacity needed to make a meaningful choice about whether to participate in treatment; Berg, Appelbaum, Lidz, & Parker, 2001).

Decision-making capacity in the medical or psychosocial treatment context includes at least the following four elements: the ability to understand the relevant information regarding the nature of treatment (including its risks and benefits and available alternatives), to appreciate the nature of one's own situation and the potential risks and benefits for one's own situation and condition, to reason with the information about the risks and benefits of the treatment alternatives, and to express a consistent choice about whether to undergo treatment (Grisso & Appelbaum, 1998).

Decision-making capacity, which should not be confused with the legal determination of *competence*, can be assessed after information is shared by a physician or other health care professional either informally by asking a series of questions or formally through a standardized and validated instrument. Informal questions might include, for example, "Can you tell me what this treatment entails? What is the purpose of the treatment? What are its risks?

What are its benefits? What alternatives are available? What are the risks and benefits of no treatment at all?"

Although it is unlikely that most infertility patients will lack decisional capacity, if they do, using a fair assessment tool, such as the MacArthur Competence Assessment Tool for Treatment (Grisso & Appelbaum, 1998), which can validate a clinician's decision not to proceed with treatment at least until a particular individual demonstrates decision-making capacity, is recommended. High levels of anxiety and depression, often reported by infertility patients, certainly can interfere with the ability to process and store information or assess risks. However, presenting information in a different manner, perhaps using perceptual aids such as printed materials, is likely to enhance the patient's decisional capacity on reassessment.

BIOETHICAL PERSPECTIVES

In the United States, the Constitution has been interpreted to protect reproductive freedom. Bioethical issues involved in decisions about denying access to fertility treatment include conflicts between the respect for individual autonomy and procreative liberty and concerns for preventing any foreseeable harm to the children who are being created; issues of justice regarding offering equal access to all who are in need of fertility treatment; the importance of treating people with dignity, including avoiding undue invasion into their privacy; and recognition and respect for differences in parenting beliefs and practices associated with socioeconomic status, race, ethnicity, religion, and other human differences (Robertson, 1994).

Welfare of the Child and Reproductive Autonomy

It is usually assumed that parents have the best interests of their children at heart. Governmental intervention into the family takes place only under the most extreme conditions (i.e., when either an incident of child abuse or neglect has taken place or a serious threat of such abuse is determined to exist). Without very serious concerns for the welfare of a child, the procreative autonomy of the individuals involved in creating a child is not threatened by outside intrusion. Whose best interests take precedence: those of the intended parents desiring to create a child or the unconceived child who has absolutely no say whatsoever in the matter of his or her creation? Yet, from the child's perspective, is it better to be born to a less than ideal parent than never to be born at all? Because the fertile population is not assessed for their ability to parent before conceiving a child, however, is it fair and equitable that the infertile population be scrutinized regarding their intended creation of their children?

There are no guidelines available to determine how to balance protection of clients' autonomy and protection of clients' and others' welfare. Therefore, when confronting the access to treatment issues presented in this chapter, we believe it is preferable to use the harm standard because it allows us to balance a prospective parent's interest in procreation with society's interest in child welfare and because in reproductive medicine, unlike in adoption or child custody disputes, the prospective parents' interests are not seen as subordinate to those of the child, as no child is yet in existence (Benatar, 2006; Storrow, 2005). Under the harm standard, a patient's decisions are honored unless there is a serious threat of harm to him- or herself or a third party, an inadequately treated psychiatric illness, or concern about the individual's capacity to provide informed consent. It must be remembered, however, that physicians are not required to violate their fundamental personal values, standards of scientific or ethical practice, or the law, although physicians may not abandon their patients. Thus, if a physician refuses to treat a patient because of his or her own personal values, the physician must take whatever measures are necessary to facilitate an effective transition of care to another physician (Quill & Cassell, 1995).

Justice

Several different bioethical concerns unrelated to fitness to parent, such as the determination of just distribution of scarce medical resources in light of the high cost of infertility treatment, limited insurance coverage in many states, and scarcity of available oocytes for egg donation, raise major ethical and social concerns regarding support for equal access to reproductive health services for all individuals regardless of their socioeconomic status or racial or ethnic origins. Older, wealthier, and more highly educated individuals are more likely to use infertility services, although those in lower socioeconomic classes actually have higher infertility rates due to poverty, poor nutrition, and increased rates of infection and sexually transmitted diseases (Robertson, 1994). Justice may also be abridged if patients who are infertile are treated differently than those who are fertile. For example, if background checks are going to be undertaken, they would need to be universal, that is, conducted on all patients requiring medical assistance for pregnancy, not just infertile individuals, single individuals, gay men, or lesbians.

Informed Consent

To obtain truly informed consent, mental health professionals involved in the evaluation of prospective fertility patients must clearly disclose this evaluation process to patients in advance of any discussions. Psychologists must make it clear to patients whether they are functioning in the role of psychoeducational consultant or evaluator, that is, gatekeeper, so as to clarify any misconceptions about the mental health professional's role that the patient may have. Lack of transparency is a barrier to fairness, as well. When functioning as a gatekeeper, mental health professionals must present a clear and honest outline of the assessment process so that patients can exercise their right to appeal psychologists' decisions or decline to sign release of information forms. An ethics committee consultation team would be useful in an advisory capacity to all programs working in this field.

EXISTING LAWS, POLICIES, AND LEGISLATION

Every state has laws regarding abuse and neglect of children, and many provide a mechanism for the termination of parental rights under egregious circumstances. In addition, every state has laws pertaining to assessing one's fitness to parent through adoption. However, ART presents a unique circumstance because physicians are placed in a position to be able to consider parental fitness in advance of helping a couple or individual procreate. In adoption, by contrast, the state has an interest in an existing child, a child for whom a placement must be made that is in the best interests of the child.

An individual's right to reproduce is constitutionally protected, although this right, like any other, is not without limitation. This right, however, might be considered to be a negative right rather than a positive right (Robertson, 1994), meaning that this is something the government cannot interfere with, but also has no obligation to provide the resources to enable reproduction by any means. The ADA (2008) states,

> No individual shall be discriminated against on the basis of disability in the full and equal enjoyment of the goods, services, facilities, privileges, advantages, or accommodations of any place of public accommodation by any person who owns, leases (or leases to) or operates a place of public accommodation. (42 U.S.C. § 12182(a))

There are exceptions, however. Under the ADA, nothing "shall require an entity to permit an individual to participate in or benefit from the goods, services, facilities, privileges, advantages and accommodations of such entity where such individual poses a direct threat to the health and safety of others" (42 U.S.C. § 12182(b)(3); 2008).

In *Bragdon v. Abbott* (1998) the U.S. Supreme Court decided that reproduction is a major life activity and that HIV substantially limits this major life activity because of the risk to the public health. Might this argument be extended to anyone who experiences infertility or must the infertility be caused by an underlying disability? Physicians are not allowed to unjustly refuse to treat a patient based solely on the person's disability category. If treatment of a disabled person is declined and the disabled individual believes that treatment has been declined on the basis of his or her disability, the physician must demonstrate clear justification. If a direct threat of risk to self or others can be shown, the charge of discrimination may be excused. It is probably prudent for infertility practices to maintain a written policy of current exclusionary guidelines that are explained during intake to all patients and applied equally to all patients. This may help to avoid future litigation. For example, in the case of *Chambers v. Melmed* (2005) a blind woman sued a fertility clinic under the ADA (2008) and the Rehabilitation Act of 1976 (2008) claiming that she was denied access to insemination by donor because of her blindness. The court ultimately concluded that blindness was not the basis for the denial, but rather the denial was based on concern for the patient's lack of social support, poor hygiene, emotional outbursts, and lack of preparations made for the care of the child. Had these criteria been initially stated, it is possible that litigation could have been avoided.

In addition to the ADA, states might also have antidiscrimination laws. In Illinois, for example, it is unprofessional conduct for a professional counselor or clinical counselor to discriminate against any person on the basis of "race, color, sex, sexual orientation, age, religion. . . . Marital status, political belief, mental or physical handicap" (Professional Counselor and Clinical Professional Counselor Licensing Act, 2008, 68 Ill. Adm. Code 1375.225).

To avoid arbitrariness and the potential for unfair discrimination, criteria for denial of services should be developed by a range of professionals, documented in writing, and discussed in advance with clients. Any nonmedical criteria for patient selection must be exercised justly, uniformly, and in accordance with existing federal, state, and local laws.

CLINICAL VIGNETTE

Joshua, 39, and Diana, 38, a Hispanic couple, enter a health care provider's office. They have been married for 5 years, trying to conceive a second child for 2 years. Joshua appears angry at having to go through IVF with its hefty price tag because they have no insurance coverage for IVF and will need to take out a loan to pay for their treatment. He has a history of substance abuse (cocaine—he reports being drug-free for 12 months), and Diana has a history of bipolar I disorder (currently treated with lithium). Diana had discontinued her medication during her first pregnancy and experienced a postpartum relapse. She subsequently attempted suicide. This couple separated briefly

1 year ago, saying that the stress of Diana's illness was responsible for the break-up, but now appear to be committed to each other. Joshua and Diana report no history of domestic abuse.

Diana also has cerebral palsy and uses forearm crutches to help her get around. Because it would be more prudent for Diana to stay on mood stabilizing medication, it has been recommended that she not carry another pregnancy. She and Joshua have decided they would like to have a gestational carrier (GC) gestate their embryo. Their home has been thoroughly adapted to enable Diana to function, and her mother, who lives nearby, is actively involved in helping her with home management and child care.

On one occasion when Diana's mother was not available to babysit, Joshua and Diana were observed speaking harshly to their 4-year-old in the waiting room. The child had become bored and fidgety as a result of waiting for her mother to be called in for an examination. Diana and Joshua had not brought any toys or books from home to entertain their daughter.

Ethical Dilemmas in the Context of Professional Guidelines

The American Psychological Association's (APA's; 2002) "Ethical Principles of Psychologists and Code of Conduct," in Principles A–E, stresses the importance for all psychologists to aspire to the general principles of beneficence (promote good), nonmaleficence (do not harm), integrity (honesty and accuracy), justice (fairness), and respect for people's rights and dignity (respect for patient autonomy and dignity, demonstrated by avoiding discrimination, maintaining confidentiality, and obtaining informed consent).[1]

In addition and relevant to the present vignette, the APA Ethics Code (2002) states that psychologists do not engage in unfair discrimination on the basis of race, ethnicity, disability, socioeconomic status, or any basis proscribed by law (APA Ethics Code Standard 3.01, Unfair Discrimination); refrain from entering into a multiple relationship that could reasonably be expected to impair the psychologists' objectivity, competence, or effectiveness (APA Ethics Code Standard 3.05, Multiple Relationships); obtain informed consent when providing assessment, therapy, or consulting services (including informing Diana and Joshua if the role of the mental health professional is psychoeducational or evaluative, that is, gatekeeper, APA Ethics Code Standards 3.10, Informed Consent, and 3.11, Psychological Services Delivered to or Through Organizations, if the psychologist is an employee of or consultant to the fertility clinic, and 9.03, Informed Consent in Assessments); maintain

---

[1]Issues related to nonmaleficence toward the gestational carrier and her family, a potential role conflict for the mental health professional, and informed consent in situations involving a gestational carrier are covered in Chapter 7, Surrogacy.

confidentiality (APA Ethics Code Standard 4.01, Maintaining Confidentiality); inform people of the limits of confidentiality (including obtaining a release to share information with others, i.e., the GC involved in this particular case, APA Ethics Code Standard 4.02, Discussing the Limits of Confidentiality); minimize intrusions on an individual's privacy (APA Ethics Code Standard 4.04, Minimizing Intrusions on Privacy); and document discussions of the reasoning behind psychologists' decisions and a treatment plan (APA Ethics Code Standard 6.01, Documentation of Professional and Scientific Work and Maintenance of Records).

To meet the ethical obligation of informed consent, the mental health professional must make certain to both provide sufficient information and provide it in a manner that is comprehensible to Diana and Joshua (APA Ethics Code Standard 3.10, Informed Consent). Federal regulations under the Health Insurance Portability and Accountability Act (U.S. Department of Health and Human Services, 2003) require that patients be given a Notice of Privacy Practices document that explains how the mental health or medical professional may use the patient's personal medical information, with whom and under what circumstances this information may be shared, as well as the patient's privacy rights in language understandable to the patient.

With regard to assessment, psychologists are expected to base the opinions contained in their recommendations and diagnostic or evaluative statements on information and techniques sufficient to substantiate their findings (APA Ethics Code Standard 9.01a, Bases for Assessments) and obtain informed consent for assessments, evaluations, or diagnostic services (APA Ethics Code Standard 9.03, Informed Consent in Assessments).

The ASRM guidelines for child-rearing ability and the provision of fertility services indicate that fertility programs may withhold services from prospective patients on the basis of well-substantiated judgments that they will be unable to provide or have others provide adequate child rearing for offspring, for example, if uncontrolled psychiatric illness, substance abuse, ongoing physical or emotional abuse, or a history of perpetuating physical or emotional abuse is present (Ethics Committee of the ASRM, 2004a). Programs, however, may provide services to all persons who medically qualify for treatment, except in clear cases of a significant harm to offspring. It is recommended that physicians and others involved in fertility treatment not assume that a history of social or psychological problems or a serious disability automatically disqualifies one from being an adequate parent. Thus, persons with disabilities should not be denied fertility services except in rare cases when a well-substantiated basis exists for concluding that they cannot provide, or have others provide, adequate child rearing for offspring. It is recommended that clinic or physician policies and procedures for determinations to withhold services be in written form and decisions be made jointly among members of a program.

In the proposed psychological guidelines for evaluation and counseling of GCs and intended parents, the Gestational Carrier Task Force of the Mental Health Professional Group of the ASRM (2000) recommends that psychological evaluation of intended parents, pre- and postcounseling of intended parents, and counseling throughout the process be available. No suggested rejection criteria are given for intended parents.

Although most mental health professionals are not members of the American Academy of Pediatrics, they may, nevertheless, find it helpful to become familiar with various professional organizations' guidelines. American Academy of Pediatrics members are informed that children do best when authoritative parenting is provided by parents who are responsive to children's needs and feelings and who combine warmth with thoughtful, firm limit setting consistently over time. Children are at special risk when their families expose them to conflict, anger, and aggression; fail to meet their emotional needs; and do not effectively discipline them or help them to internalize appropriate social norms and values. It is also noted that depression and other emotional problems of parents, marital tension, and parental substance abuse have a detrimental impact on children (American Academy of Pediatrics, 2003).

Practical Considerations

It would be important to determine whether the alterations made to Diana's home allow her to function effectively. In addition, it is essential that Diana's mother, on whom she depends for help with her child and her home, is in agreement with this process of IVF, including the assistance of a GC to enlarge her daughter and son-in-law's family.

Balancing the Multiple Perspectives

The major ethical conflict in the present case is between patient reproductive autonomy and concern for the welfare of potential children. Is it fair to assess individuals requesting assistance in reproduction for fitness when those who reproduce naturally do not undergo similar assessment? Additionally, the health care provider's obligation is to his or her patients, that is, the intended parents.

This case raises multiple specific issues, including concerns about the stability of this couple's relationship; Joshua's anger and history of drug abuse; and Diana and Joshua's ability to engage in an appropriate relationship with a GC during a pregnancy and, if all parties agree, afterward. Furthermore, Diana's mental illness and the medication needed to treat her bipolar disorder, the medications' potential teratogenic effect on developing oocytes, and the risks to her should she cease taking her medication need to be considered.

Joshua and Diana's combined ability to provide an appropriate environment for a child (on the basis of their observed harsh parenting techniques and lack of planning to anticipate a 4-year-old child's limited attention span and need for something to occupy her), Joshua's possible substance abuse, and Diana's cerebral palsy and limited mobility are additional complex factors to be weighed. Yet, are these concerns enough to consider abridging the couple's reproductive autonomy?

Society has an obligation to protect vulnerable individuals. Thus, if children are being abused or neglected within a family, they can be removed from the family by appropriate social and legal agencies. In addition, will society become responsible for the care of this couple's children should they separate or should Diana's condition deteriorate or her mother become unavailable to help her?

The Clinician or Fertility Clinic

The physicians in this situation have concerns about this couple for all of the reasons cited previously. In addition, however, they are concerned about refusing treatment for fear of being sued for violating the ADA because of the couple's disabilities (physical and psychological, including former drug abuse). They also have a duty to protect the GC involved in this situation to ensure that her well-being and that of her family is considered as important as that of the intended parents and potential child. Although fertility doctors are generally not suited to determine who will make a good parent, it appears reasonable to assess patients for their ability to safely participate in infertility treatment, become pregnant, carry a pregnancy to term, cope with unsuccessful treatment, and relate effectively with a GC. However, patients should not be disqualified for arbitrary reasons such as a disability that does not preclude pregnancy or interfere with parenting or for factors that are not medically or psychosocially relevant such as sexual orientation or marital status.

The Prospective Parents

Diana wants to have another child and provide a sibling for her daughter. Joshua is less enthusiastic about conceiving a second child through IVF with the use of a GC, raising the possibility of coercion. Joshua and Diana report that they have addressed their marital issues and that Joshua is no longer abusing drugs. Diana believes that the adaptations made to her home and the help she receives from her mother allow her to oversee household management and provide good parenting.

Although Diana and Joshua do not require medical intervention to become pregnant, on the basis of her prior postpartum experience, probably precipitated by the cessation of lithium medication during her pregnancy, the risks of a pregnancy appear greater than the risks of IVF for Diana. Thus, their consideration of this option, which includes having the assistance of a GC, appears to reflect positive problem-solving ability on their part.

The Gestational Carrier

The GC has been evaluated by a psychologist to determine her emotional stability, motivations for being a GC, and ability to carry a pregnancy for a couple and then relinquish the baby to them after delivery. The GC may believe that the IVF clinic screens prospective parents as carefully as she has been screened. Therefore, in all likelihood, she probably believes that the clinic endorses Joshua and Diana in terms of their parenting ability. If the clinic has ongoing concerns regarding Diana and Joshua, the GC has a right to be informed of this, with Joshua and Diana's consent, so that she can furnish informed consent. If Joshua and Diana are unwilling to provide this consent, treatment should not continue. Because the GC, her husband, and their children will be involved with Joshua and Diana, she needs to feel certain that her well-being and the well-being of her family are of concern to everyone involved in this process.

The Potential Children

As articulated within ASRM guidelines, the welfare of the potential child and any other children who may be affected should be taken into consideration before offering ART services. Will this child have at least a reasonable chance of having a good life being raised within this family? Is this child likely to be maltreated by his or her angry, former drug abusing father or emotionally unstable mother? Should assessment of the maternal grandmother as a caretaker be required, as it appears she will be very involved in raising this child?

The Existing Children

The welfare of Joshua and Diana's daughter and that of the children of the GC need to be considered. Will Joshua and Diana's daughter receive adequate attention from her parents after the birth of another child? How will the children of the GC feel about their mother carrying a pregnancy and then surrendering the baby to another family? Will they worry that they, too, might be relinquished, perhaps, if they misbehave or the family has financial problems?

CONCLUSION

Assessing parental fitness presents numerous challenges, not the least of which is that no reliable method exists to predict who will become a good parent, especially in advance of conception (Belsky, 1993; Budd, 2001). Research to date does not provide agreement on what constitutes good enough parenting or an adequate and reliable way of predicting this. Even risk factors for parental abuse or neglect are valid only for group prediction, not individual prediction.

Psychologists are aware that Diana, with bipolar disorder, is at high risk of relapse during the postpartum period (Viguera et al., 2000), as the additional stress and lack of sleep after the birth of the baby can precipitate mania (Ehlers, Frank, & Kupfer, 1988). This may occur even if the individual did not gestate the pregnancy. Moreover, although it may be difficult to have a bipolar parent, research suggests that if the illness is controlled with medication, bipolar parents are not universally unfit parents (Andersen & Hammen, 1993; Kahn, Brandt, & Whitaker, 2004).

However, the medication Diana needs to stabilize her may be teratogenic. It is unclear whether lithium may cause damage to a developing oocyte (McElroy, 2004). Thus, psychologists would require consultation with a knowledgeable psychopharmacologist specializing in reproduction as well as a genetic counselor to obtain information on the heritability of bipolar disorder.

They would also be concerned about Diana's ability to cope with the stresses of an IVF cycle and the mood variability that can be associated with ovarian suppression during IVF (Warnock, Bundren, & Morris, 2000), as well as her ability to effectively cope with a newborn. Thus, we would want to be sure a management strategy by Diana's psychotherapist and psychopharmacologist was in place both during the IVF cycle and for the postpartum period.

In addition, a behavioral interaction in which the parents reacted harshly to their daughter has already been surreptitiously observed in the waiting room. Although they demonstrated poor planning ability because they did not bring any books or toys to amuse their child during the time that she waited for her mother to be examined, Joshua and Diana are demonstrating good planning ability regarding an intentional planned pregnancy using a GC. A health care provider might suggest bibliotherapy and a parenting course to expand this couple's parenting skills.

Furthermore, in health care providers' ethical obligation to see that no harm comes to the individuals with whom they work, they would need to determine through interviewing Joshua that coercion is not involved. They would also screen for intimate partner violence. Because of the various issues this couple presents, health care providers would request consent from Joshua and Diana to confer with any other mental health professionals with whom they have been treated in the past (e.g., drug counselors, marital therapists, individual psychologists, psychopharmacologists). Although there are some concerns about Joshua and Diana's ability to parent adequately, none appears sufficiently severe as to suggest that treatment be denied. Assuming Joshua has been drug-free for 1 year, as he reports, and Diana is stabilized on her medications, they would be given clearance by the mental health professional to proceed to IVF. However, if their IVF cycle was postponed with the intent of transferring an embryo to a GC, the decision regarding their eligibility would be based on concerns about their ability to handle the stresses of an IVF cycle and a GC pregnancy and their capacity to maintain a warm and respectful relationship with their GC and would have nothing to do with the disability categories that these clients present nor with their inferred ability to parent.

If a health care professional recommends that treatment be withheld from these patients, careful documentation of the mental health professional's evaluation, including the reasons for exclusion, as well as specific suggestions for Joshua and Diana's future treatment would be necessary. Throughout the process, health care professionals would offer Joshua and Diana the opportunity for consultation or referral to another mental health professional for counseling so as to avoid a conflict of interest. A multidisciplinary ethics committee can be useful to clinics, both in developing their policies and in deliberating ethically contentious cases (Peterson, 2005).

Parenthood is a normative life experience for many individuals, one that can define the roles and meaning of adulthood. Few rights are as fundamental as the right to bear, beget, and raise children. It would seem that only in the most egregious cases, that is, those in which someone already has been convicted of child abuse, is suffering from uncontrolled severe mental illness (which precludes adequate self-care or child care), or has a continuing problem with substance or domestic abuse, could professionals justifiably recommend that treatment be withheld or at least deferred for psychosocial reasons until these issues can be resolved.

We do not believe we, the authors of this book, have the ability to predict who will be a fit or unfit parent in advance of the creation of a child. We also believe that because fertile individuals are not assessed for parental fitness in advance of becoming parents, it may be discriminatory to assess infertile individuals for parental fitness in advance of becoming parents. Therefore, we have determined that because of lack of sufficient evidence to the contrary, we would approve Diana and Josh for the proposed treatment.

3

EMBRYO DISPOSITION

Act in such a way that you always treat humanity, whether in your own person or in the person of any other, never simply as a means, but always at the same time as an end.
—Immanuel Kant, *Grounding for the Metaphysics of Morals*

It barely is visible to the naked eye, no larger than the head of a pin. Yet it has created controversy ranging from whether to create it to what to do with it once it is created. We are referring to human embryos, and in light of the fact that at this time (2010) well over 400,000 cryopreserved embryos exist in fertility laboratories throughout the United States alone (Hoffman et al., 2003), these issues have taken on great societal import.

Because of the inefficiency of human reproduction, reproductive endocrinologists over the years have hormonally stimulated women during in vitro fertilization (IVF) cycles to produce multiple oocytes so they could maximize the number of embryos created for multiple implantation attempts. If supernumerary embryos result, they are often cryopreserved for subsequent use. This has resulted in close to half a million embryos in cold storage throughout the United States, thus creating the dilemma of what to do with them. Although the majority of these cryopreserved embryos are awaiting future use by the couples who created them (Hoffman et al., 2003; Lyerly et al., 2008), other infertile couples, having completed their families or changed their circumstances, have found themselves confronted with a difficult decision that many of them never expected they would have to make, that is, what to do with the excess embryos that they no longer need, ironically finding themselves in

43

this situation not because they did not want a family but specifically because they did.

In addition to their own future use of the embryos, three additional options are currently available: donation to another infertile couple or individual, donation for research (which may be useful in learning more about infertility or other diseases such as Parkinson's or diabetes), or thaw without intent to transfer. Because of the difficulty in making this decision, many progenitors abandon their embryos, leaving them in a perpetual frozen state.

When individuals within a couple disagree in their disposition decisions, courts in the United States have typically favored the right not to procreate over the desire to do so. Signed advance directives regarding embryo disposition are recommended, although not always enforceable. In most states, donation of an embryo to another couple or individual is not addressed by statute. Similarly, there is no common law guidance, as only a few states have enacted legislation dealing with embryo donation.

Although fertilized eggs (ova) have usually been referred to as embryos, this is not scientifically accurate. The fertilized ovum develops into extra-embryonic structures, such as the placenta and amniotic membrane, as well as the embryo proper, and does not become an embryo capable of developing into a single person until the appearance of the *primitive streak*, which first appears at about 14 days after fertilization. At that time twinning is no longer possible, and the cells enter the embryonic period as they begin to differentiate. Thus, the fertilized ovum during the first 14 days of its existence is more accurately referred to as *preembryonic cells* or the *preembryo* (Ethics Committee of the American College of Obstetrics and Gynecology, 1994; Jones & Veeck, 2002). However, since the term *preembryo* is not uniformly accepted within the scientific community (Thorne & Kischer, 2002), the more commonly used term, *embryo*, is used in the remainder of this chapter.

In this chapter, we investigate issues involved in embryo disposition. Embryos can also be analyzed for genetic anomalies using preimplantation genetic diagnosis, which raises additional ethical issues. This is discussed in the final chapter.

MEDICAL BACKGROUND

Cryopreservation (freezing) of high-quality supernumerary embryos is routinely performed in IVF cycles. IVF cycles using cryopreserved embryos are less invasive and do not have to reexpose the female patient to additional ovarian stimulation hormones. This may be much more cost effective for those without insurance, as well, as they will not have to bear the expense of another stimulation and retrieval cycle.

At present, a significant percentage of frozen embryos do not survive the cryopreservation-thawing process (Sathanandan et al., 1991; Smith, Roots, & Dorsett, 2005; Wada et al., 1992). Vitrification (ultrarapid freezing) may increase the survival rates of cryopreserved embryos as well as improve pregnancy rates (Takahashi, Mukaida, Goto, & Oka, 2005; Wennerholm, 2000). Duration of freezing does not appear to adversely affect embryo quality or survival (Machtinger et al., 2002), and births have been reported after at least 12 to 13 years of cryopreservation (Lopez Teijon et al., 2006; Revel et al., 2004). Pregnancy success rates for frozen embryos are typically lower than for fresh embryos, however (Centers for Disease Control and Prevention, 2006).

Research suggests that neither the slow freezing process nor vitrification appears to have detrimental effects on perinatal outcomes or infant morbidity (Bankowski, Lyerly, Faden, & Wallach, 2005; Takahashi et al., 2005; Wennerholm et al., 2009). Looking at postnatal development, children conceived from frozen embryos, compared with naturally conceived children, have been found to have normal intelligence, to have comparable rates of congenital malformations, and to demonstrate no evidence of developmental delay (Olivenness et al., 1996; Sutcliffe et al., 1995; Wennerholm et al., 1998). Although it would appear that cryopreservation of embryos induces no major pathological conditions, further research is needed because studies thus far lack the methodological rigor for definitive conclusions, have only included children until preadolescence, and have had sample sizes too small to detect possible subtle problems (Sutcliffe, 2000).

PSYCHOSOCIAL LITERATURE

Disposition decisions are emotionally challenging for couples who so desperately desire a family, and many avoid making a final determination (Klock, Sheinin, & Kazer, 2001b; McMahon, Gibson, Cohen, Tennant, & Saunders, 2000; Nachtigall, Becker, Friese, Butler, & MacDougall, 2005). The sense of isolation reported in making disposition decisions (Nachtigall et al., 2005) reinforces the importance of guidance for couples in this predicament, as counseling solely at the time of cryopreservation does not adequately address the emotional and practical implications of actually having surplus embryos.

Thaw Without Intent to Transfer

Most couples choose to dispose of their excess embryos, freeze them indefinitely, or abandon them (Bangsboll, Pinborg, Yding, & Nyboe, 2004; Laruelle & Englert, 1995; Lornage, Chorier, Boulien, Mathieu, & Czyba, 1995). It is perhaps surprising that those progenitors who ascribe high importance to the well-being of the embryo, fetus, or future child are more likely to choose one of these three embryo disposition options over donation to another infertile couple or individual (Lyerly et al., 2008). It has been reported that patients often experience feelings of guilt, however, when they choose to discard their excess embryos rather than donate them to either research or other infertile couples or individuals (Laruelle & Englert, 1995).

Donation to Another Infertile Couple or Individual

The first embryo donation resulting in a pregnancy was in 1983 (Trounson, Leeton, Besanko, Wood, & Conti, 1983). Whereas many people endorse the altruistic concept of donation of one's embryos to another infertile couple or individual, few couples actually follow through and donate their embryos to others (Bangsboll et al., 2004; Hammarberg & Tinney, 2006; Hoffman et al., 2003; Newton, McDermid, Tekpetey, & Tummon, 2003; Soderstrom-Anttila, Foudila, Ripatti, & Siegberg, 2001), although some report feeling guilty for this reluctance to help other infertile couples (McMahon & Saunders, 2009). Those who are more comfortable with disclosing personal information and possible future contact with the child, who are allowed to select their recipients or specify recipient characteristics, who believe in the importance of nurture over nature, or who used donor gametes to create their embryos are more likely to donate to another couple or individual (Fuscaldo & Savulescu, 2005; Hammarberg & Tinney, 2006; Laruelle & Englert, 1995; Lyerly et al., 2008; McMahon & Saunders, 2009; Newton et al., 2003). Conversely, couples who focused on the genetic link with the embryo or its symbolic representation of their relationship, felt a responsibility toward their embryos, viewed them as full siblings to their existing children, reported being unable to stop wondering about these "potential" offspring, wished to protect the interests of their potential children, and were uneasy in not being able to have some control over whom they would donate to were reluctant to donate to others and, perhaps surprisingly, more likely to choose disposition options that resulted ultimately in the destruction of the embryo (de Lacey, 2005, 2007; Laruelle & Englert, 1995; McMahon & Saunders, 2009; Nachtigall et al., 2005; Provoost et al., 2009). The couple's view on the moral status of the embryo seemed to play a less important role in their dispositional decisions (Laruelle & Englert, 1995; Lyerly et al., 2006; Provoost et al., 2009).

It has been suggested that gamete donors should be provided the opportunity to make dispositional directives for the embryos formed with their gametes (Adsuar et al., 2005; Lo et al., 2004). Although this might be particularly important in those states with no laws regarding egg or sperm donation, conditional donation may create the potential for discriminatory practices (McMahon & Saunders, 2009). Although the Practice Committee of the American Society for Reproductive Medicine (ASRM) and the Practice Committee of the Society for Reproductive Medicine (2008) both recommend psychological assessment and counseling for embryo donors and recipients, only 28% of clinics require psychological assessment of embryo donors, whereas 64% require psychological screening of recipients (Kingsberg, Applegarth, & Janata, 2000).

Very little research has been conducted on the recipients of donor embryos. However, most recipients studied do want medical information about the donor family (Soderstrom-Anttila et al., 2001). No research has yet been conducted on either the impact of donor anonymity or on disclosure versus nondisclosure of embryo donation on offspring. Because of the increased psychological complexity of this method of family building, it is uncertain if research on offspring of gamete donation is generalizable.

Donation to Research

The percentage of couples expressing willingness to donate their embryos to research varies widely (Bangsboll et al., 2004; Hammarberg & Tinney, 2006; Hoffman et al., 2003; Jain & Missmer, 2008; McMahon et al., 2003). Couples lacking confidence in medical science were reluctant to donate to research (Fuscaldo, Russell, & Gillam, 2007; McMahon et al., 2003; Parry, 2006; Provoost et al., 2009), whereas those attributing high instrumental value to the embryo were more likely to donate their embryos to either science or to another infertile couple (Provoost et al., 2009). Some patients are given inadequate or incorrect information regarding their eligibility to donate their embryos to other couples or for research (Zweifel, Christianson, Jaeger, Olive, & Lindheim, 2007), and it can be difficult to find research institutions accepting embryos. Detailed information, guidance, and an easy pathway to embryo donation are needed to assist couples or individuals who wish to make this disposition decision. Open and directed donation may reduce donors' anxiety, as lack of control over what research would be conducted has been reported as a major deterrent (Fuscaldo et al., 2007; Fuscaldo & Savulescu, 2005; McMahon et al., 2003).

Embryos can be donated for use in many types of research. However, embryonic stem cell research has generated the most interest because it holds enormous potential to treat a host of debilitating diseases, including Parkinson's, Alzheimer's, diabetes, multiple sclerosis, and heart disease. Few other areas of science have aroused so much hope, excitement, and controversy (Chervenak & McCullough, 2008).

Timing of Dispositional Directives and Clinic Policy

Currently, most patients are being asked to make disposition decisions regarding potential excess embryos prior to undergoing their first IVF cycle, as per ASRM guidelines (Practice Committee of the ASRM and the Practice Committee of the Society for Assisted Reproductive Technology [SART], 2006), in an attempt to avoid issues of abandonment and future litigation. Patients are asked to make decisions about embryo disposition under potential conditions such as divorce, death, disagreement, mental incapacity, nonpayment of cryopreservation fees, or the inability of the clinic to contact them in the future. Individuals' initial directives, however, may not match their final disposition decisions (de Lacey, 2005; Klock et al., 2001b; Lornage et al., 1995; Lyerly et al., 2006; Newton et al., 2007), and some find currently available options unacceptable, preferring instead to participate in a ritual disposal ceremony or to thaw and transfer the embryos to the woman at a time when she is unlikely to become pregnant (Lyerly et al., 2008). However, because this latter option entails slight risks, such as the risk of infection, and expenditure of medical resources without adequate benefit, it may not be an ethically sound or medically appropriate course of action. Research on how mental health professionals can facilitate patients' moral reasoning prior to prefreeze decision making would be extremely useful, although the vast majority of individuals, at present, do not seek counseling to help them with this difficult determination (Zweifel et al., 2007).

Because the passage of time and achievement of pregnancy can profoundly affect patients' beliefs about the proper use of their surplus embryos and the importance of genetic lines, prefreeze agreements have been seen by some as an example of *uninformed consent* (Bankowski et al., 2005). After visualizing an embryo and going through the transformative experience of becoming a parent, it appears that embryo donation comes to feel more like child relinquishment than does sperm or oocyte donation (Brakman, 2005; de Lacey, 2005). Couples and individuals need to be informed that they may experience a change in their disposition decisions once they become parents and be encouraged to fulfill their obligation to maintain contact with the IVF clinic (Pennings, 2000b). Thus, most researchers in the field have recommended obtaining patient directives at two separate times, that is, at prefreeze as a tool to help couples reflect on the possible consequences of cryopreservation of preembros and immediately prior to execution of the directive (Bankowski et al., 2005; de Lacey, 2005; Klock et al., 2001b; Lyerly et al., 2006) with clinics accepting advance directives as binding only when absolutely necessary (i.e., unable to contact patients, patients unable to agree, or deceased).

There appears to be no uniform policy regarding either embryo donation or embryo disposal in the United States (Gurmankin, Sisti, & Caplan, 2004;

Kingsberg et al., 2000). Ninety-five percent of clinics report attempting to contact couples, and close to 80% of clinics require dispositional directives from both members of the couple creating the embryos prior to destruction of the embryos. Of these, 66% did not proceed with disposal if they were unable to reach the couple, thus suggesting that IVF clinic personnel are reluctant to destroy embryos without obtaining a reconsent (Gurmankin et al., 2004).

Advantages and Disadvantages of Embryo Disposition Options

Choosing a final destiny for frozen unused embryos is an enormously challenging and complex process for couples and individuals (de Lacey, 2007; Nachtigall et al., 2005). Embryo donation to other couples offers an opportunity to help other infertile couples or individuals, but donors must carefully assess their comfort level in having full genetic siblings to their own children being raised by parents with whom, in most cases, they are unfamiliar. Embryo donation for research can also be experienced as altruistic, as the eventual results may benefit others experiencing infertility as well as other diseases.

Embryo donation offers numerous advantages to recipients (e.g., control over the prenatal environment; ability to experience pregnancy, birth, nursing, and psychological bonding during pregnancy; lower costs than an entire cycle of IVF; and the possibility for an older woman to become a mother with embryos created by a younger woman). However, recipients must be made aware of the risks and disadvantages, as well. Some of the frozen embryos are unlikely to survive thawing and they yield lower pregnancy rates than fresh embryos. The couple who created these embryos may have experienced an impairment of their fertility, and the best embryos may have already been used. The child resulting from donated embryos will have no genetic connection to the recipient parents but in all likelihood will have full genetic siblings living in another family. This last issue results in greater ethical complexity with embryo donation than with oocyte or sperm donation.

BIOETHICAL PERSPECTIVES

Ethical issues abound in discussions about the embryo. For example, what is the moral and legal status of an embryo? Should an embryo be treated as a person, with implications consistent with Kant's categorical imperative as suggested in the quote at the beginning of this chapter? Is it ethical to allow embryos to be destroyed? What should be done with extra embryos, particularly if progenitors disagree? What rights do individuals have to select specific embryos for transfer and deselect (i.e., specifically choose not to transfer) others? What constitutes a *serious* genetic anomaly within an embryo meriting analysis? Should a line be drawn, and who shall decide? Do parents and/or doctors have a moral responsibility to select embryos with the best prospect of the highest quality of life (Savulescu, 1999, 2001)?

There are three main views on the moral status of an embryo:

- Embryos are persons from the moment of conception, entitled to full moral status from the time of fertilization. Those who hold this belief generally oppose embryo destruction as well as research on embryos that will lead to their destruction. To add to the controversy, there are even differences in beliefs as to when conception is deemed to have occurred, as, in contrast to the view of the Catholic Church that conception occurs at the moment of fertilization, the American Medical Association states that conception does not begin until implantation (American Medical Association House of Delegates, 2004).
- Embryos have no greater moral status than any other human tissue (e.g., blood, cornea).
- Embryos are not persons but deserve a special respect greater than that given to other bodily tissues because they have the potential to cause the development of a person and may be regarded by many as symbolic of human life. Individuals who hold this final view believe the embryo has some moral value from fertilization but less than a born human being and gradually acquires full moral status during development.

Yet, there is no general agreement as to when the embryo or fetus acquires full moral status (Steinbock, 1992).

Donating embryos for research or thawing without intent to transfer raises the two fundamental questions of when life begins and whether an embryo should have all the rights and privileges afforded to humans. When is it ethical to perform research on the excess embryos that remain from IVF? Is it ethical to create embryos specifically for research or to obtain stem cells, which results in the destruction of the embryo in the process? Do the potential therapeutic benefits outweigh the anticipated harms? Are there alternatives available yielding similar benefits at lower costs? It is important to note that it has been estimated that 50% to 80% of cryopreserved embryos, many of them low-grade, would never implant (Larsen, 1997; Sadler, 1995). This puts the number of embryos destroyed during the research process in a somewhat different perspective especially because stem cells could be harvested even from poor quality embryos (Schwartz & Rae, 2006).

Most countries do limit research on extracorporeal embryos to within the period of 14 days after initial cell division. In the United States, federal funding for laboratories developing new stem cell lines using leftover IVF embryos was banned in 2001, limiting the number of laboratories that could accept human embryos for research. At the time of this writing (2010), this policy has been reversed by the current governmental administration.

Who should have dispositional authority over embryos being used for research purposes—the individuals furnishing the gametes, the fertility doctor, the stem cell researcher, the government, or bioethicists (Robertson, 2001)? According to guidelines published by the National Academy of Sciences, all progenitors, including donors, should consent to the research use of any resulting embryos (National Academy of Sciences, Committee on Guidelines for Human Embryonic Stem Cell Research, National Research Council, 2005). Yet, these guidelines are merely recommendations and do not have the force of law.

Welfare of the Child

Embryo donation redefines the traditional relationship of a child and two parents because there is no genetic link between the embryo and future rearing parents, although there is a gestational link, one of several distinguishing characteristics from adoption. It has been suggested that being a child created by embryo donation may be preferable to postnatal adoption to both intended parents and offspring, even though there are no shared genes between the rearing parents and the child in either case. This may reflect the societal belief in an association between gestation and emotional attachment because in embryo donation the rearing mother gestates the pregnancy and the rearing father has committed to the birth of the child even before implantation (Robertson, 1995).

Should genetic disclosure to recipient couples and children be required? Do offspring have a right to access their genetic records and to know of the existence of any full siblings from the same genetic parents? Is this or should this be different than for half-siblings? Will this knowledge of their origins be informative and enlightening or confusing to the child? If parents choose to disclose to their children created through embryo donation, will they have enough information to impart, especially in case of a medical problem? Although researchers do not have the answers to all of these questions, information gleaned from oocyte and sperm donation offspring suggests that these offspring also may want this information (see Chapter 8, this volume), implying that keeping donor information in a voluntary registry for the offspring of embryo donation would best balance the needs and interests of all stakeholders involved.

Donor Welfare

In advance of consenting to donate embryos, counseling should be offered to help individuals consider potential future issues (e.g., not knowing how their genetic child might be raised, small risk of consanguinity).

Other issues are raised by the possibility of creating embryos expressly for the purpose of research. Is it ethical to put a woman through the risks of ovarian stimulation solely for the purpose of producing multiple oocytes that will be used to create embryos for research and then destroyed? Is it paternalistic to prevent adult women from consenting to this? Fewer concerns are raised by asking men to produce a semen sample for this same purpose as the risks are minimal or nonexistent. Certainly, if compensation is involved, the ethical issues of payment for body parts and potential coercion of disadvantaged women are raised. However, it is not uncommon to pay research participants for their participation and inconvenience. In fact, in June 2009, New York became the first state to allow payment to women who provide eggs for research (Empire State Stem Cell Board, 2009), with a bioethicist suggesting that it is fair and just to compensate women donating their eggs for either reproduction or research equally (Steinbock, 2009).

Informed Consent

Consent must be voluntary, comprehended, and informed. Embryo donation should be free of any pressure to donate so that donors will not feel coerced and potentially regretful later. It has been suggested that the physician responsible for treating the couple's or individual's infertility should not be the same one seeking to acquire embryos for research so as to reduce the possibility of conflict of interest (Heng, 2006; Parry, 2006). Counseling of both donors and recipients regarding the psychological, social, medical, ethical, and legal aspects of embryo donation is critical (Robertson, 1995). Recipient couples need to realize that they, in all likelihood, will not have the social support that adoptive parents enjoy. In addition, the narrative that they will need to tell their child(ren) is more complicated than had they used oocyte or sperm donation in which a genetic connection to one parent would be sustained.

Advance directives obtained by IVF centers are regarded as conditional, taking effect only if patients are unable to take part in decision making at the time an action is to be taken (Pennings, 2000b, 2002). Time is needed between the initial decision to create embryos and the decision to donate excess embryos to reduce the possibility of coercion, allow patients to reappraise their current situation and decision regarding supernumerary embryos, and provide current voluntary informed consent. Patients should also be reminded of all embryo disposition options available to them at the time of their final disposition directive and the conditions they may or may not set regarding how their donated embryos are to be used (Robertson, 1995). What happens, however, if a member of a couple changes his or her mind, cannot agree, or cannot be contacted? No universal agreement has yet been reached under these circumstances, with opinions varying (Holm, 2007; Pennings, 2000b; Robertson, 1995; Waldman, 2004).

Compensation, Commodification, and Coercion

Concern that compensation of embryo donors would result in the commodification of human life has been voiced. Currently, the consensus is that it is not acceptable to pay the donor couple for the embryo itself as this might be construed as undue influence, although reimbursement of specific donor expenses is acceptable (Practice Committee of the ASRM and the Practice Committee of the SART, 2008). This is consistent with other medical policies forbidding payment for babies or organs. Selection of specific embryos by the recipients may also encourage a consumerist approach to having children, especially if the choices being made are based on criteria of excellence. To circumvent this, it may be preferable that donors be the ones selecting the recipients of their embryos.

Embryo sharing, in which the cost of the donor's treatment is offset by the recipients in exchange for acquisition of embryos, has been suggested to reduce the costs of treatment. However, this can appear to be a form of sale of embryos, that is, commodification. In addition, it may undermine obtaining truly voluntary informed consent as the strong desire to have children may overshadow the implications of embryo donation for both the donors and the recipients. The donors may later have regrets, particularly if their own IVF cycles do not result in the birth of a child to them. For all of these reasons, we do not recommend embryo sharing.

Is It Embryo Donation or Embryo Adoption?

Embryo donation, viewed by many as a medical procedure, involves giving away a potential child wherein donors legally relinquish all parental rights and responsibilities after embryo transfer. The recipients must be medically suitable to carry a pregnancy, but the embryo has no specific rights or needs regarding parental selection because the embryo does not yet exist as a person, and thus the state has no responsibility with regard to that embryo as it would an actual child. Adoption, on the other hand, involves relinquishing physical and decisional custody of a born child, a being who already exists and whose needs must be considered when selecting appropriate parents. Widdows and MacCallum (2002) concluded that because of significant differences between embryo donation and adoption, parenting criteria should not be the same; that is, there should be more stringent criteria to adopt a child because the state has some responsibility to ensure the safety and welfare of a child as opposed to an embryo.

Use of the word *adoption* for embryos implies that the cryopreserved embryo is the equivalent of a child and has both moral and legal rights. This position is at odds with policies that allow donation for research or discarding of embryos. We fear that the word *adoption* is being used to confer personhood on embryos as a backdoor antichoice, antiabortion tactic.

EXISTING LAWS, POLICIES, AND LEGISLATION

The legal issues with regard to embryos are focused primarily in three areas: the legal status of the embryo, disposition of embryos particularly when a dispute exists between the progenitors, and use of embryos for research.

What is the legal status of the embryo? This is a question that continues to be debated and may be answered differently from a medical, legal, and/or cultural perspective. The U.S. Supreme Court has selected viability as the marker after which societal protection of the fetus is considered required (*Roe v. Wade*, 1973), and as science advances, the point of viability will shift as well. In the United States, the embryo, in most instances, does not have the same rights and protections under the Constitution as do live born children and adults. There are laws such as the federal Unborn Victims of Violence Act (2009) and the State Children's Health Insurance Program (SCHIP; 2002) in which federal laws actually define the covered *child* as existing from the moment of conception. By contrast, no laws and most legal cases refuse to define embryos as property either.

The law, by and large, regards embryos as falling somewhere between person and property and entitled to some heightened level of respect. In one of the earliest cases to consider the status of the embryo, *Del Zio v. Columbia Presbyterian Hospital* (1978), the chairman of the department of obstetrics and gynecology removed and destroyed a couple's stored embryo without their consent. The couple filed suit against the chairman and the hospital, claiming loss of property and intentional infliction of emotional distress. The court awarded the wife $50,000 in damages for emotional distress but refused the property claim made by the couple. The outcome of this case demonstrates a court's reluctance to consider embryos as property and should be recognized as having great significance.

This point was further reiterated in *Davis v. Davis* (1992), the first in a series of cases addressing dispositional disputes between progenitors of the embryos leaving open the question of whether advance directives issued prior to the creation of embryos would or should be enforceable if a later dispute arose. According to *Davis v. Davis*, Tennessee's highest court concluded that embryos are neither persons nor property but occupy an "interim category, entitling them to special respect because of their potential for human life" (*Davis v. Davis*, 1992, p. 597).

The New York case of *Kass v. Kass* (1998) addressed a dispositional dispute between the progenitors of the embryos. The issue was whether advance directives issued prior to the creation of embryos would or should be enforceable if a later dispute arose. The court determined that the couple's advance directive should prevail. However, in subsequent cases, courts around the country have generally found that the person seeking to avoid procreation should prevail. This in no way should detract from the importance of advance directives as a means to inform couples of their options and encourage them to think about future issues and document their considerations, although some process of reconsent may be beneficial for couples, clinics, and society.

Research has been another area rife with controversy, as discussed previously. Since the 1970s, long before the potential of stem cell research, a ban existed on federal funding for embryo research. During the Clinton administration, consideration of funding for such research was revisited and the conclusion was reached that although extraction of stem cells was not amenable to federal funding, research using previously extracted stem cells would be eligible for federal funds. No funds were ever awarded, however, because the administration changed and in his first national address on August 9, 2001, former President George W. Bush announced his plan to limit federal funds to the then existing 60 stem cell lines. These policies have been reversed under the current administration of President Barack Obama, thus allowing for federal funding of stem cell research, including research on cells derived from previously created embryos slated for destruction.

Even when federally prohibited under the Bush administration, states such as California, Illinois, and Connecticut took the initiative by enacting legislation to approve state funding for stem cell research. In contrast, other states, such as South Dakota enacted legislation that would make it a misdemeanor to "sell or transfer a human embryo with the knowledge that the embryo will be subjected to nontherapeutic research" (S. D. Codified Laws § 34-14-17, 2008, Medical Research).

CLINICAL VIGNETTE

Anita and Ralph created 15 embryos when they were ages 34 and 37, respectively. After two unsuccessful IVF attempts, seven embryos remain. In their prefreeze disposition, Anita and Ralph agreed that in case of divorce, death of either partner, disagreement between partners, or inability of the clinic to contact them, the embryos should be destroyed. Now, 8 years after creating their embryos, Anita and Ralph have divorced. In addition, in the interim, Anita has undergone chemotherapy and radiation for ovarian cancer, which has rendered her sterile. Now, cancer-free at age 42, these embryos are her only chance for a pregnancy with her own eggs. Ralph does not want the embryos used because he does not want to parent a child with Anita. The clinic director asks the mental health professional to help the couple resolve this dilemma.

Ethical Dilemmas in the Context of Professional Guidelines

The major question raised in the case of Anita and Ralph is whether advance directives are binding, particularly when there are tensions and a current disagreement between the individuals who created the embryos and the parties' circumstances have changed dramatically. Can individuals truly give informed consent regarding embryo disposition options prior to initially freezing their embryos, especially when the possibility of unpredictable life-changing circumstances exists?

As indicated in the American Psychological Association's (2002) "Ethical Principles of Psychologists and Code of Conduct," psychologists are to be guided and inspired by the ethical principles of beneficence and nonmaleficence, fidelity and responsibility, integrity, justice, and respect for people's rights and dignity (Principles A–E). Although, in fairness to Anita, mental health professionals may wish to allow her to have access to embryos containing her eggs, the rights of her ex-husband must also be given equal and due respect. The American Psychological Association's Standard 3.11 (Psychological Services Delivered to or Through Organizations) may also come into play should the decision of the infertility clinic staff differ from that of the embedded mental health professional.

The Practice Committee of the ASRM and the Practice Committee of the SART (2006) and the Ethics Committee of the ASRM (2009b) recommend that individuals and couples be provided full information regarding disposition options for their excess embryos, which is necessary for voluntary informed consent. This would include being informed of the risks and benefits of each option, the psychological and ethical issues, and being counseled that there will be the opportunity to reevaluate disposition decisions after the conclusion of reproductive attempts. As was done in the case of Anita and Ralph, advance disposition directives should be obtained for the following contingencies: death of one or both partners, divorce or dissolution of the partnership, mental incompetence, loss of contact with gamete providers, disagreement between partners, and arrears in paying storage fees.

Couples may jointly agree to alter their advance disposition directives at a later time and submit new written directives to the assisted reproductive technology program. However, there is no universal agreement about what an IVF center should do regarding disposition of embryos if members of a couple do not agree jointly either to change their decision or follow the original disposition decision.

Practical Considerations

As previously mentioned, we know from research and clinical experience that patients often change their minds from prefreeze to postfamily completion about what they wish to do with their excess embryos. Some couples may even agree to donate their embryos to avoid paying for freezing and then request that their embryos be returned to them if they did not become pregnant through the IVF cycle.

Even if this couple could agree that Ralph would have no responsibilities, financial or otherwise, for any children created through transfer of the embryos under discussion and each party's competing reproductive interests could be addressed, an agreement stipulating that Anita could have the embryos transferred to her may be difficult to accomplish legally as in all states the right to child support belongs to the child and not to Anita.

Balancing the Multiple Perspectives

Society has an interest in children being born with clear designation regarding who will be responsible for them. If Anita experiences a relapse of her cancer and Ralph has no parental rights or responsibilities, the child might become a ward of the state. This is a concern to society because the state then becomes responsible for the child.

The Clinician or Fertility Clinic

Once Anita contacted the IVF program to use her stored embryos, the clinic should approach Ralph to see if he is willing to allow Anita to transfer their excess embryos despite their divorce in light of the fact that Anita has undergone treatment for cancer. The physician would need to assess Anita's current health status as it relates to her undergoing a pregnancy.

It has been suggested that advance directives be adhered to only if the clinic has made a concerted effort to contact the couple and was unable to do so (Pennings, 2002). Yet, in this case, the possibility of one partner no longer being able to create embryos with her own gametes had not been anticipated. What if Ralph still wants to dispose of the embryos? Whose directive or which directive takes precedence? The program may have the ability to thaw and discard excess embryos, per the original disposition agreement, if Anita and Ralph cannot agree. However, they would probably be reluctant to do so without both parties agreeing to this decision, and the program would not have the legal right to offer a transfer of the embryos to Anita without the agreement of her ex-husband, despite the extenuating circumstances.

The Prospective Parent

In the present case, unforeseen circumstances have occurred, which have caused Anita to reconsider the original prefreeze disposition option. It is unclear from the presentation of the scenario whether Ralph would be willing to allow the cryopreserved embryos to be transferred to Anita at this time as this is her only opportunity to have a child with her own oocytes. Who has the right to make the decision about how the remaining embryos will be used? Does Anita have priority in this scenario both because of the woman's greater contribution to the IVF process and because this is her only chance to have a child who is genetically related to her? Should the changes in Anita's life circumstances allow her to render her advance directive null and void? Does Ralph have priority because he does not wish to have children born of these embryos, which were created with his gametes, and wishes, instead, to adhere to his and Anita's original embryo disposition agreement? Should Anita and Ralph's prefreeze disposition directive be held binding if Anita and Ralph cannot agree to any changes? Where does one individual's right to avoid unwanted parenthood end and another individual's right to bear their genetic child begin?

The Potential Child

There are issues involved regarding the potential child who may be created if Anita is allowed to transfer the remaining embryos. Is it fair to allow a child to be born to a single parent who has had cancer? That may depend on Anita's current health and prognosis. In addition, is it fair to allow a child to be born when his or her genetic father did not want him or her to be born and may agree to the child's creation only if he has no involvement with or responsibilities toward that child? However, Ralph may be unable to avoid his legal—including financial—obligations to a child created from his gametes. Because many children born to single mothers who strongly desire their birth seem to fare well despite having uninvolved or unknown fathers (see Chapter 8, this volume), this concern seems of less merit.

CONCLUSION

The magnitude of decisions regarding surplus embryos should be stressed to couples undergoing IVF. Mental health professionals have not frequently been called on to resolve differences between partners or former partners in embryo disposition decisions. However, mental health professionals may be able to help couples clarify their thoughts and feelings about excess embryos and come to a final, mutual agreement regarding disposition of their excess embryos, thus circumventing involvement of the legal system.

Prior to making prefreeze decisions, intended parents should be made aware that those with excess embryos often change their perspectives as they mature. They should be given the choice for disposition options both before the embryos are cryopreserved, in case they are unavailable for recontact by the IVF program, and postembryo creation after they have completed their family. Although ASRM guidelines (Practice Committee of the ASRM and the Practice Committee of the SART, 2006) suggest that prefreeze decisions could be adhered to if couples are unable to agree or the clinic, following a diligent effort, is unable to recontact them after they have completed their family, experience suggests that this is rarely done. Annual reconsent regarding embryo disposition decisions when storage fees are collected may help to preclude a situation such as the one illustrated in the vignette.

In the present clinical dilemma, the mental health professional may be asked to meet with Ralph, with Anita's consent, to explain the current circumstances and determine his wishes. Ralph would be helped to clarify his feelings about the importance of nurture and nature, his concerns about the welfare of any potential children created through the use of these embryos and raised by Anita, his possible legal and financial responsibilities for the child, and his current feelings about destruction of the remaining embryos. In a separate meeting, Anita, too, would be assisted to think through her feelings about these issues as well as the option of adoption as a single parent. Documentation of these meetings is important. If Ralph is unwilling to agree to Anita's request, past legal precedent suggests that if this entered the legal system, the courts would likely decide that the desire not to become a parent supersedes the desire to become a parent in this type of situation. However, the fact that this would be Anita's only opportunity to reproduce with her own gametes may be a fact that has not been addressed in prior cases, except *in dicta*, that is, in the opinions of the judge that do not embody the resolution or determination of the court, in the New York case of *Kass v. Kass* (1998). The clinic would probably be required, however, to follow the prefreeze agreement of this couple and discard the excess embryos (Ethics Committee of the ASRM, 2004b; Robertson, 2001) but may wait for a court order before pursuing this.

While emotions, perspectives, and life circumstances certainly can change for those individuals contributing to the creation of embryos, it is preferable to minimize the need for state intrusion into private reproductive choices. If Anita and Ralph could not come to a mutual agreement, at present, it is likely that the right not to procreate will trump the right to procreate, even in situations that are heartbreaking.

4

MULTIFETAL PREGNANCIES

Morality, like art, means drawing a line someplace.
—Oscar Wilde, *The Picture of Dorian Gray*

An epidemic of multifetal pregnancies has taken place in industrialized nations within the past few decades as a result of the increased availability and success of assisted reproductive technology (ART). The Centers for Disease Control and Prevention (2007) reported that close to one third of in vitro fertilization (IVF) births in the United States resulted in multiple births, compared with 3% in the overall population. Human ovulation is designed to ensure singleton gestation, and the human uterus, sometimes humorously referred to as an SRO (single room occupancy), clearly is not designed to carry a high number of multiple fetuses to term. Iatrogenic multifetal pregnancies caused by the superovulation induction common with ART can, in fact, be considered an adverse outcome from the perspective of both maternal and fetal health.

Higher order multifetal pregnancies most commonly result from the administration of fertility drugs and inseminations to women. No one can predict just how many eggs will become fertilized once sperm is introduced into the uterus. Canceling an intrauterine insemination cycle during which a woman has produced more than two or three oocytes or converting the cycle to an IVF cycle and limiting the number of embryos transferred to a woman during IVF can successfully reduce the likelihood of a multifetal pregnancy. In the United States, the decision regarding the number of embryos transferred is not legislated and, in general, is left to the individual physician and program. The American Society for Reproductive Medicine (ASRM) does, however, suggest age and prognosis-dependent guidelines for limiting the number of embryos to transfer (Practice Committee of the Society for Assisted Reproductive Technology [SART] and the Practice Committee of the ASRM, 2008). Nevertheless, physicians may sometimes feel pressure from their patients as well as from their own desire to increase the success rates of their program to attract future patients because as the number of embryos transferred increases, ART programs' success rates may increase as well. However, so does the risk of multifetal pregnancies (P. M. Martin & Welch, 1998).

Should multifetal pregnancies be discouraged? If there is either patient or physician opposition to transferring fewer embryos to reduce the possibility of a multifetal pregnancy, what should the role of the mental health professional be?

MEDICAL BACKGROUND

A multifetal pregnancy is often desired by intended parents as a way to complete their family through undergoing only a single IVF cycle, which saves women from additional exposure to ovarian stimulant drugs and the surgical removal of oocytes and also saves money if the couple or individual lacks insurance coverage for infertility treatment. The potential risks to both the health of the mother and the resulting offspring are often overlooked, however.

Risks to Maternal Health

A multifetal gestation increases maternal risk throughout the pregnancy, labor, and delivery (Mackay, Berg, King, Duran, & Chang, 2006). Increased risks include pregnancy-induced hypertension (Day, Barton, O'Brien, Istwan, & Sibai, 2005; Hernandez-Diaz, Werler, & Mitchell, 2007; Luke & Brown, 2008; Sibai et al., 2000), preeclampsia (a toxemia of late pregnancy that is potentially life threatening; Santema, Koppelaar, & Wallenburg, 1995; Senat, Ancel, Bouvier-Colle, & Brerat, 1998), and gestational diabetes (Adler-Levy, Lunenfeld, & Levy, 2007; Sibai et al., 2000; Wen, Demissie, Yang, & Walker, 2004). Although several recent studies have found no significant differences in these maternal complications when comparing assisted conception to spontaneously conceived (SC) twin pregnancies, the risks do remain elevated in multifetal pregnancies (Huang et al., 2006; Luke et al., 2004).

Women carrying multiple fetuses have a 2 to 3 times higher rate of caesarean section delivery than women carrying singletons, which carries with it higher risks of morbidity and mortality for women (Adler-Levy et al., 2007; Luke & Brown, 2008; Simoes, Kunz, Bosing-Schwenkglenks, & Schmahl, 2005).

The maternal death rate associated with caesarean section is 2 to 4 times higher than with vaginal deliveries (Deneux-Tharaux, Carmona, Bouvier-Colle, & Breart, 2006), although it must be kept in mind that the risk of caesarean delivery is higher among all IVF pregnancies compared with SC pregnancies (Huang et al., 2006; Tan et al., 1992).

Women carrying multiple fetuses also may require extensive time on bed rest, and are sometimes unable to get up other than to void and shower. This can result in health risks for the woman that may endure beyond the pregnancy, such as muscle atrophy. Being restricted to bed rest can cause economic consequences if the woman must miss work or is unable to care for other older children. In addition, it may put stress on the marital relationship as husbands may resent having to both financially support the family as well as to take on the additional household responsibilities that their wives assumed prior to bed rest.

All of the previously stated risks may appear magnified when a couple is asking a surrogate or gestational carrier to bear a multifetal pregnancy for them as she is being asked to accept these additional risks to her health. In their quest to have children, patients, already minimizing the potential risks to their children and themselves, are often insensitive to the ramifications for the gestational carrier and her family.

Multiple gestations are also common in older women conceiving through egg donation (Paulson et al., 2002; Sauer, Paulson, & Lobo, 1992, 1996). There has been a tenfold increase in triplets born to 35–44-year-old women and a fiftyfold increase to women over age 44 from 1971 to 1998 (Aliyu, Salihu, Blankson, Alexander, & Keith, 2004; Kiely & Kiely, 2001). The maternal health risks of a multifetal pregnancy remain high for women of advanced maternal age (at or above age 40) conceiving by ovum donation as well (Simchen, Shulman, Wiser, Zilberberg, & Schiff, 2009).

Risks to the Health of Potential Children

One of the concerns for a multifetal pregnancy is premature birth, commonly defined as delivery before the 37th week of pregnancy. As the average gestational age for a singleton pregnancy is 40 weeks, an accepted clinical axiom for multifetal pregnancies is that gestational age at delivery is approximately 3 weeks less for every additional fetus, that is, 37 weeks for twins, 34 weeks for triplets, and 31 weeks for quadruplets. Twins, in general, have a ninefold increased risk of low birth weight (below 2,500 g) compared with singletons (Alexander, Hammond, & Steinkampf, 1995). Results have been conflicting in comparing ART twins with SC twins, with some studies reporting that ART twins have similar or better outcomes than SC twins (Boulet et al., 2008; Putterman, Figueroa, Garry, & Maulik, 2003), with even lower rates of perinatal mortality (Helmerhorst, Perquin, Donker, & Keirse, 2004), whereas other studies have reported that ART twins have greater risks of preterm birth, low birth weight, death, admissions to a neonatal intensive care unit, and hospital admissions in the first several years of life than SC twins (Daskalakis, Anastasakis, Papantoniou, Mesogitis, & Antsaklis, 2009; Hansen et al., 2009). However, ART twin pregnancies do, in general, have higher risks than ART singletons, including higher risks of preterm birth, stillbirth, caesarean section, neonatal intensive care unit admittance, total malformations (although not major malformations), and cerebral palsy (Pinborg, Loft, Rasmussen, et al., 2004; Stromberg et al., 2002). Mean gestational age at delivery and birth weight are also lower for ovum donation twins gestated by women over age 40 than for SC twins (Simchen et al., 2009).

In triplets, the incidence of low birth weight has been estimated to be approximately 91% and that of very low birth weight (below 1,500 g), almost 34% (Luke & Keith, 1992). Triplets also experience higher infant mortality rates, more preterm labor, premature birth, lower gestational age, higher rates of severe handicaps, longer hospital stays, and lower Apgar scores (which assess skin color, heart rate, reflex irritability, muscle tone, and respiration at birth; Luke, Brown, Hediger, Misiunas, & Anderson, 2006; Ziadeh, 2000). However, the average birth weight is lower (by approximately 480 g) and the gestational age shorter (by 1 week) for babies of a multifetal pregnancy following ART than matched controls conceived spontaneously (Glazebrook, Sheard, Cox, Oates, & Ndukwe, 2004; Tallo, Vehr, Oh, Rubin, & Haning, Jr., 1995).

In the United States, there has been an 8% increased risk of cerebral palsy in children born after IVF, attributable primarily to the rise in multiple births (Stromberg et al., 2002), with a lower gestational age highly associated with a greater risk (Yokoyama, Shimizu, & Hayakawa, 1995). In addition, twins are 4 times more likely to die within the first month of life than singletons, and triplets are 10 times more likely to die in this time period (Martin & Park, 1999). Multiples may also experience increased risks of congenital anomalies and birth defects compared with singletons (Glinianaia, Rankin, & Wright, 2008; Y. Tang et al., 2006).

A further area of interest regarding risks is the impact of both spontaneous reduction and multifetal pregnancy reduction (MFPR) on the remaining fetuses. If a woman is carrying a higher order multifetal pregnancy, MFPR is often recommended. Performed late in the first trimester of pregnancy, the hope is that MFPR will lower risks to the remaining fetuses by reducing the frequency of preterm birth and neonatal morbidity and mortality. There appears to be consensus on the decision to reduce pregnancies of four or more fetuses. Although the benefit of reducing triplets to twins may exceed the risks involved in the procedure and outcome parameters tend to be improved in the twin gestation in comparison with the triplet pregnancy (Lipitz et al., 1996), not all studies find clear obstetric benefit (Cheang et al., 2007; Papageorghiou, Avgidou, Basoulas, Sebire, & Nicolaides, 2006). Some studies have found an increased risk of preterm labor and lower gestational age when twins reduced from triplets are compared with nonreduced twins (Leondires, Ernst, Miller, & Scott, 2000; Luke et al., 2004; Silver et al., 1997). However, other studies have found that twins reduced from an original triplet pregnancy have lowered risks of prematurity, low and very low birth weight, neonatal morbidity, and fewer pregnancy complications, although gestational age at delivery appears to be inversely correlated with the starting number of fetuses (Antsaklis et al., 2004; Boulot et al., 2000; Dodd & Crowther, 2004; Luke et al., 2004; Papageorghiou et al., 2006). Thus, the decision to reduce a triplet pregnancy remains controversial. Additionally, there are inherent medical risks to the remaining embryos after MFPR as approximately 8% of procedures lead to spontaneous abortion of all fetuses for triplet or quadruplet pregnancies, and this figure rises to 14%–23% when it is applied to sextuplets or more (Coffler, Kol, Drugan, & Itskovitz-Eldor, 1999; Evans et al., 1996; Timor-Tritsch, Bashiri, Monteagudo, Rebarber, & Arslan, 2004).

In every case of a multiple gestation, there is the possibility of a spontaneous loss of one or more of the fetuses. A Danish study estimated that one in 10 IVF singleton pregnancies originates from a twin gestation in which one of the twins vanishes early in the pregnancy. In a comparison of a group of IVF with intracytoplasmic sperm injection (ICSI) singleton survivors of a vanishing cotwin to IVF/ICSI twins and IVF/ICSI singletons, no excess risk of neurological sequelae was found when comparing the two groups of singletons (Pinborg, Lidegaard, la Cour Freiesleben, & Andersen, 2005), although those surviving a vanishing cotwin have been found to demonstrate an increased risk of premature delivery, small size for gestational age, low and very low birth weight (Luke et al., 2009a; Pinborg, Lidegaard, la Cour Freiesleben, & Andersen, 2007; Shebl, Ebner, Sommergruber, Sir, & Tews, 2008; Spandorfer, Davis, & Rosenwaks, 2007), and cerebral palsy (Pharoah & Adi, 2000; Pinborg et al., 2005). Live-born twins who survived early fetal loss in an ART pregnancy (i.e., more than two fetal heartbeats visualized on early ultrasound) also have been found to have significantly higher risks of preterm birth and low birth weight (Luke et al., 2009b). To ensure that consent is informed, prospective parents should be educated about these possibilities if more than one embryo is being transferred during an IVF cycle.

In the United States, voluntary professional guidelines recommending the transfer of fewer embryos have been associated with reductions in the number of embryos being transferred and a reduction in high-order multiple pregnancies (Stern et al., 2007), but it has been difficult to completely eliminate multiple births because of currently inadequate methods of embryo selection as well as both social and economic issues that pressure patients and physicians to transfer multiple embryos. However, when used under appropriate circumstances (i.e., considering patient age and the grade of the embryos), elective single-embryo transfer has been found to reduce the rate of ART twin pregnancies to approximately 5% and triplets to fewer than 1% (Neubourg et al., 2006; Strandell, Bergh, & Lundin, 2000; Tiitinen, Unkila-Kallio, Halttunen, & Hyden-Granskog, 2003) often without reducing pregnancy rates (Criniti et al., 2005; Fiddelers et al., 2006; Gleicher & Barad, 2006; Styer, Wright, Wolkovich, Veiga, & Toth, 2008).

PSYCHOSOCIAL LITERATURE

Although announcement of a multifetal pregnancy is often accompanied by great excitement on the part of parents who have experienced infertility, how do families with multiples actually cope in the long run, especially after having already possibly depleted their emotional and financial resources from the experience of infertility? What is the reality for the family as well as the children who will have to share parental attention, stimulation, and love with another person or persons of their same age? In addition, how do other children already in the family fare and how do the increased caregiving responsibilities impact on the family, especially if the children have special needs?

Impact on Families

The intense desire for children and the overwhelming fear of treatment failure may result in infertile couples and individuals overlooking, minimizing, or denying the increased medical risks of a multifetal gestation (Lacey, Davies, Homan, Briggs, & Norman, 2007). When given a choice between having one or two embryos transferred, Swedish patients who were younger, had a previous childbirth, had spare embryos to freeze, and were more worried about having twins were more likely to choose one embryo, whereas those having had previous IVF failure and who believed they had a higher chance of pregnancy if multiple embryos were transferred chose to transfer two (Blennborn, Nilsson, Hillervik, & Hellberg, 2005). Infertile individuals have been found to have a rather positive attitude toward the possibility of a multiple birth over a singleton pregnancy, however, with the preference for multiples increasing with increasing parental age (Gleicher et al., 1995; Hojgaard, Ottosen, Kesmodel, & Ingerslev, 2007; Ryan, Zhang, Dokras, Syrop, & Van Voorhis, 2004). Yet, approximately half of the infertile women in these studies were not fully aware of the increased risks of infant mortality and cerebral palsy in twin pregnancies. Lack of insurance coverage for fertility treatment may also induce people to try to complete their family in the fewest number of very expensive IVF cycles possible, in effect, attempting to get "the most bang for the buck" and ignoring the risks inherent in a multiple pregnancy (Reynolds, Schieve, Jeng, & Peterson, 2003). Yet, many patients who are given information about the problems with multiple births remain hopeful that they will conceive a higher order pregnancy.

The majority of controlled studies of IVF twins have found that mothers of both infants and preschoolers report higher levels of parenting stress and depression than mothers of singletons (Ellison & Hall, 2003; Glazebrook et al., 2004; Luke et al., 2006; Olivennes, Golombok, Ramogida, Rust, & the Follow-up Team, 2005; Pinborg, Loft, Schmidt, & Nyboe Andersen, 2003) and were more frequently on sick leave from work or hospitalized during pregnancy than IVF singleton or non-IVF twin mothers (Pinborg, Loft, Schmidt, Langhoff-Roos, & Andersen, 2004). Only approximately one quarter of those mothers reporting moderate to severe depressive symptoms at 9 months after delivery of a twin, triplet, or higher order multifetal pregnancy, however, reported talking about the emotional or psychological problems that they were experiencing with either a medical provider or a mental health professional (Choi, Bishai, & Minkovitz, 2009). It is likely that twin parenthood, rather than ART, however, contributes to the negative impact on parental mental health.

Mothers of premature twins have also been found to be less responsive to their babies than mothers of premature singletons (Ostfeld, Smith, Hiatt, & Hegyi, 2000). If confirmed by other controlled studies, this finding would be of particular concern because of the high risk of prematurity in multifetal pregnancies.

Regarding marital distress, research has been equivocal, with some studies finding that parents of twins experience more marital distress than parents of singletons (Pinborg et al., 2003), although others do not (Baor, Bar-David, & Blickstein, 2004; Olivennes et al., 2005; Tully, Moffitt, & Caspi, 2003). The reason for these dissimilar findings may be that the impact of a multiple birth on marriage can vary; some mothers have reported feeling that they were losing touch with their husbands, whereas others have felt that their marriage was strengthened by the need to pull together as a team to cope with the demands of the children (Ellison & Hall, 2003).

In general, marital distress and divorce rates tend to be low in ART twin families (Ellison & Hall, 2003; Pinborg et al., 2003; Sydsjo, Wadsby, Sydsjo, & Selling, 2008). However, although reports of divorce rates specific to ART multiples families with disabled children were not found, more marital distress has been reported among families of children with special needs (Hodapp & Krasner, 1995; Seligman & Darling, 2006; Taanila, Syrjala, Kokkonen, & Jarvelin, 2002). Additionally, we have observed that after giving birth, some couples, in ministering to the multiple needs of their multiple babies, appear joyless, sleep-deprived, irritable, and stressed. Their communication often suffers, and many report that their sex lives are nonexistent.

Mothers of 1-year-old triplets have reported considerable fatigue, stress, social isolation, marital strain, and inability to give either adequate attention to all three of their children at the same time or to enjoy their presence, and 25% were prescribed antidepressants (Garel & Blondel, 1992). By the time their triplets were 4 years old, one third of the mothers of multiples were clinically depressed and on antidepressant medication. The mothers reported that their relationship with their children was the main source of their distress (Garel et al., 1997). In a more recent study, Golombok and her colleagues (2007) also found mothers of triplets experienced more distress in parenting than mothers of singletons, although they were no different than mothers of ART twins. Mothers raising multiples have also reported feeling judged because they believe others have negative opinions regarding their infertility and decision to use ART to have their children (Ellison & Hall, 2003). At present, there are no reported studies of family adjustment in quadruplet and higher order multiple families.

Studies of the psychosocial impact of MFPR on parents are rare and mostly retrospective. At 1 year postpartum, women with twins reduced from an originally higher order multifetal pregnancy demonstrated a similar incidence of depression as women with nonreduced twins (McKinney, Tuber, & Downey, 1996). By 2 years after birth, a higher percentage of mothers of triplets reported considerable fatigue and stress compared with mothers of reduced twins (73% vs. 21%; Garel et al., 1997). All of the mothers of triplets reported that parenting three children of the same age at the same time created marital difficulties, though no divorces were reported in either group of parents, and all mothers of triplets voiced concern about their inability to cope effectively with their children's behavior and felt both frustration and guilt at not being able to enjoy their intensely desired children as much as they had hoped. These sentiments were not expressed by the mothers of twins. Mothers of twins did report, however, that the decision to reduce their pregnancy to twins was stressful, but the decision was easier for women who had been given detailed information about the risks of a multiple pregnancy and pregnancy reduction as well as nonreduction and who had received support from their doctor. This suggests the great importance of informed consent in this process. Younger women, those who are more religious, those who saw the multifetal pregnancy more often on ultrasound, or those who lost the entire pregnancy may be at higher risk of psychological distress (Bergh, Moller, Nilsson, & Wikland, 1999; Britt, Risinger, Mans, & Evans, 2003; Garel et al., 1997; Kanhai et al., 1994; McKinney, Downey, & Timor-Tritsch, 1995; Schreiner-Engel, Walther, Mindes, Lynch, & Berkowitz, 1995). The possibility of MFPR is a necessary topic for physicians and mental health professionals to discuss with patients considering ovarian stimulation cycles with insemination or IVF. However, we have encountered patients who have merely had the ASRM patient fact sheet included in their IVF information packets without verbal explanation from their medical team.

Impact on Children

The psychosocial implications of being a twin, triplet, or higher order multifetal gestation have not received a great deal of study. However, decades of research have demonstrated the importance for infants and small children of developing a strong, close relationship with one caring person during the first year of life. This early relationship, dependent on the sensitivity of the primary caretaker, creates a secure attachment to the caretaker and forms the basis for future social interactions and emotional growth (Ainsworth, 1985; Bowlby, 1982). In addition, the sensory stimulation provided by an available person speaking directly to the child is thought to be important for cognitive, language, and emotional development. When parents have more than one infant of the same age at the same time, the exclusive parenting available to a singleton is likely reduced.

In a comparison of ART twins with singletons, delays in language and cognitive development as well as behavioral problems are more pronounced in multiples (Luke et al., 2006; Olivenness et al., 2005; Pinborg, Loft, Schmidt, Griesen, et al., 2004; Rutter, Thorpe, Greenwood, Northstone, & Golding, 2003). In addition to low birth weight, however, differential parental responsiveness to twins compared with singletons may also contribute to these poorer childhood outcomes (Ostfeld et al., 2000). Twins also appear to be at higher risk of attention-deficit/hyperactivity disorder (Levy, Hay, McLaughlin, Wood, & Waldman, 1996).

Triplets are a growing population with their rates increasing tenfold since 1980 (Blickstein & Keith, 2000). However, very few studies have investigated the psychosocial development of triplets or higher order multiples, the majority of whom are created through ART. Luke and her colleagues (2006) found that 18-month-old triplets scored lower on both mental and motor scales than twins. In comparing ART singletons, twins, and triplets, Golombok and her colleagues (2007) found no differences in emotional or behavioral problems among these groups, however, the triplets and twins showed mild language delays when compared with singleton children.

Older siblings are also more adversely affected and more likely to show behavioral disturbances by the arrival of multiples than a singleton sibling (Hay, MacIndoe, & O'Brien, 1988). Further research is needed on the impact that multiples have on already existing children in the family, especially if one or more multiples suffer from a disability.

Mental health professionals know that infertile patients are often unrealistic in their assessment of the additional burdens of conceiving and raising multiples, even twins, although, after being giving information concerning the risks of specific perinatal and developmental complications, women have been found to be less positive regarding their desire for a twin pregnancy (Grobman, Milad, Stout, & Klock, 2001). In addition, to make informed decisions, patients need the absence of overwhelming emotion (Newton, Feyles, Tekpetey, & Power, 2007). It is unlikely that this condition can be met at the moment that a woman is awaiting embryo transfer. Regrettably, this is often the first time that physicians and patients discuss the number of embryos that will be transferred. Because a large proportion of the public has difficulty understanding numerical risk information (e.g., odds, percentages; Mayhorn, Fisk & Whittle, 2002; Tversky & Kahneman, 1981), patients seldom believe that the risks faced by others apply to them (Weinstein, 1999) and if experiencing negative emotions, they may demonstrate increased risk taking in decision making (Leith & Baumeister, 1996; Newton, Feyles, et al., 2007). It is important to assess patients' mood state as well as their understanding of the risks involved in multiple-embryo transfer. Potential parents should be informed that their intense desire for a child may result in their underestimating the realistic difficulties of raising multiples, especially when one or more of the children may have special needs.

BIOETHICAL PERSPECTIVES

The bioethical issue that dominates in discussion of iatrogenically produced ART multifetal pregnancies is nonmaleficence. Either patient or physician autonomy may be compromised, however, in an effort to "do no harm."

Beneficence and Nonmaleficence

Health care providers have a duty not to cause unnecessary harm to their patients, which certainly includes those patients whom reproductive endocrinologists treat; but does it also include the children they help to create? This is a quintessential example of the maternal versus fetal conflict. Some have suggested that physicians, in their ethical obligation of beneficence (promoting health), have an obligation to the fetus but only when the fetus is a patient (Chervenak & McCullough, 2000).

Since physicians are currently aware of the strong possibility of adverse outcomes increasing with a multifetal pregnancy; reducing the number of multifetal pregnancies would reflect this goal of nonmaleficence. Competition among infertility clinics to have the highest success rates along with the profit motive contributes to this problem. Some have recommended that reporting pregnancy rates for fertility clinics in the United States be banished in favor of reporting implantation rates and average number of embryos transferred to reduce the incentives to programs to transfer excess embryos (Criniti et al., 2005; Goldfarb, 2006).

Patient Autonomy

Patient resistance to single-embryo transfer in the United States, where most patients self-pay for ART procedures and equate more embryos transferred with higher pregnancy rates, remains high (Ryan et al., 2004). Pregnancy rates remain higher when two embryos are transferred instead of one. However, if a second embryo is frozen after single-embryo transfer and pregnancies from the return of that frozen embryo are also included, pregnancy rates between single- and double-embryo transfer for women under 36 years of age who have at least two high quality embryos available for transfer are comparable (Lukassen et al., 2005) or somewhat, but not substantially, lower (Pandian, Templeton, Serour, & Bhattacharya, 2005; Thurin et al. 2004), but all studies demonstrated significantly reduced multifetal pregnancy rates. The need to focus on what we believe to be the most important goals (i.e., the birth of a healthy child and the continued good health of the gestating woman) is apparent, as is the need for research on appropriate patient selection for elective single-embryo transfer and further education of patients about elective single-embryo transfer.

The issue of autonomy also arises in terms of who determines the number of embryos to be transferred to a woman's uterus. Patients need complete and specific information to make informed decisions, and physicians need to take responsibility both for the health of their patients and for predictable outcomes of their interventions. Out of respect for the patient's right to self-determination, in the United States it has been suggested by some that the decision regarding the number of embryos to transfer after the patient has received full and complete information regarding risks should be given to the female patient (Chervenak & McCullough, 2000). However, as reviewed previously, infertile women often underestimate the risks of a multifetal pregnancy, and many patients report that they will leave it in the hands of their physician to know what is best for them given the quality of the embryos on the day of transfer. If this is indeed the case, physicians, although given the ultimate authority on the number of embryos to be transferred, are in a unique position to prevent multiples. Mental health professionals, however, can also prepare patients to make informed decisions for themselves and their potential children.

Financial pressures often induce patients to request transfer of more than one embryo, and because the incidence of multiple pregnancies is lower in countries that provide public subsidies for ART (International Committee for Monitoring Assisted Reproductive Technology, 2006), advocacy across the United States for a policy to cover a reasonable number of IVF cycles so as to reduce the number of multiple pregnancies and protect future children seems warranted to eliminate discrimination against couples not having access to this coverage.

Physician Autonomy

Physicians, too, have the right to autonomy. A physician is not required to participate in any activity he or she finds morally unacceptable (e.g., MFPR), nor is he or she obligated to perform a procedure that he or she does not believe to be necessary or appropriate. However, regarding MFPR, the physician would be expected to make a referral to a colleague for whom such incompatibility does not exist and would be expected not to judge the patient for making an autonomous decision regarding her pregnancy.

Justice

Injustice may exist because wealthy individuals may be able to pursue more than one IVF cycle if necessary to conceive a child, and those individuals with fewer financial resources may be unable to do the same. As a result, less affluent individuals and couples may feel compelled to take greater risks, namely, transferring more than one embryo per cycle in an attempt to ensure a pregnancy.

EXISTING LAWS, POLICIES, AND LEGISLATION

Informed consent has long been the embodiment of respect for persons and reflects both a bioethical and a legal construct. "Every human being of adult years and sound mind has a right to determine what shall be done with his own body" (*Schloendorff v. Society of New York Hospitals*, 1914, 105 N.E. 92.93). Informed consent requires that prospective parents be made aware of the risks involved in a multifetal pregnancy that may arise for the mother and the infants as well as loss rates should a decision for MFPR be made. Prospective parents must also be made aware not only of the immediate risks to the infants but also of the long-term consequences for the developing children. Also, the potential family disruption and stress caused by a multifetal pregnancy needs to be presented. Although this information might be outside the realm of the typical informed consent, which usually consists of medical risks, benefits, and alternatives, it is significant enough to warrant discussion in advance of treatment.

This discussion, although primarily medical, also has many psychosocial elements, which would and should be elucidated in a consultation with a mental health professional.

Without informed consent, one legal question that may arise is whether any liability may result if higher order multiples are born, with their attendant health difficulties and the health difficulties for the mother, not to mention the increased financial burdens of caring for the children if they suffer any disability as a result of the multiple gestation. If the consent is flawed, parents may attempt to raise a wrongful birth action asserting that if they had received the necessary information, they would not have continued with the higher order pregnancy. Wrongful birth suits have been filed, albeit rarely, and with great disfavor by courts, and they have not yet centered on issues of multifetal pregnancy. As with any negligence action, the parents would need to prove that they were harmed.

Similarly, although this is disfavored by courts and legislatures, the children may assert a wrongful life action against not only the physician but also their parents. As an Illinois Appellate Court reasoned in 1963, such suits are disfavored because

> one might seek damages for being born of a certain color, another because of race; one for being born with a hereditary disease, another for inheriting unfortunate family characteristics; one for being born into a large and destitute family, another because a parent has an unsavory reputation. (Zepeda v. Zepeda, 1963, p. 260)

The disruption that this might bring on the family is unspeakable. The mere potential of such action may be sufficient to elicit a discussion of the impact of a multifetal gestation on the children.

In the United States, no law currently exists to limit the number of embryos to be transferred and/or created. Other countries, however, have imposed such limitations (see Appendix B, this volume). Given that medicine is, by and large, a self-regulated field, laws limiting the number of embryos to be created may interfere with the expertise of physicians as well as with the physician–patient relationship. Additionally, professional society guidelines have suggested transferring fewer embryos to reduce the number of higher order multiples (Practice Committee of the SART and the Practice Committee of the ASRM, 2008).

Physicians do have autonomy, but they must also adhere to standards of beneficence. It has been argued that clinicians have a duty to withhold treatments that threaten harm and probably will not achieve their intended goal (Ethics Committee of the ASRM, 2004a). Because the patient and physician may not always agree on the appropriate course of action, it becomes important for a physician to clarify for patients in advance of treatment when the physician will proceed with a course of action and when he or she will not and to apply the same standard to all patients in making such a decision. This is particularly important with regard to the number of embryos to be transferred in any given cycle and truly is part of the informed consent process.

CLINICAL VIGNETTE

Given the heightened risks of multifetal pregnancy for families, mothers, and children, it would seem preferable to encourage single-embryo transfer, particularly if factors such as maternal age, quality of embryos, and prior IVF history are favorable. However, the following dilemma is not uncommonly faced by physicians and mental health professionals working in the field of reproductive medicine.

Ed (36 years old), a computer salesman, and Camille (34 years old), an insurance adjustor, both Catholic, wanted desperately to have a large family. They had been trying to conceive for 2 years before considering ART. Their budget left little extra after paying their monthly expenses, and their insurance had a $10,000 lifetime cap on infertility treatment. During an IVF cycle, Camille produced seven eggs; all were retrieved, six fertilized, and four continued dividing to blastocyst stage and were rated as very good quality as they approached the day of transfer. They hoped to conceive triplets or at least twins and requested on the day prior to transfer that their reproductive endocrinologist transfer all four embryos. The reproductive endocrinologist was reluctant to follow their wishes because of Camille's age, the quality of the embryos, and his awareness of their opposition to multifetal pregnancy reduction because of their religious backgrounds. After hearing their desire to transfer all four of their embryos, the reproductive endocrinologist quickly referred them to a mental health professional for immediate counseling.

Ethical Dilemmas in the Context of Professional Guidelines

How can the interests of all parties involved in this case be resolved in a mutually acceptable manner? Multifetal pregnancies pose known additional risks to both mothers and children. Thus, a psychologist condoning the transfer of a larger number of embryos than is medically advisable according to the unique circumstances of the woman's situation and professional guidelines goes against the American Psychological Association's (2002) "Ethical Principles of Psychologist and Code of Conduct" principle of beneficence and nonmaleficence (Principle A). Yet, the psychologist is placed in a bind with regard to respect for people's rights and dignity (Principle E) if, after being fully informed of the risks, the patient still chooses to transfer a higher number of embryos than is medically advisable.

The Practice Committees of the SART and the ASRM (2008) in their "Guidelines on Number of Embryos Transferred" recommend transferring two or fewer embryos for patients under age 35 in the absence of extraordinary circumstances. Patients with the most favorable prognosis (i.e., first IVF cycle, good quality embryos, and with excess embryos of sufficient quality to warrant cryopreservation) have been advised to consider transferring only a single embryo. These guidelines are totally voluntary, however, and the rate of twin pregnancies may continue to be too high with the transfer of two embryos, whereas it is all but eliminated with single-embryo transfer (Neubourg et al., 2002).

Practical Considerations

The continuing high incidence of iatrogenically produced multifetal pregnancies and their intrinsically higher risk for the resulting children and families represents a clear public health concern. Although MFPR is available, it is certainly not a highly desirable solution for most couples who have experienced infertility because of its psychological ramifications as well as indications that the originally higher order pregnancy still has detrimental effects (i.e. higher rates of prematurity) on the remaining fetuses.

Balancing the Multiple Perspectives

Society at large may be asked to take on the financial burden of antenatal care for the babies of a multifetal pregnancy and, possibly, lifelong care for babies requiring costly medical intervention because of health problems or disability. Average hospital charges alone have been reported to be 4 times higher for a twin delivery and 11 times higher for a triplet delivery than for a singleton (Callahan et al., 1994). The rise in multiple birth rates has also had an impact on the educational system. Schools may not be equipped to separate either a large influx of twin siblings or higher order multiples into different classrooms, a pattern often followed to help each child develop his or her own individual identity. Nor may a school system be prepared to manage the range of special needs that may arise.

The Clinician or Fertility Clinic

Reproductive endocrinologists have the responsibility of informing patients of the risks of multifetal pregnancies prior to their undergoing treatment. If, in fact, the IVF program has a policy about the number of embryos to be transferred based on the age of the recipient, her prior IVF history, embryo quality, and number of embryos produced, the patient should be informed of this prior to giving informed consent and undergoing any intervention for infertility because good decision making begins with accurate information.

The physician and other medical staff involved in Camille and Ed's case may experience conflict between their respect for patient autonomy in decision making and their sense of responsibility toward the children they help to create (beneficence and nonmaleficence). The professional's duty to try to do no harm, especially when the possibility of a reasonably high risk of harm is known in advance of offering an intervention, appears to be breached in this case by the concerns raised about the safety to both the mother and the potential babies being conceived. The reproductive endocrinologist does have the right to veto a patient's wishes and follow his or her professional guidelines and clinical judgment. Potential harm to the medical staff themselves may occur if they are expected to go against their own professional standards or personal consciences. To reduce charges of paternalism in cases of conflict between physicians and patients, the European Society of Human Reproduction and Embryology has recommended that the lowest number of embryos indicated by either party should be followed so that no more embryos are transferred than wanted by either the physician or the parents (European Society of Human Reproduction and Embryology Task Force on Ethics and Law, 2003).

Although the focus of concern must be the multiples and their families, clinics are more marketable when they report high pregnancy rates. Therefore, it has also been suggested that a new standard of success be used, that is, instead of percentage of cycles resulting in a live birth, report either births per embryo transferred or implantation rates to reduce the incentives for programs to transfer excess embryos (Goldfarb, 2006; Pennings, 2000a). Advocating for the same insurance coverage for IVF as may often be available for superovulation cycles may prove to be in everyone's best interest, including the insurance companies, as limits to the number of embryos transferred may be more acceptable to patients when insurance is available (Jain, Harlow, & Hornstein, 2002; Reynolds et al., 2003), and this policy would have the potential to save money by reducing the costs of care of multifetal preterm babies in intensive care units.

The Prospective Parents and Children

Do patients have a right to choose what to do with their embryos, including the transfer of the number of embryos they wish, even if it conflicts with existing guidelines and the reproductive endocrinologist's adherence to these guidelines, which he or she sees as in the best interest of the prospective parents? In transferring four embryos as requested by Camille and her husband, there exists a potential risk to the prospective mother of a difficult pregnancy, to the parents of having a high order multifetal pregnancy, and to the potential children of being born preterm of low or very low birth weight with possible health problems and having to share parental time and attention with a same-age sibling or siblings. The infertility center wishes to provide quality service, do no harm, help patients reach their goal of pregnancy, and have success rates that attract future patients. However, by following guidelines in an attempt to reduce the rate of multifetal pregnancies from the potential parents' perspective, it runs the risk of depleting the parent's insurance allotment without having a baby to bring home.

CONCLUSION

Although this is an age of unprecedented emphasis on patient autonomy, multiple interests need to be balanced, including the infertile couple's desire to have a family, the potential children's interest in being born healthy, the physician's interest in his or her decision-making autonomy and ability to be innovative, and society's interest in reducing rising health care costs and in protecting the health and welfare of its citizens (Elster & the Institute for Science, Law, and Technology Working Group on Reproductive Technology, 2000).

In this particular situation, mental health providers fill the role of psychoeducational consultants to Camille and Ed, educating them on the advantages and disadvantages of a multifetal pregnancy, including the issues that can arise regarding the pregnant woman's health; the long-term consequences for her health; the physical and psychological health of the potential children; the psychosocial issues of raising multiple children of the same age at the same time; the potential financial hardships; and the availability, risks, and benefits of MFPR.

We recommend that the ASRM patient fact sheets on *Complications and Problems Associated with Multiple Births* (ASRM, 2008a), *Challenges of Parenting Multiples* (ASRM, 2003), and *Fertility Drugs and the Risk of Multiple Births* (ASRM, 2008b) be given to all patients undergoing ovarian stimulation and/or embryo transfer and that they be referred to information such as that available in *InFocus: The American Fertility Association Magazine* (American Fertility Association, 2003) because they are all at increased risk of a multifetal pregnancy if more than one embryo is transferred. Having patients list the advantages and disadvantages of each treatment option (e.g., single-embryo transfer, double-embryo transfer) and explaining their understanding of risk factors that may modify or enhance their own susceptibility to a multifetal pregnancy may be ways of determining whether they can provide informed consent (Almashat, Ayotte, Edelstein, & Margrett, 2008; Paling, 2003; Weinstein, 1999). All discussions with Camille and Ed regarding the risks and benefits of fertility treatment should be carefully documented in the patients' medical and psychological records.

In the present case, one would hope that after receiving objective and complete information about the risks of a multifetal pregnancy, Camille and

Ed would choose to transfer no more than two embryos and cryopreserve the remainder. If they still insist on transferring all four embryos, although health care providers respect patient autonomy, in light of the potentially serious medical risks to Camille as well as to possible children created by the intervention, as presented in the preceding literature review, it would be appropriate for the mental health professional to support the physician in following his or her professional practice standards because they represent the current standard of care within the United States.

5

OOCYTE DONATION AND RECIPIENCY

It has been said time heals all wounds. I do not agree. The wounds remain.
In time, the mind, protecting its sanity, covers them with scar tissue and
the pain lessens. But it is never gone.

—Rose Kennedy, 1974

The majority of oocyte donation is conducted in the United States, and
as of 2005, there were 134,260 assisted reproductive treatment cycles reported
to the Centers for Disease Control and Prevention (V. C. Wright, Chang, Jeng,
& Macaluso, 2008). The popularity of this procedure may be a result of certain practical issues because in the United States, unlike some other countries,
it is not illegal to compensate donors for their efforts.

During the 1980s, Drs. Buster and Bustillo performed a uterine lavage
of a donor using the recipient's husband's sperm. This included washing the
embryos from the donor's uterus and transferring them to the sperm donor's
wife's (the recipient's) uterus (Buster et al., 1983; Bustillo et al., 1984). Although
the groundbreaking procedure was successful, the process of oocyte donation
has been refined, and currently in vitro fertilization (IVF) is used. In the mid-
1980s, the first pregnancy using the retrieved eggs from a healthy young woman
and fertilized through IVF, which were subsequently transferred to the uterus
of a woman with primary ovarian insufficiency (POI), was reported in Australia
(Lutjen et al.,1984).

Even though the first successful oocyte donations using IVF occurred
in the 1980s (Glazer & Sterling, 2005; Klein & Sauer, 2002), the procedure has
remained controversial. Although sperm donation has been quietly conducted

79

for over 100 years, the early oocyte donations were widely publicized. The introduction of a conspicuous third party into the reproductive technologies continues to draw criticism. Selecting a specific woman to mix her unique 23 chromosomes with those of someone to whom she is not wed suggests both eugenics and adultery. Oocyte donation involves the creation of novel and thus unconventional types of families. Equality of access to medical treatment using oocyte donation and the commodification of, if not payment for, body parts raises both ethical and legal dilemmas. Concern for the children conceived with donated ova remains. Before we expand on the ethical issues involved in oocyte donation and recipiency, we first review the medical background and protocols.

MEDICAL BACKGROUND

Several years ago the American Society for Reproductive Medicine (ASRM) began a campaign to educate the public regarding the preservation of fertility for women of all ages. Thus far, their goals have not been met, and the general public remains uninformed. Until such educational goals are attained, physicians may continue to find it necessary to counsel women who suffer from declining or ceased ovarian function, advanced age, and poor quality eggs to use donated ova.

Candidates for Oocyte Recipiency

Women are born with a finite number of immature eggs. Approximately two million eggs are found in a female infant's ovaries. As a teenager, 300,000 to 400,000 remain, with about 1,000 dying each month. By age 37, most women will have approximately 25,000 eggs remaining in their ovaries and will start to become infertile. There are exceptions to this estimate, with some women becoming infertile in their 20s and others remaining fertile well into their 40s (Silber, 2005). When no eggs remain, a woman's ovaries will cease producing estrogen, and she will go through menopause. A woman will likely become infertile 10 to 13 years prior to the onset of menopause. Some women will go through menopause prior to age 50 and suffer from POI, also referred to as *premature ovarian failure*. The process of ovarian failure is intermittent, rather than a sudden or abrupt event, thereby rendering it difficult to diagnose (Taylor, 2001).

In any given month the probability of a woman in her early 20s conceiving is about 25%. This probability is reduced to approximately 15% by her late 20s and reduced again to about 10% in her early 30s. By the time a woman reaches her late 30s, she has about an 8% chance of conceiving per month, and it will probably take 12 months to accomplish (Silber, 2005).

The need to use donated ova is ironic in that these same women, when in their teens and early 20s, were probably trying to avoid getting pregnant. Regrettably, to date, efforts to disseminate information about the age-related decline of fertility and fertility preservation appear to be inadequate, and many women believe IVF can reverse the delay of childbearing (Maheshwari, Porter, Shetty, & Bhattacharya, 2008).

Other problems can lead to the cessation of ovulation, such as cancer treatment protocols that have improved the long-term survival rates of adolescents and young women (Lutchman Singh, Davies, & Chatterjee, 2005). Nevertheless, the very treatments that save women's lives may trigger the onset of premature menopause. The two major determinants of ovarian damage following cancer treatment are the woman's age and the class of chemotherapeutic agent used (Abdallah & Muasher, 2006). It has been recommended that prior to treatment, young women and their families consult not only with their oncologist but also with specialists in biological reproduction and psychology to learn about options for fertility preservation (Rosenblum & Rampenaux, 2005). As better educational materials and professional guidelines for fertility preservation are developed, women who have had cancer will require donated ova with less frequency (Oehninger, 2005; Schover, 2005; see Chapter 2, this volume).

Women over age 40 may also find their ovarian function further reduced as a result of past surgeries, infection, or endometriosis. After patients have met with their physicians and medical team, mental health professionals, too, may ensure that recipients have been fully informed and understand the various aspects of their medical treatment. Therefore, psychologists are expected to be familiar with patient protocols, fertility medications and their side effects, as well as the emotional quandaries possibly arising as a result of such diagnosis and/or treatment.

Once it has been established there are no sperm quality issues or implantation problems, women in their 20s and 30s will be tested for POI, Turner's syndrome (a rare chromosomal disorder occurring when part of or the entire X chromosome is deleted), fragile X, and aneuploidy (which occurs when there is an extra or missing chromosome) and will be questioned to ascertain whether they have been exposed to toxic chemicals (Crisostomo & Molina, 2002; Mlynarcikova, Fickova, & Scsukova, 2005; N. Tang & Zhu, 2003; Watson & Money, 1975). Should they be unable to use their own eggs, women will be asked to consider using a donated ovum.

Despite the fact that a woman's chances of conceiving may seem remote, many women insist on attempting one IVF cycle using their own eggs before attempting oocyte recipiency (Scott, 2004). This is just one of the many conundrums in the field of infertility that confront psychologists and ethicists alike. Most reproductive endocrinologists (REs) would prefer to have patients with POI use donated oocytes to maximize their chances to conceive. However, in our experience, we find that patients are often not psychologically prepared to accept this alternative.

Even though the prognosis for conception is very poor, Scott (2004) advised REs to candidly counsel their patients and allow them access to treatment using their own eggs. Although the odds of conceiving with their own eggs are low, women may feel a sense of closure knowing they have exhausted all possibility of using their own gametes prior to moving on to oocyte recipiency. However, women 40 years of age or older with impaired endometrial receptivity, decreased oocyte quality, or a combination of the two will have an increased likelihood of miscarriage and may decide to receive donor ova.

The Practice Committee of the ASRM and the Practice Committee of the Society for Assisted Reproductive Technology (SART; 2008) have suggested women with hypergonadotropic hypogonadism, diminished ovarian reserve, or who are known carriers of or are affected by a significant genetic defect are good candidates for oocyte recipiency. Also, women who have a family history of a medical condition, even if not verifiable, as well as women with poor oocyte and/or embryo quality, are appropriate patients for using donated ova (Carson, Casson, & Shuman, 1999). Women who have experienced multiple failures through assisted reproductive technology are also good candidates. We believe those mental health professionals who are aware of the medical facets of oocyte recipiency are better equipped to assist these patients psychologically.

Medical Procedures for Oocyte Recipients

To use donated eggs, both the donor's and the recipient's menstrual cycles are synchronized, and the ovum recipient's endometrial lining is made ready for the transferred embryos (Sauer & Kavic, 2006). Progesterone injections or suppositories will be given to the ovum recipient beginning 1 day prior to the donor's egg retrieval and continuing on a daily basis until the 8th to 12th week of pregnancy, or should a pregnancy not be achieved, the progesterone injections will cease (Jun, Racowski, Fox, & Hornstein, 2001; Kliman, Copperman, Honig, Walls, & McSweet, 2005; Muasher, Abdallah, & Hubayter, 2006).

Concurrently, the laboratory staff processes the sperm, which capacitates (activates) them, so they can penetrate the eggs. The ova are fertilized with either the partner's sperm or a donor's sperm. The eggs are placed in a container with the culture medium, and after several hours the processed sperm are added to the microenvironments under oil. Once the sperm enter the eggs and fertilization occurs, the embryos are allowed to develop prior to embryo transfer. The laboratory dishes are kept in an incubator at the temperature a woman's body would provide. The embryo(s) are transferred into a catheter and deposited into the recipient's or gestational surrogate's uterus 3 to 5 days later (Balaban et al., 2001).

The recipient will have a blood test 10 to 12 days after embryo transfer to determine whether she is pregnant (Sher, Davis, & Stoess, 2005). Patients have characterized the difficult wait for the pregnancy test as the most trying phase of the protocol (Martins, Ferriani, Nastri, dos Reis, & Filho, 2008). Excess embryos that were not transferred can be cryopreserved for another IVF cycle. Issues related to cryopreservation of embryos are discussed further in Chapter 3.

Candidates for Oocyte Donation

There are four possible types of oocyte donors. *Known donors* are those known to the recipient at the time of conception and are usually family members or friends who are often approached to act as potential donors; at times they themselves approach the recipient(s). Recipients may opt to use a known donor because her genetic background and health history are familiar and, in the case of family members, are similar. Friends may proffer their assistance on learning of the couple's plight. However, family members and friends usually have rather naive expectations of the commitment involved in acting as a designated donor. The rigors of the medical protocol, the possible long-term consequences of the medications, and the time involved are often minimized by known donors (Gurmankin, 2001). Both the fertility clinic and the recipients must scrupulously describe the donation process so the potential known donor can make a truly informed choice.

A couple may prefer to use *anonymous donors* who indicate that their identities should never be revealed to the recipient couple or their potential offspring. Anonymous donation avoids changes in the dynamics of the family or friendships. Additionally, anonymous donation does not necessarily cause the child the social or relational confusion believed by some to be inherent in known donation (Raoul-Duval, Letur-Konirsch, & Frydman, 1992). Using unknown donors avoids any future interference from the oocyte donor because the relationship is time limited and clear boundaries exist between the anonymous oocyte donor and the recipients. Most families prefer to be free from donor interference (Karpel, Flis-Treves, Blanchet, Loivennes, & Frydman, 2005; Sheldon, 2005). However, we have observed an increasing interest by recipients to at least meet or speak with their egg donors.

Other oocyte donors may be classified as *identified donors*. These women permit their identities to be released to the children conceived from their eggs or agree to meet the intended parents prior to the donation. Typically, personal contact with identified donors can be made once the offspring have reached the age of legal majority.

Both anonymous and identified donors can be recruited by oocyte dona-tion agencies or IVF programs and clinics. Women also may be invited to par-ticipate in the donation process as egg sharers. Egg sharers are women who are already in treatment for fertility problems unrelated to their egg quality or quantity and are usually anonymous. Whether anonymous, identified, egg sharing, or known, oocyte donors have infrequently been the subjects of psychological or sociological investigation.

Medical Procedures for Oocyte Donors

The medical facets of egg donation merit discussion. One month prior to stimulation of her cycle, the ovum donor is directed to either abstain from sex or use barrier contraception. IVF with donated oocytes entails ovulation induction for the donor so she can produce many eggs, which increases the likelihood there will be an adequate number of good quality eggs to fertilize to form healthy embryos (J. Cohen, 2003). The egg donor may be placed on one or more of the following medications: human menopausal gonadotropins to induce ovarian follicle growth, human recombinant follicle stimulating hor-mones to induce ovarian follicle growth and maturation, and gonadotropin-releasing hormone for ovulation control (Al-Inany, Aboulghar, Mansour, & Serour, 2005; Lee, Couchman, & Walmer, 2005; Sauer & Kavic, 2006). In preparation for IVF, a donor's ovaries will be scanned on an ultrasound to monitor the development of her follicles. Also, blood will be drawn to mea-sure her hormone levels (Ben-Schlomo, Geslevich, & Shalev, 2001). Once the donor has enough adequately sized follicles she will receive an injection of human chorionic gonadotropins to trigger the release of her eggs.

Approximately 2 days later she will be sedated, and her eggs will be removed from her ovaries, a procedure called *oocyte retrieval*. When the eggs are ready to be harvested, the donor will have transvaginal ultrasound aspiration in which a needle is guided to enter each of the follicles that have adequately matured. The follicles are emptied and both their fluid and the mature eggs are retrieved and evaluated by embryologists (Sher et al., 2005).

The medical risks for oocyte donors include ovarian hyperstimulation ovarian torsion, and rupture of ovarian cysts (Maxwell, Chlost, & Rosenwaks, 2008). However, except in the case of egg sharing, because an embryo itself is not transferred to the donor's uterus, the risk of mild ovarian hyperstimulation and/or paracentesis, a procedure that removes the fluid accumulated in the abdominal cavity, occurs in 1% to 14% of donors, and severe ovarian hyper-stimulation occurs in approximately 1% of the women donating their eggs (Human Fertilisation and Embryology Authority, 2006; National Academies of Science, 2007; Schneider & Kramer, 2009).

Anesthesia is used during the removal of the donor's oocytes. The use of anesthesic agents presents a 1 in 10,000 risk to an egg donor. Serious pelvic infections resulting from ova extraction occur in fewer than 1 in 500 women and uterine bleeding in approximately 1 in 2,500 (R. Kennedy, 2005). Donors are usually told not to exert themselves for 1 week postsurgery. Often our patients report they experience bloating and abdominal discomfort during and briefly after the egg donation process.

Researchers have studied oocyte donors to evaluate whether multiple and/or sequential stimulation cycles affect pregnancy rates for the recipients (Jain et al., 2005; Mendes-Periera et al., 2005; Opsahl et al., 2001). It appears fertile women can donate oocytes between three and six times without adversely influencing themselves or the outcomes of IVF (Practice Committee of the ASRM, 2006).

Unlike a sperm donor, who masturbates to collect his semen, a young, healthy egg donor not only takes medications but will also need to undergo a surgical procedure that is of no physical benefit to her unless she is participating as an egg sharer. Egg sharing occurs when IVF patients who are in need of medical intervention unrelated to egg quality or ovarian reserve, divide half of their retrieved eggs with an oocyte recipient in exchange for a reduced treatment fee. The National Advisory Board on Ethics in Reproduction (NABER; 1996), an independent, multidisciplinary panel, recommended the practice of egg sharing be discouraged because the donors' participation may result from coercion.

PSYCHOSOCIAL LITERATURE

Some patients arrive at the decision to use donated oocytes after other assisted reproductive techniques have failed. An extended period of time may have transpired between their first efforts to conceive and the time when oocyte recipiency is recommended to them. Other, usually older, patients may consult with REs after 6 months of trying to conceive without medical intervention, only to be told outright their only viable alternative is to use donated ova. Regardless, we have found this suggestion, which prevents the woman from being biogenetically linked to her child, frequently results in feelings of loss, grief, frustration, regret, guilt, ambivalence, and anger at life's injustice.

Oocyte Recipients

Those clinics following the published practice and ethical guidelines in the field of reproductive medicine send their oocyte recipients for psychological evaluations and/or psychoeducational consultations. In many of the countries that regulate IVF, such counseling is actually mandated (European Society of Human Reproduction and Embryology Task Force on Ethics and Law, 2002).

We believe that prior to beginning medical treatment an oocyte recipient will need to address whether she feels unequal within the parenting unit. Many of our oocyte recipient patients fearfully fantasize that one day their children will state aloud they are not the "real" mother. These women are distinguishing the difference between being a genetic, rather than gestational mother. A mental health professional can help sort through these emotions and help the oocyte recipient come to terms with this differentiation. A psychotherapist can also attempt to help recipients avoid triangulation and the possibility of a shadowed relationship caused by the memories of infertility (Bowen, 1966; R. B. Miller, Anderson, & Keala, 2004; M. P. Nichols & Schwartz, 2001). Psychologists can have the egg recipient acknowledge and accept that for 9 months of pregnancy she will nourish, protect, and in all likelihood, bond with this child. Moreover, the oocyte recipient can come to see herself as a caring mother even prior to embryo transfer by her efforts to eliminate caffeine, alcohol, or any drugs that might harm the fetus and to eat well-balanced meals and take prenatal vitamins.

The Oocyte Donor

Within the fields of psychology and sociology, the aspects of oocyte donation most frequently studied are the egg donors' motivations to donate, their satisfaction with the process, and the level of information with which they are provided in the recruitment process.

Motivations to Donate

Oocyte donors, both anonymous and known, are motivated by one or more predominant factors: altruism, personal relationships, or financial compensation (Braverman, 2001). Some donors wish to help couples or individuals who otherwise could not have children because of their familiarity with friends or family members who experienced infertility in the past. Other altruistic women believe their donation is analogous to giving a gift (Fielding, Handley, Duqueno, Weaver, & Lui, 1998; Klock, Stout, & Davidson, 2002; Lindheim, Chase, & Sauer, 2001).

Known ovum donors typically state they are motivated by their personal relationship with the recipients (Baetens, Devroey, Camus, Van Steirtaghem, & Ponjaert-Kristoffersen, 2000; Braverman, 2001; Fielding et al., 1998). We have found, and research supports, that almost all donors who report being motivated by monetary gain also cite altruism and/or their relationship with the recipient(s) as important factors (Braverman, 2001; Klock et al., 2002; Lindheim et al., 2001). Women who have donated two or more times, whether they were enlisted by agencies or IVF clinics, emphasize the importance of the interactions with their recruiters (Klock et al., 2002).

Attempts to recruit donors for substantial amounts of money through student newspapers or the Internet are discouraged by ASRM, the Mental Health Professional Group of ASRM, and more generally, by society. The current compensation for their time and efforts paid to oocyte donors typically ranges from $6,000 to $20,000. The practice of paying donors an unequal amount of money for their physical or intellectual attributes or the number of eggs they produce rather than equitably compensating women for their time and effort has raised not only eyebrows but ethical questions as well.

Satisfaction With the Donation Process

Oocyte donors report various levels of satisfaction with the donation process (Yee, Hitkari, & Greenblatt, 2007). Some donors who were motivated by financial gain regretted donating their oocytes and expressed dissatisfaction with the lack of availability of outcome information (Patrick, Smith, Meyer, & Bashford, 2001). Oocyte donors who are motivated by altruism generally feel moderately to extremely satisfied (Klock, Braverman, & Rausch, 1998), and many would donate again (Rosenberg & Epstein, 1995; Schover, Rothman, & Collins, 1992). However, many of the women who reported satisfaction with the donation process expressed a desire to know the outcome for their recipients (Jordon, Belar, & Williams, 2004; Kalfoglou & Geller, 2000; Kalfoglou & Gittleson, 2000; Klock et al., 2002).

Although no long-term studies exist on the psychological effects of oocyte donation, it is conceivable that oocyte donors may experience emotional problems as a result of donation. Young women donating prior to bearing children of their own may be at increased psychological risk. Maturity, coupled with life experience, may cause donors to view their donation somewhat differently with the passage of time. Donors may feel unexpected biological attachment to the children conceived with their oocytes, especially if they confront their own fertility issues at some future date, which is a real possibility given that infertility impacts nearly one in six couples each year (Cooper-Hilbert, 1998). Despite their former lack of concern, donors may discover they have become preoccupied with thoughts about these children at some time in the future, wondering how the children developed and whether the recipients are good parents. Additionally, egg donors may be concerned their own children will have inadvertent sexual relations with offspring conceived with their gametes.

Oocyte donors also may be concerned with the consequences of taking ovulation stimulating drugs and whether their own fertility was affected. Donors uninformed of the recipients' treatment outcomes or donors inadequately stimulated in prior cycles may be especially at risk for worry, wondering if they themselves are fertile. Because oocyte donation is in its infancy, there are no longitudinal studies that provide information about the long-term psychological or physical effects of oocyte donation.

BIOETHICAL PERSPECTIVES

Most bioethical discussions regarding egg donation address the commodification of donors, their oocytes, and the children created with their ova. The Practice Committee of the ASRM and the Practice Committee of SART (2008) guidelines state that monetary compensation of the donor should reflect the time, inconvenience, and physical and emotional demands and risks associated with oocyte donation. Craft (1997) suggested donors be given an "inconvenience allowance." Steinbock (2004) wrote that payment for the burdens of the egg retrieval process is ethically sound but opined payment for the number of eggs retrieved, their quality, or the donor's characteristics is objectionable.

Commodification of Oocytes

Donor egg recipients are considered by some ethicists to be the *purchasers* of a *commodity*. Macklin (1996) questioned why payment to egg donors is ethically suspect when compensation has been so readily accepted. Attempting to enlist intellectually gifted oocyte donors, couples have advertised on several Ivy League university campuses. Several metropolitan newspapers publish personal ads asking young women to act as designated ova donors (Blyth, 1994). However, it is recommended that compensation should minimize undue inducement of donors and should not suggest payment for oocytes (Shanley, 2002). Some ethicists argue that in the current U.S. society, which respects personal autonomy and procreative liberty, people are permitted to select their mates according to their personal preferences, and it is reasonable to allow them to enhance the characteristics of their offspring (Strong, 1996).

The ethical concern, however, is whether one should pay a premium for certain characteristics and if such a practice is tantamount to the practice of eugenics. Recipients wish to receive good genes and select oocyte donors who physically resemble themselves and who, after genetic testing, prove to be healthy. Many disparate products and services in our economy are sold, however, and some may even argue it is more exploitative not to pay donors for the time and effort they exert in the process (Macklin, 1996).

Dickenson (2002) examined the ethical problem presented when altruistic women donate their ova without compensation, although the biotechnology industry, researchers, and IVF clinics profit from their reproductive materials. One might conclude it seems reasonable to commodify oocytes, as almost everything in our society is dominated by market forces.

A significant question is whether commodification diminishes human dignity, and further, whether the offspring who are created from allegedly commodified oocytes then become the equivalent of objects or products (J. Cohen, 1995). Those opposing commodification fear treating oocytes like a commodity may result in psychological damage to the offspring.

Sauer (1997) posed an important ethical dilemma when he asked whether the benefits to one group (viz., the recipients) should be allowed to outweigh the physical and emotional risks to the other group (viz., the donors). In their study, Kalfoglou and Gittelsohn (2000) found that egg donors did not believe their best interests were of primary concern to the staff of the medical facilities. We believe oocyte donors are commodified when they are treated as merely a means to the recipients' and physicians' ends.

Currently, uniform standards govern the methods used for egg donor recruitment and care. When society applies rights to egg donation, donors have the prerogative to be left alone in their pursuit to donate ova as a matter of respecting their autonomy and should be provided access to the medical intervention necessary to facilitate the process.

However, the lure of financial reward may cause some oocyte donors to distort their medical histories, thus potentially endangering the recipients and/or the recipients' child(ren) and even the donor herself. Because most aspects of reproductive medicine are not regulated, an oocyte donor wishing to pay off educational loans, qualify for a mortgage, or eliminate credit card debt may be tempted to misrepresent her medical information or intentionally underreport the number of times she has previously donated.

Clinics or recruitment agencies, striving to be competitive, may feel compelled to raise donors' compensation, and consequently, access to medical treatment may be available only to wealthy recipients. Medical providers, who attract better qualified donors, report increased success rates, and therefore their clinics become more marketable (Sauer, n.d.).

Many eligible women recruited by egg donation agencies are college students. Agencies remain unregulated and are not required to disclose to ovum donor candidates the potential physical or psychological risks. However, this does not obviate the duty of the medical providers to provide adequate informed consent. Does this negate the notion of respect for the individual, and turn the ova, if not also the donors, into commodities to be *brokered*?

Should a uniform tracking system be implemented to ensure donors recruited by agencies are given adequate medical information and psychological counseling prior to donation?

Egg Sharing

Some IVF programs offer the option of egg sharing. The terminology in the literature can be somewhat confusing. Many clinics refer to *egg sharing* as the process by which an anonymous donor provides her oocytes for two different recipients during one stimulation cycle. Both recipients' cycles are then timed to coincide with that of the oocyte donor. This is considered by some to be ethically sound, provided the donor is made aware two separate couples will receive her ova. However, opponents question whether the division of the eggs will be equitable not only in numbers but in quality. Furthermore, this type of egg sharing increases the risk of inadvertent consanguinity because there are potentially more children who are conceived from the same donor.

Sharing the oocytes between two recipient couples has been found to reduce their financial burden without compromising treatment results (Check, Fox, Deperro, Davis, & Krotec, 2003). Clinics adopting a policy of egg sharing between two different recipients will have more available oocyte donors. However, recipients will have half the number of oocytes and possibly few, if any, frozen embryos.

Other clinics use the term *egg sharing* to describe the process requiring the recipients to pay their own medical fees in addition to most of the costs incurred by their egg donor who will simultaneously be going through IVF. Many couples are unable to receive fertility treatment because of the high costs. Through egg sharing, donors already receiving gonadotropins as part of their IVF treatment can reduce the cost of their medical care by providing half of their oocytes to an oocyte recipient. However, should their cycle be unsuccessful, they will need additional gonadotropins in future IVF treatments because they are less likely to have been able to freeze embryos. Furthermore, many of these egg donors have been diagnosed with unexplained infertility, making the quality of their donated eggs questionable. Would the lowered fees for their own treatment unduly influence egg donors to assume some risks they ordinarily would not undertake?

The recipient's treatment results are rarely disclosed to egg sharing donors. When IVF fails for the oocyte donors, they may wonder whether the recipients received the better quality eggs and may subsequently experience resentment or remorse. Should the oocyte donor's cycle result in a positive pregnancy, she might worry or be concerned the recipient was unsuccessful. It has been found that despite fears about giving away half of their eggs, women remain hopeful of a successful treatment outcome and will undergo multiple attempts in their pursuit of a child (Rapport, 2003).

Despite the NABER report, many medical ethicists believe egg sharing is the only ethical method of oocyte donation because it does not subject healthy women to medical or surgical risks. Some researchers report pregnancy rates in egg-sharing programs are comparable to those found in other types of egg donation protocols (Ahuja & Simmons, 1996; Blyth, 2002).

Egg sharing is believed to be advantageous to both women because without the reduction of medical costs some donors might not have the opportunity to receive IVF treatment and some recipients might find it difficult to find suitable donors (Ahuja, Mostyn, & Simons, 1997; Ahuja, Simons, & Edwards, 1999). The subsidization of the medical fees is viewed differently than paid egg donation. Some ethicists believe social justice is promoted through the mutual act of sharing between the two patients especially because both are similarly diagnosed (Ahuja & Simons, 1996; Ahuja et al., 1999). However, egg sharing remains controversial because the egg sharers are a subfertile population.

Is it not in a woman's best interest to retain all of her eggs? Should she retain all of her ova, during a second IVF cycle using her frozen embryos, the non-egg-sharing donor would not have to inject herself with additional drugs to stimulate her ovaries or be subjected to further surgery to harvest her eggs. Presently, the long-term consequences of gonadotropins are unknown. Subjecting a woman to the additional medical risks of repeated donation cycles is viewed by many as unethical (Johnson, 1999). Who will be responsible for assessing and caring for the donor should she learn or fantasize her recipient has conceived when she has not?

Informed Consent

The provision of sufficient information to oocyte donors regarding the potential risks of the donation process has been considered a critical antecedent to obtaining informed consent (Charlesworth, 1992; Pearson, 2006). However, Gurmankin (2001) determined the majority of the oocyte donor programs she studied provided incomplete or inaccurate information at the initial point of contact regarding the risks related to the medications used for ovarian stimulation, the egg retrieval surgery, and ovarian cancer. R. Kennedy (2005) suggested that all potential donors be given detailed information about the potential risks and long-term consequences associated with the drugs that are used to stimulate egg production; the surgical risks associated with the harvesting of ova, including those attendant to sedation and anesthesia; the possibility of damage to the structures surrounding the ovaries; and the likelihood of pelvic infection. He also wrote that an explanation of the psychological and emotional risks should be provided prior to obtaining informed consent from egg donors. Moreover, we endorse the recommendation made by NABER (1996) that donors be given a cooling-off period of at least 24 hours to consider whether to sign the consent forms for oocyte donation.

Sauer (1997) questioned whether 21-year-olds had gained enough life experience to enable them to make informed decisions, notwithstanding that oocyte donors of legal majority are being permitted to make autonomous choices. It is possible a young woman in financial need may be unable to make objective decisions about oocyte donation because it may be difficult for her to sort through her emotions and adequately evaluate the possible long-term consequences of having genetically related offspring whom she probably will never have the opportunity to meet. Will the egg donor later suffer the "ambiguous loss" noted by Boss (1999), or will she become a bereaved parent, as described by Schiff (1977)? Yet, if a young woman is old enough to vote, drink alcoholic beverages, and make her own medical decisions, as long as she is informed of these possibilities, should she be denied the opportunity to choose to donate her gametes?

Some believe students do not have a sufficient level of maturity to understand the risks related to the medical and surgical procedures or the psychological and sociological sequelae of producing offspring whom they may never know (Papadimos & Papadimos, 2004). However, this may be seen as paternalistic given the law recognizes at age 18 individuals are mature enough to enter into legally binding contracts and serve in the military. Incomplete or insufficient disclosure negates informed consent of those individuals who may not comprehend or give credence to the existing risks. Are students really exploited if they are sufficiently compensated for their time and efforts, notwithstanding their lack of fully informed consent? Given the high cost of college education, will the *sale* of ova appeal to some women regardless of the risks? Another important consideration, given these women are competent adults, is where do we draw the fine line between respecting autonomy and being overprotective?

The National Institutes of Health (1994) also reported inadequate informed consent protocols were given to oocyte donors. Braverman, Benward, and Scheib (2002) found most consent forms distributed to gamete donors omitted information regarding the duration their records would be kept, the storage location, and the potential offspring's access to such records. Consent forms provided to the recipients, however, included such information. Consideration of the moral and legal rights of donors has led us and others to conclude both full disclosure about and increased control over the donation process should be provided (Kalfoglou, 2001; Kalfoglou & Geller, 2000).

Some ethicists have suggested informed consent and disclosure issues should be handled exclusively by physicians, medical personnel, and other qualified professionals (Strong, 2001). Although some donors have been given information over the telephone by receptionists at IVF clinics, ethicists have disparaged this practice (Gurmankin, 2001). Those professionals possessing the requisite knowledge have both the legal and ethical obligation to disclose and should do so in person (Berg, 2001; C. B. Cohen, 2001). Essentially, this is a multidisciplinary endeavor with each professional providing the information relevant to his or her discipline to ensure donors are receiving all of the necessary medical, legal, and psychological facts to make a more informed choice.

Daar (2001) and Dresser (2001) concluded it is unethical to permit women to donate their oocytes without full disclosure. Potential donors, according to these experts, are not given adequate information or choice regarding the recipients of their oocytes or the manner in which their genetic material may be disposed of in the future. This issue is of increasing concern as stem cell research expands and the need for donated embryos and eggs may intensify.

Recently, the Ethics Committee of the ARSM (2009) published a report discussing the obligations and rights of gamete donors. They proposed a multilevel approach to information sharing that includes providing the recipients with nonidentifying information, nonidentifying contact with the donors for medical updates, nonidentifying personal contact, and identification with personal contact. Responding to the atmosphere of greater advocacy for donors, they suggested making available information regarding whether a pregnancy and birth resulted from the gamete donation.

The European Society of Human Reproduction and Embryology Task Force on Ethics and Law (2002) concluded that all gamete donors should receive counseling about the disposition of their genetic materials. The task force members also suggested informing ovum donors that the meaning they attach to donation may possibly be affected as a result of maturity and personal life events.

Lo et al. (2004) suggested treating physicians not have the responsibility of asking egg donors to donate the excess embryos created with their ova to research. Would it be ethically permissible to have an outside consultant obtain consent? Should only Mental Health Professional Group members of the ASRM be permitted to conduct the psychological evaluations of potential donors because they are conversant with all of the previously described issues, including embryo disposition, which must necessarily be considered to ensure consents are truly informed? Would nonmembers of the ASRM be familiar with all of issues involved in egg donation to enable them to confirm informed consent?

Historically, directives for disposition of donated oocytes have been made exclusively by recipient couples or individuals. In the past, many egg donors have waived their rights to their genetic material once retrieval has taken place (Adsuar, Pritts, Olive, & Lindheim, 2003). Others may not waive such rights until their eggs have been combined with sperm. One study found fewer than 50% of ovum donors supported giving their recipient couples total dispositional authority over the embryos created from their oocytes (Kalfoglou & Geller, 2000). Given the dearth of qualified oocyte donors, is it not desirable to make the donation process more satisfactory for them? Donors have stated they would be more likely to donate again if they were more involved in the process, were provided more follow-up care, could have more input regarding who would receive their oocytes and the method of their disposition, and knew the outcome for the recipients (Adsuar et al., 2003; Fielding et al., 1998; Kalfoglou & Gittelsohn, 2000; Kump et al., 2003; Rosenberg & Epstein, 1995; Schover, Collins, Quigley, Blankstein, & Kanoti, 1991). Many of the relevant issues regarding disposition can be addressed in contracts between donors and recipients so all parties are aware of and adhere to the concerns of those with whom they are matched.

Research has found donors' desires change posttreatment (Kalfoglou & Geller, 2000; Kalfoglou & Gittelsohn, 2000; Klock, Sheinin, & Kazer, 2001a; Kump et al., 2003; Zweifel et al., 2006). What should be done with the genetic material of oocyte donors who, after having children of their own, change their minds regarding the disposition of the oocytes and embryos created from their oocytes? When should oocyte donors be contacted to ascertain whether their original disposition options remain unchanged? Because women often change their minds after having their own children, should nulliparous women be prohibited from oocyte donation?

Kalfoglou and Geller (2000) proposed three alternatives to IVF centers whose donors wished to impose stipulations regarding the disposition of their genetic material or who can receive their oocytes. The donors can be rejected; they can be accepted and their conditions accepted; or they can be advised they will be required to relinquish their rights to their oocytes or embryos created from their genetic material. This raises some concern, however, about whether the donor's participation can then truly be said to be voluntary. These researchers determined 25% of donors did not want their oocytes or embryos used for research.

Furthermore, most donors believed recipients would be as thoroughly screened as they, and they wanted the recipients to undergo background checks for criminal or violent behavior. Donors, it seems, desired some assurance the recipients would make good parents. Oocyte donors wanted to know the outcome of the donation process because they wanted to "feel good" should a pregnancy occur; they wanted to prevent consanguinity; and several donors wished to find out whether they themselves were fertile. Among the known donors studied, Kalfoglou and Geller found they were satisfied permitting the recipients to set the boundaries in their relationships.

Both we and numerous other researchers concluded there are potential ethical and legal problems if oocyte donors believe their eggs are being used for one purpose and are appropriated for other purposes without their signed permission or consent.

EXISTING LAWS, POLICIES, AND LEGISLATION

In the United States, egg donation is largely unregulated. Currently, few states have laws addressing egg donation in the context of family building. Fla. Stat. § 742.14 (2008) and Okla. Stat. tit. 10, § 554 (2008) are two examples, both of which release the donor from parental rights or responsibilities. The laws recognize the intended parents, that is, the recipients, as the legal parents of any child conceived and assert the donor has no parental rights or obligations for any child conceived using the donated gametes. These laws, however, do not address the issue of donor compensation. The existing statutes primarily address the issue of parentage but do not consider such issues as future contact; inadvertent consanguinity; or the when, where, how, and what of the informed consent process.

Many other nations, including Canada and the United Kingdom, prohibit payment for gametes (Storrow, 2006). Donor compensation seems to be somewhat of an oxymoron and has been the focus of many ethical concerns. Donation of a woman's eggs for research has the potential to assist countless individuals, whereas donation for reproductive purposes may only help a select few (Steinbock, 2009).

Recently, bills have been introduced to address concerns regarding payment of donors who may be donating their oocytes for research practices. In Connecticut, for example, any person seeking to donate unfertilized eggs for stem cell purposes shall not receive direct payment for such eggs (Conn. Gen. Stat. sec. 19a-32d [2008]). It is likely similar legislation may be introduced regarding compensating donors who donate for reproductive purposes. Legislative restrictions on donor compensation is an issue often discussed in the literature and the popular press especially when recipients place ads offering tens of thousands of dollars to donors with certain qualifications.

Case law addressing these issues has been limited. To date, no cases of donors seeking custody or visitation of a child conceived as a result of the donation process have been reported. This does not mean no such attempts have been made, but it does suggest any such conflicts have been resolved without resort to the appellate courts.

One way to address some of the concerns that might arise in the context of egg donation is through private ordering, that is, contracts between donors and recipients. This can be accomplished even when donors are anonymous. Contracts can enhance informed consent and define the rights and obligations of the donors and recipients, clarifying each party's expectations of the other, presently and in the future. The mental health professional can assist each party in determining what he or she expects from such an arrangement so that the information can be shared with his or her independent counsel.

Although not unique to oocyte recipiency, yet another ethical topic was labeled by Knoppers and LeBris (1991) as "procreative tourism." This term is used to describe the traveling of citizens from one country where treatment is not available to another less restrictive country to obtain assisted reproductive treatment. Inhorn and Patrizio (2009) suggested that the phrase "reproductive exile" would more accurately reflect the despair infertility patients feel when unable to receive medical treatment within the country in which they reside. The main causes of cross-border reproductive care, also known as reproductive travel, are as follows:

1. A type of treatment is forbidden by law.
2. A treatment is unavailable because of the lack of equipment or expertise.
3. A treatment currently is not available because it is considered experimental.
4. Patients in certain categories are ineligible; the waiting lists are too long; and the costs of treatment are too high (Cook, 2003; Knoppers & LeBris, 1991; Lee, 2005).

Some ethicists believe each individual should make decisions regarding treatment according to his or her personal and moral convictions. Other ethicists argue this position negates the opinions of those who support the denial of some specific types of treatment. In any given country then, policies imposed by the majority may cause the minority to travel elsewhere for medical treatment. Reproductive travel allows those in the minority to pursue their dream of parenthood.

In the eyes of the law, egg donation is a relatively new procedure, and the evolution of law on this issue is in its infancy. As egg donors age and build their own families and as the children of oocyte donation become adults and begin to reproduce, more and more questions may come to light. Given the reactive nature of the law, legislation and/or case law may not emerge until or unless disputes arise. Mental health professionals can play a very active role in helping to reduce or ameliorate disputes by attempting to keep the lines of communication open for all of the participants involved.

CLINICAL VIGNETTE

Brooke, a practicing attorney, was scheduled to be seen with her husband, Scott, a forensic psychologist, for their psychoeducational interview prior to beginning their first oocyte recipient cycle. At age 33, Brooke was diagnosed with POI. Brooke's diagnosis came as a surprise because she had been able to conceive her two children from her first marriage with relative ease. Brooke's sister Julia, age 30, would be their oocyte donor. Julia and her husband, Justin, were also scheduled for their psychological session 1 hour before Brooke and Scott's interview. Julia would be taking the Minnesota Multiphasic Personality Inventory-2 (MMPI-2; Hathaway & McKinley, 1989), while her sister and brother-in-law were scheduled to speak with the psychologist. Following the two couples' psychological sessions, a third interview was to convene with all four participants meeting with the psychologist to discuss and resolve any problems that might have been identified during their previous interviews.

During the psychological appointment with Brooke's sister, the donor, Julia, a high school graduate and mother of two, disclosed she was approached by the women's mother to act as the designated oocyte donor for her sister. Julia reported her sister was happy to have her act as the donor because their genetics are similar and their health histories known.

Julia, who has a prior history of dysthymia and severe postpartum depression after the birth of her younger child, had been placed on a selective serotonin reuptake inhibitor (SSRI) by her gynecologist. Although the possible outcomes had been disclosed to Julia, she was not concerned about the need for her to discontinue her psychotropic medication or the potential side effects of the gonadotropins necessary for controlled ovarian hyperstimulation.

Although both Julia and Brooke were raised in a fairly strict Catholic home, Julia was always less devout than her sister. Brooke and Scott remain religious, and her two children from her first marriage are matriculated in the school located in an annex of the same Catholic Church where they regularly attend services.

Brooke and Scott's interview revealed some unexpected and disconcerting information. When the likelihood of creating and cryopreserving more than the two embryos Brooke wished to have transferred was mentioned, she stiffened. Brooke explained it went against her religious beliefs to create more "lives" than would be needed for transfer to her uterus. Additionally, should Broke conceive triplets, she would not be in favor of participating in fetal reduction, even though the IVF nurse at the clinic had reviewed and distributed the ASRM patient fact sheet regarding the complications and problems with multiple births.

Furthermore, Brooke disclosed to the psychologist over the telephone before their appointment that she would prefer not to participate in IVF but felt obligated to do so because her husband, Scott, did not have any children. Brooke also disclosed she felt peculiar having Julia act as their oocyte donor for several reasons. Brooke was fearful her and Scott's child might suffer from depression. Moreover, Brooke believed, after disclosing the details of the child's conception to her son or daughter, the child might wonder who actually was his or her "real" mother.

Ethical Dilemmas in the Context of Professional Guidelines

In the American Psychological Association's (APA's) "Ethical Principles of Psychologists and Code of Conduct," Principle C, Integrity, encourages psychologists to promote accuracy, honesty, and truthfulness. Mental health professionals owe this duty to donors and recipients, alike. Therefore, the psychologist should avoid misrepresentation of the information disclosed by Brooke and consider the harmful effects that could be caused by possible collusion with her.

The psychologist should, according to APA Ethics Code Standard 3.07, Third-Party Requests for Services, clarify the nature of his or her role to Julia and Justin. At the outset of their interview the mental health professional should explain theirs will be an evaluative assessment, one that might result in gatekeeping, that is, the prevention of their participation in medical treatment.

APA Ethics Code Standard 3.11, Psychological Services Delivered to or Through Organizations, might be interpreted to mean that if the mental health professional will be obtaining information for a physician or fertility clinic where he or she is employed, is acting as a paid consultant, or will be evaluating the egg donor couple at the request of an oocyte recipient couple or egg donor agency, this information should be provided to the clients prior to the commencement of services. Furthermore, the psychologist should inform Julia and Justin about (a) the nature and objectives of the services, (b) the intended recipients of the information, (c) which of the individuals are considered the clients, (d) the relationship the psychologist will have with each person and the clinic, (e) the probable uses of the services provided and the information obtained, (f) who will have access to the information, and (g) the limits of confidentiality.

To practice in accordance with APA Ethics Code Standard 9.03, Informed Consent in Assessments, the psychologist should explain that Justin and Julia's evaluations could lead to a psychological diagnosis. Furthermore, it should be disclosed that Brooke and Scott will participate in a psychoeducational session, which is dissimilar to their interview in both length and substance.

The most common type of nonanonymous oocyte donation is sister to sister. According to the Ethics Committee of the ASRM (2004c), the appearance of or an actual consanguineous relationship must not exist between gamete recipients and donors. Sister-to-sister donations are therefore acceptable. Sometimes the sisters' physical proximity makes it easy for them to be patients at the same IVF center; however, neither should be assigned to the same RE, if possible. Sisters may be too emotionally close to each other to permit autonomous and fully informed decision making as contemplated by ASRM guidelines. During the donor sister's psychological session, the mental health professional will need to inform Julia the results of her MMPI-2 (Hathaway & McKinley, 1989) test, and the psychological session may disqualify her from acting as Brooke's oocyte provider.

The Practice Committee of the ASRM and the Practice Committee of the SART (2008) guidelines state a potential oocyte donor's current use of psychotropic medication is cause for exclusion. Furthermore, the Ethics Committee of the ASRM (2004d) warns against the coercion of participants in the assisted reproductive technologies. Some well placed, open-ended questions could help the mental health professional ascertain whether others, in this case Julia and Brooke's mother, exercised undue influence on the donor's willingness to participate in intrafamilial reproductive collaboration. The psychologist also needs to determine the significance that Julia attaches to the financial compensation.

Recipient sisters often express concern that their children might be confused as a result of the donor sister's multiple relational roles. In the vignette, Brooke verbalized apprehension about the ramifications that her child might experience if Julia was identified as her oocyte donor.

Religious oocyte recipients might resolve their reservations regarding pregnancy reduction by electing to have a single-embryo transfer; however, that would not address the issue of supernumerary embryo disposition. Brooke expressed extreme discomfort regarding the creation, not to mention disposition, of excess embryos. Further discussion of the alternatives may not assuage the recipient's misgivings. Ultimately, a religious oocyte recipient's participation in IVF may possibly be detrimental to her, her partner, and other family members. This potential outcome is addressed by both the Ethics Committee of the ASRM (2004c) guidelines and by the APA's Ethics Code Principle A, Beneficence and Nonmaleficence.

None of this book's authors is a member of the American Association of Christian Counselors; however, when one's clients are particularly religious, it may become necessary to review the ethical code and beliefs of their religion (Ohlschager, 2004). Participation in all assisted reproductive technologies is forbidden by the Catholic Church (Colliton, 2004). Abortion, and therefore, fetal reduction, are also prohibited. Because most Christians, including Catholics, believe life begins at conception, the creation and destruction of embryos is not permitted (Engelhardt, 2006). Mental health professionals practicing in the area of reproductive medicine may erroneously assume clients participating in IVF have previously resolved all religious conflicts. However, this often is not the case, as illustrated in this chapter's clinical vignette.

Practical Considerations

Fortunately, Brooke and Scott have established careers and earn sufficient income to cover the cost of oocyte recipiency. The procedure is usually very expensive because the recipient couple is responsible for not only their own physical evaluations, psychological assessment, medications, and surgery but also for those of the donor couple. Also, both couples reside in an area of the country that has numerous qualified, well-respected REs and IVF centers.

Balancing the Multiple Perspectives

A review of the literature suggests society is more supportive of familial oocyte donation than the procurement of anonymous donors from either an IVF center or oocyte donor agency. Society, it seems, deems sister-to-sister donation as less offensive because coercion, commodification, and anonymity are rarely involved (Lessor, Rietz, Balmaceda, & Asch, 1990).

The Clinician or Fertility Clinic

Most REs endorse sister-to-sister oocyte donation. Research reveals physicians frequently request that oocyte recipients solicit relatives who might be willing to act as a designated donor (Baetens et al., 2000; Greenfeld & Klock, 2004; Lessor, Rietz, Balmaceda, & Asch, 1990; Sauer & Kavic, 2006). Conveniently, Brooke and Julia reside near each other, thus simplifying arrangements for physical evaluations, monitoring, oocyte retrieval, and embryo transfer.

Because it was Brooke and Scott who initiated the appointment with the clinic, it might be assumed both were eager to have a child and had previously considered the religious implications of IVF; however, this should be verified. Furthermore, the staff at an IVF clinic might believe a sister-to-sister donation would be less financially burdensome for the recipients rather than resorting to an egg donor agency.

The Prospective Parents

This is Scott's first marriage, and he generously adopted Brooke's two children from her previous marriage. Scott has assumed emotional and financial responsibility for Brooke's children, and he has demonstrated that he is an excellent father. Is Scott not entitled to experience the joys of parenting a child from infancy through adulthood? However, must Scott have a biogenetic link to the potential child? Could Scott's desires be met through the adoption?

Mental health professionals should inform clients from the outset that anything discussed individually during their psychoeducational interview will be divulged to their partner. Scott is unaware Brooke is only considering having an additional child out of a sense of obligation to him. It would be better if Scott knew of Brooke's motivation. Although Scott may be disappointed, the couple will need to resolve whether to proceed with IVF.

Brooke and Scott are active members of the Catholic Church, which has concluded assisted reproductive technologies are contrary to its moral teachings (Blois & O'Rourke, 1995). Meilaender (1998) suggested the assisted reproductive technologies take the most intimate area of a couple's life, that is, their sexual relations, and infuse it with procedures involving additional partners. Furthermore, most Catholic ethicists report that the introduction of an oocyte provider violates the recipients' marital union.

If Brooke believes IVF is morally reprehensible and compromises her religious convictions, the couple should not participate in oocyte recipiency. However, Brooke might be satisfied if the RE agrees to single-embryo transfer and the embryologist creates and possibly cryopreserves only enough embryos for one fresh and one frozen IVF cycle. However, further discussion of the alternatives still might not assuage Brooke's misgivings.

Although Brooke may decide to use IVF to have an additional child, her reservations about having her sister act as the donor may be insurmountable. Ultimately, Brooke's participation in IVF may possibly be detrimental to her, Scott, and other family members.

The Donor

The most significant variable to be determined is whether Julia's mother coerced her to act as Brooke's oocyte donor. Julia will be excluded from potential candidacy if coercion is confirmed.

Weaning Julia off of her psychotropic medication may have undesirable consequences. She and Justin have two children for whom they are responsible, and the discontinuation of Julia's antidepressant may adversely impact the entire nuclear family. Additionally, the side effects of the gonadotropins that would be administered to Julia may exacerbate her predisposition toward additional psychological problems.

Usually potential candidates are prohibited from oocyte donation if they are currently taking medication for a diagnosed mood disorder (Practice Committee of the ASRM and the Practice Committee of the SART, 2008). In the circumstance of sister-to-sister donation, women are not categorically rejected because their genetics are already known to the recipients. Julia's cavalier attitude regarding the need to discontinue her SSRI is troubling, especially if coercion is tainting this decision. However, unless the act of donating one's oocytes is potentially harmful to Julia or others, she might be permitted to participate in assisted reproductive technology. The consequences of cessation of Julia's antidepressant medication and the potential side effects of gonadotropins must be medically and psychologically assessed and disclosed to Julia and her husband, Justin.

Both the ASRM's guidelines and APA's Ethics Code Principle A, Beneficence and Nonmalificence, guide the psychologist to counsel Julia so that she will not experience harm as a result of her participation in oocyte donation. Would Julia blame herself if IVF was unsuccessful? If so, how would her possible feelings of culpability impact not only her but her entire family? The mental health professional will need to discuss with Julia the possibility that she may be disappointed and assess her commitment to donate should her expectations and wishes not come to fruition.

The Potential Child

A genetic counselor could provide the adults in this collaborative reproductive arrangement with information regarding the heritability of Julia's dysthymic disorder.

Relational confusion possibly experienced by Brooke and Scott's potential child might be time limited. The child's cognitive and emotional adaptation would probably be contingent on his or her developmental age as well as the reactions and responsiveness of the child's parents, extended family, and peer group. In sister-to-sister oocyte donation we doubt very young children would question whether the oocyte provider was their mother or their aunt. As they age, children can more easily understand the role that an oocyte donor played in their conception, hopefully without experiencing uncertainty, insecurity, or hostility.

After having learned the details of conception, Brooke and Scott's child may discuss it with friends, relatives, and teachers. Friends in parochial school may in turn disclose this information to their parents, putting in motion a chain of events that may possibly be injurious.

The child conceived with a donor's ova may feel secure because he or she was desired by the parent(s) who went to extraordinary lengths to have him or her. Grandparents, aunts, uncles, and other relatives who are aware of the parents' struggle to conceive may be especially warm and loving because this child may seem like a miracle to the family members.

Conversely, the child, lacking a total biogenetic link to both parents, may feel unequal to children of his or her age. Because there are older siblings in this nuclear family, the child conceived with a donated ovum may believe his or her parents love those children more. Furthermore, should some of the child's relatives be disapproving of third-party reproduction, the child may feel rejected. Eventually children conceived from donated ova may experience more distress in adolescence when being similar to one's peers becomes extremely important.

The Existing Children

Existing children in a family that used donated oocytes to enlarge their household may wonder whether they were inadequate in meeting their parents' needs. In adolescence, Brooke's existing children may be self-conscious of their family's uniqueness and wonder whether they are the subjects of gossip. The children who are fully biogenetically related to each other born prior to the donor oocyte child may feel more entitled and beloved than their younger sibling, which has the potential for negatively impacting the dynamics of the household.

The birth of another child might be perceived by the existing children as a loss of their parents' attention. On the other hand, having a third child might act as a catalyst for psychic healing and cement their family ties, although this does not negate the potential for sibling rivalry. Additionally, Brooke's existing children, who exclusively know Julia as their aunt, may experience relational confusion, as might Julia's existing children. Conversely, the cousins may become more close-knit as a result of Julia's donation of her oocytes to Brooke.

Brooke's existing children may feel confused as a result of their educational experiences at Catholic school, where they might be taught all assisted reproductive technologies are prohibited. They may believe their parents participated in a sinful activity. Moreover, the two children may perceive their parents as having engaged in a medical procedure that conflicts with their religious beliefs, resulting in an erosion of the parent–child relationship as a result of what they believe is hypocritical behavior.

CONCLUSION

We believe Brooke is not ready to proceed to oocyte recipiency and, in fact, may never actually want to participate. Brooke lacks the desire to have additional children, and furthermore, she has disclosed she is uncomfortable with IVF on moral and religious grounds.

It is crucial to note that Brooke is being dishonest both to her husband, out of a sense of obligation, and her sister, not wishing to hurt Julia's feelings. Brooke's unwillingness to be assertive may originate from a desire for approval and/or an eagerness to be well liked. Conversely, she simply may be deceitful, duplicitous, or passive aggressive. We would consider Brooke's misrepresentations when drawing conclusions pertaining to her appropriateness as an oocyte recipient candidate.

The likelihood that Brooke would need to participate in fetal reduction would be minimal if no more than one embryo was transferred. However, the creation of more than one embryo during an IVF cycle is prudent. Because IVF, fetal reduction, and the creation of embryos through oocyte recipiency are all prohibited by the Catholic Church, it seems likely participation in these procedures would cause Brooke to experience inner turmoil. Should Brooke eventually reconcile all of the previously mentioned factors, we might urge her to consider potential oocyte donor candidates other than Julia. This alternative would likely be in the best interest of both sisters.

Brooke's fear that her potential child might experience relational confusion is understandable. However, if Brooke remained unconvinced after being presented with the various methods of disclosure found to be useful to children born after assisted reproductive technology, the need to exclude Julia would be enhanced.

Julia might actually benefit from being disqualified to act as Brooke's oocyte donor because discontinuation of SSRIs after experiencing a mood disorder for almost a lifetime is contraindicated. Julia's role as homemaker would almost certainly suffer should she become even temporarily depressed and therefore less responsive to her family's needs. On the other hand, the 4- to 6-week period of time necessary to titrate and experience the positive effects of an SSRI may seem inconsequential when compared with the gift Julia might provide her sister and brother-in-law. However, because Brooke does not seem enamored of receiving Julia's eggs, the possibility of her sister's depression can be avoided altogether.

Mental health professionals may never know with any certainty whether Julia was self-motivated to donate or if she did so as a result of coercion. If it was discovered Julia was directly or indirectly coerced, she should not be permitted to act as her sister's oocyte donor.

This chapter's scenario, while complex, is not uncommon. Sister-to-sister donations, however, usually are slightly more straightforward. Brooke's opposition to IVF and fetal reduction on religious and moral grounds is compelling, and participation might be detrimental to her and, eventually, to her relationship with Scott. We would recommend Brooke participate in both individual and couples counseling with Scott in the hopes she could resolve her ambivalence.

Moreover, if they proceeded with medical treatment, we would suggest that Brooke and Scott select another oocyte donor for several reasons. First, Brooke is far too critical of Julia's mood disorder. Second, we oppose colluding with Brooke and misleading her sister. Third, should Brooke and Scott proceed with oocyte recipiency, the use of another unrelated donor would eliminate Brooke's concerns regarding her child's relational confusion.

Furthermore, our assessment of Julia may reinforce our opinion. We would not wish for Julia to participate in oocyte donation and become depressed should Brooke and Scott fail to conceive and/or to give birth to a healthy child.

Although Julia's genetics are similar to Brooke's and we are fairly certain she would not ingest alcoholic beverages, smoke, misuse prescription or non-prescription drugs, or have indiscriminate sexual relations, her history of dysthymia renders her only marginally appropriate to act as an oocyte donor. Marital counseling is strongly advised for Brooke and Scott prior to either known or anonymous oocyte recipiency. Many conditions would have to be met before reconsidering them as oocyte recipients and Julia as their oocyte donor.

6

SPERM DONATION AND RECIPIENCY

It doesn't help matters when prime time TV has Murphy Brown, a character who supposedly epitomizes today's intelligent, highly paid professional woman, mocking the importance of fathers by bearing a child alone and calling it just another lifestyle choice.

—Former Vice President Dan Quayle,
Poverty of Values: The Murphy Brown Speech

When giving a speech about the erosion of traditional values and the breakdown of the American family, then Vice President Dan Quayle attacked an extremely popular character in a television series and made headlines. More than 15 years later it is difficult to describe an average American home and impossible to speculate on what is the best method to create a family.

As of 2008, approximately 6 in every 10 children, or nearly 45 million, lived with their biological mother and father, and approximately 19.3 million, or 26%, lived with one parent (U.S. Census Bureau News, 2008). It is difficult to determine how many children are living with gay or lesbian parents. Patterson (1992) reported there were approximately 2–8 million gay or lesbian parents in the United States and approximately 4–14 million children living with gay or lesbian parents. However, Gates and Ost (2004) published significantly lower findings in which they stated there were only 250,000 children under age 18 raised by same-sex couples in 1999.

In this chapter, we focus on sperm donation and sperm recipiency, specifically in three types of families: households headed by heterosexual couples, lesbian couples, and single women. Although most heterosexual couples who use donated sperm to have children have a medical need, women without male partners, that is, lesbian couples and single women, frequently choose to become sperm recipients so that they too may become parents.

MEDICAL BACKGROUND

Medical interventions are often attempted prior to suggesting that the partners of male patients use donated sperm. A discussion of some of these methods follows. One method available to assist conception is *intracytoplasmic sperm injection (ICSI)*, which injects the sperm directly into the egg so fertilization may take place (Friedler et al., 2002; Gabrielsen, Fedder, & Agerholm, 2006). Also, ICSI is used with men who have a low concentration of sperm in their ejaculate (De Croo, Van der Erst, Everaert, De Sutter, & Dhont, 2000). If the male partner can produce some sperm, most heterosexual couples would prefer to use ICSI in conjunction with in vitro fertilization (IVF) to preserve a genetic link to both parents, although those procedures may be cost prohibitive (Schover et al., 1996). The sperm can be collected after ejaculation or extracted in the various ways mentioned in the following paragraph (De Croo et al., 2000; Heidenreich, Altmann, & Engelmann, 2000; Mansour et al., 1997).

Sperm aspiration refers to the group of microsurgical procedures used to retrieve viable sperm from the male reproductive tract. Sperm can be aspirated from the vas deferens, testes, or epididymis (Heidenreich et al., 2000). Aspiration is used to acquire sperm from those men who have no sperm in their ejaculate (azoospermia), whose sperm have poor motility, or whose sperm, once ejaculated, are dead (Kolettis, 2002). Often sperm aspiration is used to treat men with blockages, retrograde ejaculation (Herslag, Schiff, & DeCherney, 1991; Meacham, 2005), spinal cord injuries (DeForge et al., 2005; Hovav, Almagor, & Yaffe, 2002), and Klinefelter's syndrome (Brandes & Mesrobian, 2005; Denschlag, Tempfer, Kunzem, Wolff, & Keck, 2004; Osborne, 2006).

Currently, aspiration is widely used in conjuction with IVF (M. Licht, personal communication, April 15, 2006). However, these methods can be expensive. IVF with ICSI may cost in excess of 5 times the cost of an intrauterine insemination (IUI) cycle using donor sperm. Consequently men with azoospermia, an absence of sperm resulting from obstructive and nonobstructive causes, as well as females without male partners may consider donor insemination (DI) an appropriate method for conception.

Candidates for Sperm Recipiency

Potential sperm recipient candidates include single or lesbian women, women who are partnered with men who either do not wish to submit to or cannot afford other medical interventions, or those for whom alternative medical treatments would not assist.

Medical Procedures for Receiving Donor Sperm

Prior to using DI with a heterosexual couple, both members must be medically evaluated, that is, complete detailed medical histories and medical examinations. In lesbian couples, only the female to be inseminated will complete a medical evaluation.

Insemination can be performed without the use of ovulation-stimulating drugs, but timing of a woman's menstrual cycle is critical. DI is synchronized with a woman's menstrual cycle to coincide with ovulation. Often medications for controlled ovarian hyperstimulation are administered in conjunction with DI to maximize the likelihood of conception. IUI can also be used with clomiphene citrate or gonadotropins and is referred to as IUI with controlled ovarian hyperstimulation.

Controlled ovarian hyperstimulation is used with women who do not ovulate and will increase the number of eggs produced by the ovaries, which allows multiple eggs to be exposed to the sperm. Women with cervical factor infertility can benefit from IUI as the sperm bypass the cervix and are placed directly into the uterus.

DI is conducted with thawed semen that is drawn into an insemination catheter with a syringe attached to its end. The syringe is inserted through the woman's cervix and into her uterine cavity where the semen is deposited. If DI is successful, the sperm will travel into her fallopian tubes where fertilization will occur (Goldstein, 2004).

Donated sperm used in IVF with ICSI will have to survive the thawing process. The success rates for this procedure can be influenced by many factors, including the quality of the sperm, the ova, and the woman's uterine environment (Silber, Nagy, Devroey, Camus, & Van Steirteghem, 1997).

Candidates for Sperm Donation

The potential sperm donor and his family's health histories are scrutinized. Those whose histories include such problems as cleft lip, cleft palate, congenital heart malformation, spina bifida, clubfoot, hypospadia, transmittable spongiform encephalopathy (infection of the brain), or Creutzfeld-Jakob disease (a rare, degenerative, fatal brain disorder) are eliminated from consideration. Additional disqualifiers are hemoglobin disorders, asthma, juvenile diabetes, epilepsy, rheumatoid arthritis, cystic fibrosis, thalessemia, or Tay-Sach disease (Practice Committee of American Society for Reproductive Medicine [ASRM] and Practice Committee of the Society for Assisted Reproductive Technology [SART], 2008).

The guidelines of the Practice Committee of the ASRM and the Practice Committee of the SART (2008) call for careful record keeping. Those who donate are asked to provide the sperm bank with up-to-date health information. Additionally, they are responsible for disclosing any subsequent donations of their sperm. All of this information, however, is self-reported and is not legally required. The sperm donor's records should be maintained so the medical information would be available to any offspring, yet anonymity should be preserved for all but known donors. All sperm donor records should be confidential (Practice Committee of the ASRM and the Practice Committee of the SART, 2008).

Medical Procedures for Sperm Donation

Although a man's sperm count might enable him to impregnate his partner, it may be insufficient to qualify him as a sperm donor. Currently, in anonymous sperm donation, sperm are quarantined and frozen for a period of no less than 6 months to check for contagious diseases. Approximately 50% to 80% of sperm do not survive the thawing process (Jimenez, 2005).

Sperm donors should be of legal age but no older than age 40 because increased age is associated with a decline in semen volume, sperm motility, and sperm morphology (Kidd, Eskenazia, & Wyrobek, 2001). Additionally, the frequency of Down syndrome, malformations of the extremities, and syndromes of multiple systems are more prevalent with increased paternal age (Zhu et al., 2005). Increased risks of schizophrenia, autism, and bipolar disorder have also been reported ("Children of Older Fathers," 2008; Feldman, 2007; New York University Medical Center and School of Medicine, 2001). Fecundity, the time it takes to achieve a pregnancy, also declines as men age (Ford et al., 2000).

Before having their sperm tested, potential donors must sign informed consent forms (Barrat, Englert, Gottlieb, & Jouannet, 1998). However, typically they are not provided any counsel with regard to the legal ramifications of their participation as sperm donors nor, in most instances, are they provided with a psychoeducational consultation (Childress-Beatty, 2009). Donors are instructed to abstain from ejaculation for 2 to 3 days prior to providing their samples. Potential sperm donors produce semen samples that must meet the minimal standards (Jimenez, 2005). Donors are requested to provide several samples, and all should have a volume of above 2 ml (Borrero, 2001). Should the sperm donor be accepted, he will be asked to continue to provide several samples, usually in 6-month intervals (Practice Committee of the ASRM and the Practice Committee of the SART, 2008). At least 50% of the sperm in each sample should be moving in an actively purposeful direction (Borrero, 2001). A minimum concentration greater than 50% of the potential donor's sperm should be motile when multiplied by 10 to the 6th power per milliliter

(Borrero, 2001). Additionally, the donor's sperm morphology (shape) needs to be within the normal range (Carson, Casson, & Shuman, 1999).

Every potential sperm donor should be in good physical and psychological health, produce quality sperm, and be free from any known genetic abnormalities (Practice Committee of the ASRM and the Practice Committee of the SART, 2008). The use of fresh sperm is prohibited as it could transmit HIV and other infectious diseases before the donor is seropositive (Practice Committee of the ASRM and the Practice Committee of the SART, 2008).

The Practice Committee of the ASRM and the Practice Committee of the SART (2008), the European Society of Human Reproduction and Embryology Task Force on Ethics and Law (2002), and the British Andrology Society (1999) have published guidelines for the qualification of potential sperm donors. Men who have sexual relations with other men; who have hepatitis B or C or are intravenous drug abusers; or who are suspected of being HIV positive or test positive (with verification by a second test) for HIV-1, HIV-2, HTLV-1, and HTLV-2 are excluded from sperm donation. Sperm donors who have or have had certain sexually transmitted diseases, for example, chlamydia trachomatis, gonorrhea, syphilis, genital warts, genital herpes and genital ulcers, or urethral discharge, are prohibited from donation. Seropositive sperm donors infected with the cytomegalovirus or herpes virus Type 5 are also barred from donating. Those men who have had acupuncture, body piercings, or tattooing from instruments that might not be sterile are not permitted to donate their sperm for a period of time after undergoing such procedures. In addition, many states have laws requiring particular testing of any tissue donors, and these laws include sperm donors.

PSYCHOSOCIAL CONCERNS

In the past, the mixing of semen from an anonymous donor with the semen from an infertile male was used in an attempt to stave off negative emotional sequelae (Baran & Pannor, 1993; Friedman, 1980). Moreover, physicians recommended couples have intercourse just prior to insemination so they would not know whose sperm was responsible for fertilizing the egg (Grace & Daniels, 2007). Many of our patients who had previously mixed their sperm with that of a donor continue to hope their offspring resulted from their own gametes. Even in the face of indisputable evidence to the contrary, a great number of men remain in denial and refuse to accept that their children were conceived with donor sperm. Many of these fathers scrutinize their sons and daughters well into their teens for any physical resemblance to themselves. Thankfully, mixing of sperm is now disfavored.

Sperm Recipients

Blaser, Maloigne-Katz, and Gigon (1988) studied whether the need to use donor sperm was detrimental to the infertile male. Though they found no support for their hypothesis, other researchers have reported men's sexuality, virility, and masculinity were compromised once they were diagnosed as infertile, which may be due, in part, to the concomitant social stigma (Berger, 1980; Daniels, 2004, 2005; Daniels, Thorn, & Westerbrooke, 2007; Daniluk, 1988; Nielsen, Pedersen, & Lauritsen, 1995; Petok, 2006; Thorn, 2006).

Numerous studies have found additional psychological and emotional reactions are directly related to the need to use DI. These responses include stress and anxiety (Carr, Friedman, Lannon, & Sharp, 1990; Clarke, Klock, Geighegan, & Travassos, 1999; Hart, 2002; Petok, 2006; Van Thiel, Mantadakis, Vekemans, & Gillot de Vries, 1990), depression (Baran & Pannor, 1993; Van Thiel et al., 1990), shame and lack of confidence (Daniels et al., 2007), and significant lowering of the male partner's self-esteem (Berger, Eisen, Shuber, & Doody, 1986; Daniels, 2004; Nachtigall, Becker, & Wozny, 1992), among other negative emotions.

Interestingly, we have observed and research supports that even when the need to use DI was due to male factor infertility, the female partners reported experiencing increased emotional distress (Daniluk, 1988; Nachtigall et al., 1992; Prattke & Gass-Sternas, 1993; J. Wright et al., 1991). We have also noticed that whether or not pregnancy occurred after DI, many female partners attributed the outcome of the procedure to their own emotional well-being or fragility during the insemination procedures (Reading, Sledmere, & Cox, 1982).

Despite the negative emotions they experienced while proceeding through infertility treatment, many patients preferred DI over adoption (Baran & Pannor, 1993; Daniels, 1994). Furthermore, some individuals and couples perceived children conceived from DI differently than adopted children, whereas others did not distinguish between the two alternatives to family building (Tyler, Nicholas, Crockett, & Driscoll, 1983).

Historically, opinions regarding the use of psychological interviews to assist and evaluate individuals and couples as they decided whether to use DI have been divided. Although Waltzer (1982) believed psychological interviews were unnecessary, others have found mental health professionals helpful for their DI patients (Daniels, 2004; Klock & Maier, 1991; Thorn, 2006). The Ethics Committee of the ASRM (2004c) issued guidelines strongly suggesting all gamete recipients receive at least one psychoeducational interview.

Initially physicians advised their patients to keep DI a secret (Daniels & Taylor, 1993). However, researchers have concluded that lack of discussion about one's use of DI inhibits the healing process through the defense mechanism of denial (Berger, 1980; Berger et al., 1986). The individual's or couple's acknowledgement of the need for infertility treatment in general, and donated sperm in particular, can assist in the individual's or couple's coming to terms with the decision. However, despite the psychological benefits, many of the physicians with whom we consult continue to counsel their patients not to disclose.

Boivin, Scanlan, and Walker (1999) examined why infertile patients seldom used psychological counseling. They found that this population relied on loved ones for emotional support. However, the more distressed individuals and couples did not know whom to contact, that is, a mental health professional who specialized in working with infertile patients, and/or they were financially unable to afford psychotherapy.

We believe reproductive endocrinologists may be hesitant to refer their patients for psychological assistance for several reasons. First, the reproductive endocrinologists may wish to be financially competitive and do not want their patients to incur additional expense. Second, those patients who believe a referral for psychological consultation is analogous to calling them mentally unstable would be offended and might possibly discontinue medical treatments with the referring reproductive endocrinologist.

Candidates for Sperm Donation

There is no one specific type of man who becomes a sperm donor (Daniels, 2004), although generally sperm donors are found to be emotionally stable, extroverted (Nicholas & Tyler, 1983), above average intelligence, considerate, disciplined (Taus & Gerzova, 1991), and better educated than the average male (Daniels, Curson, & Lewis, 1996). This last finding seems reasonable because many sperm donors are recruited from universities. Although many potential sperm donors do not consider themselves to be altruistic, their acquaintances often perceive them as compassionate and unselfish (Sauer, Gorrill, Zeffer, & Bustillo, 1989).

Financial compensation and altruism are the primary motivators among men who donate their sperm (Daniels, Curson, & Lewis, 1996; Pedersen, Nielsen, & Lauritsen, 1994). Many donors are motivated by altruism alone (Daniels, Blyth, Crawshaw, & Curson, 2005; Lalos, Daniels, Gottlieb, & Lalos, 2003; Lui et al., 1995). However, others would not donate without financial compensation (Daniels, 2000; Daniels, Curson, & Lewis, 1996; Lui et al., 1995). Sperm donors' compensation ranges from $30 to $200 per donation, and the donors are asked to commit to a 6- to 12-month period of time during which they will collect their semen one to two times per week (California Cryobank, 2007; Fertility Cryobank, 2009; "Sperm Bank Basics," 2009).

Some men who already have children of their own elect to donate sperm because they wish to help others experience parenthood. Others have family members or friends who have experienced fertility problems, and hence they are sensitized to the emotional ramifications of infertility (Daniels, Curson, & Lewis, 1996; Lalos et al., 2003).

Few, if any, anonymous sperm donors have any psychological counseling prior to their donation process (Shenfield, 1998). Mental health professionals meet with sperm donors who are known to the recipients before an open donation process. Otherwise, sperm donors are interviewed by employees of the various sperm banks.

BIOETHICAL PERSPECTIVES

Currently, there are more than 500 licensed sperm banks in the United States and tens of thousands of donors (Wanjek, 2006). The first published reports regarding the practice of insemination using donor sperm appeared in 1945 (ASRM, 2006). However, therapeutic DI had already been practiced for well over 100 years. In 1884, Dr. William Pancoast, without the permission of his patients, inseminated the wife of an infertile male (Corea, 1985).

The media bombard the public with sensational news stories about sperm donation. Headlines blaze with titles such as "Sperm Donor Fights Order to Support 2 Children" (White Stack, 2005) and "Sperm Donor Must Pay Maintenance" (Ananova, 2006). Electrifying stories report gay activists demanding the Food and Drug Administration rescind its rule prohibiting men who have had homosexual sex from donating their sperm to prevent the spread of HIV and AIDS, calling the rule discriminatory and scaring away potential recipients (Fumento, 2005). Plotz (2005) documented the history of the Repository for Germinal Choice, dubbed the Nobel Prize Sperm Bank, which promised to provide recipients with sperm exclusively acquired from genius donors. However, most sperm donations are neither lurid nor shocking.

Single Heterosexual and Lesbian Sperm Recipients

Within the past 15 years, physicians have been receiving more requests for DI from single heterosexual and lesbian women (Baetens, Camus, & Devroey, 2003; MacCullum & Golombok, 2004; Robinson, 1997). Whereas the use of DI with heterosexual couples provides them with an opportunity to be a more "normal" family, the use of DI with two-mother families results in distinguishing them as "less similar" (Brewaeys, Ponjaert-Krisstoffersen, Van Steirteghem, & Devroey, 1993).

As might be expected, researchers have found that most lesbian couples prefer using sperm provided by identified donors (Brewaeys, de Bruyn, Louwe, & Helmerhorst, 2005). Some lesbian mothers wished to obtain more information about the donors, especially identifying data, whereas others, usually the social mothers, wanted no information at all (Baetens et al., 2003; Brewaeys, Devroey, Hemerhorst, Van Hall & Ponjaert, 1995).

It has been suggested that the counseling lesbian couples receive prior to DI should be similar to that provided to heterosexual couples (Baetens & Brewaeys, 2001). However, we believe psychologists can respectfully discuss the different experiences children may encounter in two-mother households, such as preparing the children for the possibility of prejudicial treatment from their classmates and schoolteachers, and the benefits of having a good support system and good male role models.

Anonymous Versus Open Donation

Mature sperm donors are more amenable to open donation and seem less motivated by the financial compensation they receive than younger sperm providers (Daniels, 2004; Daniels, Lalos, Gottlieb, & Lalos, 2005). As the younger sperm donors age, they may favor greater openness (Baran & Pannor, 1993; Daniels, 2004). However, there is some concern that younger men, whom neuropsychologists have found to have less fully developed brains (Packard, 2007; Rosso, Young, Femia, & Yurgelun-Todd, 2004), may be unable to consider the long-term ramifications of providing sperm (Daniels, Lewis, & Gillet, 1996).

Researchers have reported the majority of potential sperm donors require confidentiality and anonymity (Lui et al., 1995; Pedersen et al., 1994; Sauer et al., 1989), especially if they are young (Daniels, 2004). However, many potential sperm donors are willing to provide nonidentifying information about themselves to the recipients and offspring (Lui et al., 1995; Mahlstedt & Probasco, 1991; Pedersen et al., 1994). Some sperm donors have permitted their identities to be released when their offspring reach the age of majority (Daniels et al., 2005; Mahlstedt & Probasco, 1991; Purdie et al., 1992). Recently, it has been suggested the providers' attitudes toward openness reflect the attitudes held by the recruitment centers (Daniels, 2007), suggesting sperm bank personnel may be influential in encouraging either openness or secrecy.

Like their female counterparts, that is, oocyte donors, many sperm donors are interested in the outcome of the process (Crawshaw, Blyth, & Daniels, 2007; Daniels, 2004; Daniels et al., 2005), although others do not desire any future contact by the clinics after they have donated (Cook & Golombok, 1995).

Should anonymity be removed, donors are concerned they might be forced to become financially, morally, and emotionally, if not legally, responsible for their offspring. Some sperm donors are fearful that contact from the children conceived with their sperm might negatively impact their own family members, especially their spouses (Blyth, Firth, & Farrand, 2005). Yet, Rowland

(1985) found that most sperm donors did not object to having personal information disclosed to their recipients. Furthermore, over half of the surveyed
donors indicated they would accept contact from their adult offspring. Some
stated they would be willing to participate in a voluntary sperm donor registry,
especially if they were afforded some control over the information released to
the offspring and could obtain advice from professionals knowledgeable of the
search and reunion process (Crawshaw et al., 2007). Should those in the field
of reproductive medicine lobby for change and require open sperm donation?

Known and Intrafamilial Sperm Donors

Those unable to conceive with their own sperm infrequently tell others
they are infertile. Male friends and family members only occasionally volunteer
to donate their sperm.

Advantages

Sperm donors who are known by their recipients are motivated to
donate because of their existing emotional bonds. Sperm providers who know
their recipients, especially in intrafamilial donation, already know what type
of home life their offspring will experience (Adair & Purdie, 1996). Furthermore, in known donation, the genetic background of the sperm provider is
available to the recipients and is similar to the recipients in intrafamilial
gamete donation. Sperm provided by family members preserves the recipient's
genetic link. In intrafamilial donation, the donors, recipients, and their offspring may enjoy a closer relationship than if sperm had been provided from
a nonfamily member (Ethics Committee of the ASRM, 2004c; Nikolettos,
Asimakopoulos, & Hatzissabas, 2003).

Disadvantages

Known sperm providers are seldom approached to donate their sperm,
and intrafamilial sperm donors are less often used. Therefore, because of the
sheer lack of numbers, known donation is very difficult to research. Although
the appearance of consanguinity is prohibited in intrafamilial sperm donation
(Ethics Committee of the ASRM, 2004c), other disadvantages exist.

Known donors, including family members, are required to submit to the
identical medical, genetic, and psychological testing required of anonymous
donors. Should the medical staff determine the known potential donor's sperm
quality is poor, how should this finding be revealed? How might this impact
the man who previously believed he was fertile? What if the results indicate
he is HIV positive? Known sperm donors, especially family members, might
experience guilt if a pregnancy does not occur or if their offspring suffers from

an inherited disease. From an ethical perspective there is also the consideration that a family member may be donating as a result of familial pressure, which might call into question the actual voluntariness of his participation.

Intrafamilial and known sperm providers and their recipients may encounter emotional problems as a result of the donation process. Researchers have reported that those who provide their gametes to family members may experience changes in their family dynamics (Marshall, 2002; Nikolettis et al., 2003), bringing some family members closer, whereas others may experience a deterioration of relations usually associated with the partner or wife of the sperm donor (Adair & Purdie, 1996). Although mental health providers want family members to make autonomous decisions, should psychologists be held responsible for potentially negative consequences of sperm donation?

Number of Sperm Donations

DI programs vary with respect to the number of times that they permit sperm providers to donate (Daniels, 1987). Ethicists advise clinics to reduce the risk of inadvertent consanguinity between the offspring of sperm recipients of the same donor (Borrero, 2001) and/or between the recipients' children and the sperm providers' own children (Curie-Cohen, 1980). The use of a variety of mathematical formulas regarding the number of donations recommended per capita has been suggested (de Boer, Oosterwijk, Rigters-Arsis, 1995; Practice Committee of the ASRM and The Practice Committee of the SART, 2008; Wang et al., 2007) to limit the number of children conceived with a single sperm donor. Purdie, Peek, Adair, Graham, and Fisher (1994) found couples objected to the male partner becoming a sperm donor partially as a result of their concern about possible incest. Of the individuals surveyed, 20% believed each sperm donor should be permitted only one recipient. Another 50% suggested one sperm provider should be limited to three or fewer families. The risk of inadvertent consanguinity is greater when anonymous sperm donors are involved and the resulting offspring are uninformed about the method used in their conception.

EXISTING LAWS, POLICIES, AND LEGISLATION

With regard to sperm donation, both statutory and case law tend to focus either on screening requirements and/or parentage. In Indiana, the Burns Indiana Code Annotated, section 16-41-14-5 (2008), for example, states that "a practitioner shall test each donor of semen for the following diseases before the donor provides a donation: (1) syphilis, (2) hepatitis B surface antigen and core antibody, and (3) HIV antibody" (Ind. Code Ann. § 16-41-14-5, 2007).

The vast majority of states have laws addressing DI. In most of these states the sperm donor is released from any and all parental rights and obligations, and all legal rights and responsibilities for the child are vested in the consenting husband and/or the woman inseminated. However, at least 13 of these state statutes are only protective of married heterosexual couples using sperm donors (Swink & Reich, 2007).

These laws, though, do not address a donor's rights and/or obligations in the event he passes on genetic or other health problems to the child. This issue came to the fore in *Johnson v. Superior Court* (2000). This California case concerned a child who suffered from a rare kidney disease allegedly transmitted from a sperm donor. Her parents sought to depose the sperm donor to learn more about his medical history. The California appellate court held that

> the alleged sperm donor in this case must submit to a deposition and answer questions, as well as produce documents which are relevant to the issues in the pending action, but that his identity should remain undisclosed to the fullest extent possible. (*Johnson v. Superior Court*, 2000, p. 1056)

In dicta, that is, in the opinions of a judge that do not embody the resolution or determination of the court, however, the court did indicate that under some circumstances anonymity may not be protected and the donor's interest in privacy may give way to the child's best interests.

In 2006, the press reported a sperm provider passed on a rare genetic condition to five children born from his donation (Grady, 2006). This case raised and continues to raise questions about how much information is and should be available about donors. In the instance of a rare disease such as this, however, one must also consider whether such information could even have been known about an intimate partner. Who bears responsibility is a daunting question and unfortunately one that might not be answered except in the context of litigation or legislation.

Much of the existing case law primarily addresses the rights and/or obligations of a sperm donor. In *In re Parentage of J.M.K.* (2005), the donor was having an ongoing relationship with the mother while he was married to someone else. The woman underwent IVF with his sperm. Although he accepted parentage of the first child, he denied any obligation to support the second child conceived using excess embryos because he did not have input in the decision to have the second child. The man asserted that he was the equivalent of a sperm donor and thus should have no obligations of support. The court found that under the former parentage statute the man was the father of the children despite the fact that the couple was not married.

In *Ferguson v. McKiernan* (2007), while married to another man the plaintiff had an affair with a coworker whom she convinced to provide sperm for IVF. He agreed, but only if she would not claim any support from him. He had little or no contact with the children for 5 years until the mother sought to obtain support from him. The trial court found the man to be responsible, and the agreement between him and the mother to be unenforceable because it sought to bargain away rights that did not belong to either of them, but to the children. On appeal, however, the court found the agreement to be legally valid, holding that "absent the parties' agreement, however, the twins would not have been born at all, or would have been born to a different and anonymous sperm donor, who neither party disputes would be safe from a support order" (*Ferguson v. McKiernan*, 2007, 940, A. 2d 1236, 1248).

In *In the Interest of H.C.S.* (2006), the donor sought to be involved in the child's life. In this case, the court found that an unmarried man who provided sperm used for assisted reproduction and who did not sign and file an acknowledgement of paternity did not have standing to pursue suit to determine paternity.

In the Kansas case, *In the Interest of K.M.H* (2007), a known sperm donor asserted that he was being denied his constitutional rights by not being able to share in parenting of the children conceived. The couple never entered into a written agreement before the insemination and disagreed as to what was intended. At issue was a state statute that denies a donor parental rights unless otherwise agreed to in writing by the parties. The court found the donor's constitutional rights were not violated as no written agreement existed between the parties.

As this brief overview illustrates, both case law and statutory law with regard to sperm donation tend to focus primarily on questions of parental rights.

CLINICAL VIGNETTE

Thus far, the information discussed has addressed the more common situations arising in collaborative reproductive arrangements involving the assistance of sperm donors. The following case study, however, represents some of the more unusual circumstances that may present and the typical instances in which a mental health professional would become involved in the arrangement.

Michael, a well-known professional football player, wished to become the designated sperm donor for his father, Zack. Michael, at age 32, had never married and had no children of his own. Zack, a famous football coach, age 60, had recently married Stephanie, age 33. This was Stephanie's first marriage and before becoming engaged both agreed they wanted to have children.

Zack did not disclose to Stephanie he previously had been treated for testicular cancer and had not banked his sperm. Zack wanted to have Michael surreptitiously act as his sperm donor and had previously arranged this with the IVF clinic. Additionally, Zack is hoping to have a child with exceptional athletic ability. After 6 months of unsuccessful attempts to conceive, Stephanie was informed by the clinic's staff that she and Zack would need to participate in IUI to have a child. Unbeknownst to Stephanie, 8 months prior Michael submitted to the extensive physical evaluations and had frozen his sperm. However, Stephanie was told by her husband they would be using his, Zack's, banked sperm. Although the clinic was willing to conspire in this arrangement, they required individual and joint psychoeducational interviews with both father and son prior to insemination. These were to be conducted by the mental health professional employed by the IVF clinic.

Ethical Dilemmas in the Context of Professional Guidelines

The American Psychological Association's (APA's; 2002) "Ethical Principles of Psychologists and Code of Conduct" Principle A, Beneficence and Nonmaleficence, guides psychologists to benefit their clients and do no harm. Certainly Stephanie would be deceived if it is not disclosed that Michael's sperm and not her husband's will be used in the insemination procedure. Two synonyms of the word *harmed* that have sexual connotations are abused and molested, which is exactly how Stephanie may feel if violated by her husband, her physicians, and her husband's psychologist.

APA Ethics Code Principle B, Fidelity and Responsibility, encourages psychologists to establish relationships of trust with those with whom they work as well as managing conflicts of interest that could lead to harmful consequences. Accordingly, the psychologist should act in the best interest of the patients, including Stephanie (even though she was not referred for psychological counseling), as well as the fertility practice.

APA Ethics Code Principle C, Integrity, guides psychologists toward truthfulness, accuracy, and honesty in the practice of their profession. Should the psychologist intentionally misrepresent the actual facts of this family's particular medical protocol, he or she would be engaged in deliberate subterfuge.

APA Ethics Code Principle D, Justice, entitles Stephanie to access to and benefits from the same type of psychoeducational counseling her husband, Zack, will receive. The failure of the psychologist to do so would be tantamount to condoning Michael and Zack's deceit.

APA Ethics Code Principle E, Respect for People's Rights and Dignity, acknowledges the rights of individuals to self-determination. If the truth of the circumstances of her potential child's conception is withheld, Stephanie would be unable to render an autonomous decision. One could argue her gender and role as the homemaker and trophy wife place her at a disadvantage because she has neither the power nor celebrity of her husband, the renowned coach, or her stepson, the charismatic and highly paid professional football player.

APA Ethics Code Standard 1.03, Conflicts between Ethics and Organizational Demands, entrusts the psychologist with a duty to inform the medical practice of his or her commitment to the APA Ethics Code and if feasible, to come to a resolution that would result in adherence to the Ethics Code. APA Ethics Code Standard 3.04, Avoiding Harm, requests a psychologist take the necessary steps to avoid harming Stephanie. APA Ethics Code Standard 3.06, Conflicts of Interest, might require the psychologist to refrain from accepting this case because his or her objectivity or effectiveness may be impaired as a result of the need for financial security and employment retention.

Finally, it would be impossible for the psychologist to obtain Stephanie's informed consent, as written in APA Ethics Code Standard 3.10, Informed Consent, because she could not give such consent in the absence of full disclosure by her husband. Stephanie's lack of informed consent would negate all of the decisions regarding the couple's possible fertility treatment.

The Ethics Committee of the ASRM (2004c) guidelines regarding intrafamilial and intergenerational gamete donation cannot be followed in this vignette because of the deliberate deception of Stephanie. Zack wishes to use Michael as his sperm donor to preserve his family's genetic inheritance. Furthermore, although he is hopeful of producing a son capable of displaying outstanding athletic capability, will he be bitterly disappointed if his child does not inherit this characteristic? Does this wish constitute eugenic manipulation? What if the child were female?

Under the circumstances described in this vignette, Zack would be not only the rearing father but also the genetic grandfather. Michael, the genetic father, would be the offspring's social half brother. And, as if this were not sufficiently complicated, Zack's ex-wife would be the genetic paternal grandmother. One might wonder what dynamics would occur should Zack prematurely die leaving his young and attractive wife alone to cobble together a relationship with his son Michael who was the biogenetic provider for her child. Would Michael disclose the deception, not wanting to be excluded from a role in his offspring's life? Would this disclosure wreak havoc on Stephanie and her child?

The ASRM (2004c) guidelines state a family member should not provide gametes if it results in a relationship that appears incestuous or consanguineous. A son who provides sperm for his father does not give the impression of incest or a consanguineous relationship with his father's wife. However, when the second wife is approximately the same age as the son, the donation may be perceived as peculiar. Also, ASRM acknowledges intergenerational familial collaborative reproduction presents potential risks to autonomy. Although intergenerational in nature, father-to-son donations are looked on more favorably than the reverse.

Free and fully informed consent cannot be given in this vignette because Zack has orchestrated the situation so his wife will be unaware sperm donation was used for the conception of their child and has enlisted his son Michael in this charade.

The Ethics Committee of the ASRM (2004c) has written that all parties should be adequately protected when familial donors are used. There would be no opportunity to provide psychological assistance to Zack's wife, and therefore, Stephanie could not emotionally or cognitively prepare herself for the use of her stepson's gametes or for any negative sequelae that might befall her potential children. The inherent duplicity of the scenario presents an abundance of unhealthy family dynamics. Moreover, the essential legal advice and documentation required in son-to-father gamete donation is absent. Additionally, given that a legal arrangement would be necessary in some states and/or explicit consent of the recipient (i.e., Stephanie), there may be no legal protection of the relationship. Arguably, Zack might not be recognized as the legal father if the facts were brought to light and/or if Michael ever sought to assert his parental rights.

Practical Considerations

As Garceau et al. (2002) reported, intrauterine insemination with donor sperm is extremely cost effective. Although Zack would be able to afford more expensive treatment technologies, he did not bank his sperm prior to cancer treatment. Therefore, using Zack's sperm in an IVF cycle with ICSI is not an option.

There can be no cooperation among the parties because the truth has been withheld from Stephanie and she has not provided truly informed consent to this procedure. However, the entire situation would be more acceptable if Zack and Stephanie discussed whether she would be comfortable using Michael's sperm to achieve a pregnancy. If Stephanie declines, they could certainly consider using sperm from an anonymous provider. Stephanie and Zack also have the financial ability to adopt a child, or they could decide their marriage would remain child free.

Balancing the Multiple Perspectives

Reproductive libertarians believe society is best served when use of assisted reproductive technologies is governed primarily by a respect for procreative liberty (Robertson, 1994). However, we believe it is advantageous to consider all of the stakeholders, especially the children who will be conceived, as they are the most vulnerable individuals. Although some people may find the conditions under which the child was conceived to be objectionable or unseemly, it is doubtful whether society would benefit from or be injured by Michael and Zack's ruse.

The Clinician or Fertility Center

Although most IVF clinics adhere to the guidelines promulgated by the ASRM, Stern, Cramer, Garrod, and Green (2001) found attitudes vary considerably among fertility clinic directors with respect to access-to-treatment issues. Many IVF centers have published written policies, but currently there are no laws governing the assisted reproductive technologies in the United States.

Gurmankin, Caplan, and Braverman (2005) reported that IVF programs refuse to treat approximately 4% of their potential candidates each year. About 3% of patients were not accepted for medical reasons, whereas only approximately 1% were denied access to treatment as a result of psychological, emotional, or social causes. Physicians must honor refusals of medical care, that is, when a patient declines treatment, but doctors are under no obligation to honor all requests for procedures using assisted reproductive technologies.

As in all professions, there exist those clinics that strictly follow professional guidelines as well as those known for their willingness to bend accepted standards to meet their patients' demands. Those who ignore practice standards may take the position that any individual who has a strong desire to have a child should not be denied medical treatment. Should participants experience negative consequences as a result of their treatment, those same doctors may believe the recipients have the responsibility to avoid risks (Stern, Cramer, Green, Garrod, & DeVries, 2003).

Physicians may question whether they possess the wisdom or the right to make decisions for their patients and may prefer to defer to patient autonomy. Undoubtedly, wealthy and famous Zack will be able to find a physician willing to collude with him and deceive Stephanie. Doctors, like many people, may enjoy associating with celebrities.

Nevertheless, fertility centers could decline to accommodate Michael and Zack by exercising their right to physician autonomy. Reproductive endocrinologists are under no legal or ethical obligation to treat all who request their services (New York State Task Force on Life and the Law, 1998), and in this situation may actually be violating the law.

The Prospective Parents

Zack, who never disclosed to Stephanie that he is a cancer survivor, may wish to appear vigorous and robust in the eyes of his young wife. Should Stephanie discover Zack is infertile, the balance of power between them might change (Turner & Coyle, 2000). Alternatively, the choice not to disclose his need to use donated sperm may originate from his fear of the stigma of infertility (Daniels & Taylor, 1993; McWhinnie, 1995; Nachtigall, 1993).

Optimally, in heterosexual couples, procreational decisions are made between the husband and the wife, rather than the husband, his sperm donor son, and their urologist or reproductive endocrinologist. The arrangement illustrated in this vignette undermines an honest marital relationship, which most spouses aspire to and expect, and the arrangement precludes Stephanie from autonomous decision making. Moreover, the introduction of a known sperm donor may subvert feelings of sexual and procreational exclusivity and cause one or both partners to view their medical treatment as a form of adultery (Pennings, 1996b).

The Sperm Donor

Zack's recruitment of Michael potentially would present a conflict because it is difficult to eliminate the possibility of coercion and/or undue influence in intergenerational and intrafamilial gamete donation (Ethics Committee of the ASRM, 2004c).

Pennings (1995) wrote that sperm donors should have the right to choose their recipients. In this vignette, Michael is acting in accordance with Pennings's position. However, other than helping his father, little else in this scenario seems to benefit Michael.

Currently, Michael is a single heterosexual male who has no partner whose wishes need to be considered (Pennings, 1996b). However, should the sperm donation be disclosed to his future spouse, she may view Michael as Stephanie's adulterous partner, and this knowledge, might adversely affect their relationship. Should he meet a prospective partner or marry prior to Stephanie's conceiving, will Michael feel entitled to request his father discontinue using his sperm (Pennings, 1996a)?

How will Michael feel if fertility treatment is unsuccessful? If Michael's semen reveals pathology, should he be informed of the results (Shenfield, 1998, 1999)? If Zack's offspring have chromosomal or structural abnormalities, will Michael feel tremendous guilt and responsibility (Kuller, Meyer, Traynor, & Hartmann, 2001)? Would Zack blame Michael for these problems, and if so, would it irreparably damage their relationship? What might occur if Michael cannot have children of his own?

The Potential Children

The screening of potential gamete donors and recipients entering assisted reproductive technology clinics varies. However, almost universally, the most important consideration is the safety and welfare of the potential child, followed by attempts to limit the risks to the health and well-being of the prospective mother (Gurmankin et al., 2005).

Intrafamilial and intergenerational gamete donation has implications for the dynamics of the family, which could impact the emotional health of the donor's offspring (Walker & Broderick, 1999). In this chapter's vignette, information regarding the child's conception will have been withheld from both Stephanie and the potential child. However, children frequently sense something or some information is being kept secret (Baran & Pannor, 1993; Ehrensaft, 2005). The exact consequences of such lack of disclosure are unknown (see Chapter 8, this volume).

Should the child learn about the method used for his or her conception, especially under negative circumstances, both the child and Stephanie would be at risk of psychological injury (Baran & Pannor, 1993; R. Snowden, Mitchell, & Snowden, 1983). In addition, the child's identity might be threatened (Breakwell, 1987, 1998), and other family relationships might be damaged.

Even if the truth is revealed in a neutral manner, the potential child would likely experience relational confusion. Suddenly his or her half brother Michael would become the biogenetic father. Zack, the child's social father, would abruptly be thrust into the role of genetic grandfather. From the child's perspective, Stephanie could erroneously be sexually partnered with the child's half brother and biogenetic father. Since this scenario is confusing to those within the field of reproductive medicine, one can only imagine the bewilderment a child might experience.

The Existing Children

Zack's two other children, Laura (age 36) and Leigh (age 34), aware of his previous cancer treatment, would probably not have difficulty with Michael acting as their father's sperm provider if the facts were disclosed to them. Were his children significantly younger, though, they might experience relational confusion similar to a potential child conceived from DI using a relative's sperm.

However, although no one intends to disclose the true facts and circumstances, Zack's daughters might still detect the unspoken secret. They might feel betrayed by both their father and their brother, especially if the truth were revealed at an inauspicious time. Consequently, Zack's relationship with his daughters might deteriorate, as might Michael's relationship with his sisters.

Anger about having the truth withheld from them might be played out in the financial and legal arenas, as are many primarily emotional conflicts. Should Zack die intestate, his daughters might challenge the child's claim to any inheritance as a result of the irregularity of his or her conception (P. Broderick & Walker, 2001).

CONCLUSION

Familiar with the psychological stresses encountered by cancer survivors, mental health professionals would not wish to cause Zack additional pain by stigmatizing him with the label of infertility. Moreover, there is no reliable method for psychologists to predict to what degree, if any, Michael's family dynamics might suffer. However, the duplicity of the situation presents a potential minefield.

Stephanie is not only unaware Michael's sperm will be used to conceive her child, but she is also unable to provide informed consent for the procedure or make autonomous treatment decisions. Furthermore, she will receive paternalistic medical treatment unequal to that provided to her husband and his son, the sperm donor. If a physician believed Zack and Michael were entitled to procreative liberty at Stephanie's expense, there is little likelihood, approximately 1% according to Gurmankin et al. (2005), that access to treatment would be denied for the psychological, emotional, or social sequelae that might occur.

The risks to Stephanie's mental health, should she learn Michael's sperm was used to impregnate her, are great. Her marriage to Zack might not survive because she might feel violated and betrayed. The potential risks to Stephanie do not justify a procedure that the physicians are not legally obligated to perform (Stern, Cramer, Garrod, & Green, 2002).

Additionally, the dynamics between Michael and Zack, Stephanie and Zack, Stephanie and Michael, and finally, those of the entire family, including Zack's children from his first marriage, might be irrevocably damaged. The potential for negative consequences is great.

Nevertheless, positions for mental health professionals within IVF clinics are highly desirable. Postings for job openings within an IVF center are rare and once announced, very competitive. The benefits of employment include paid vacation time, sick leave, health insurance, pension plans, and frequently, fully or partially paid expenses for attendance at the ASRM annual meetings. Often the perks are so advantageous it becomes difficult to rationalize confronting one's employer and possibly getting fired.

However, being employed by an IVF clinic can be challenging when the mental health professional disagrees with a decision made by his or her employer. Whereas independent psychologists in private practice are free to decline referrals for cases that they believe are unethical, the embedded mental health professional runs the risk of losing his or her job if he or she refuses to meet with the IVF center's patients. The employee might verbalize his or her disagreement with the reproductive endocrinologist's decision to accede to Zack's wishes, however, such communication may be futile. Furthermore, might it not be in the mental health professional's best interest to meet individually and jointly with both father and son? The doctor obviously is aware of the irregularity of inseminating Stephanie with Michael's sperm under the guise that Zack was providing a fresh sample or had the foresight to freeze his sperm prior to cancer treatment.

Both the ASRM and the APA guidelines promote the concept of autonomous decision making for their professional members. Regardless of psychologists' employment, they should adhere to APA's Ethics Code. In this vignette, the psychologist risks bringing harm to the participants in a situation in which medical and psychological treatment may be inappropriate and could be withheld on ethical grounds.

In conclusion, mental health professionals in private practice could, and probably would, decline the referral of Zack and Michael. An embedded psychologist might feel powerless if assigned the psychological component of treatment for Michael and his father. Unfortunately, a mental health professional's ability to make autonomous decisions might be compromised by his or her employment situation. However, psychologists could rightfully argue that impregnating Stephanie with Michael's sperm is in violation of both ASRM's guidelines and APA's Ethics Code and emphasize the potential emotional complications that might arise for all involved. Therefore, the psychologist could refuse to become involved in this highly irregular situation. Additionally, because there are myriad legal considerations, all parties should be referred for legal consultation.

7

SURROGACY

We must be willing to get rid of the life we've planned so as to have the life that is waiting for us.

—Joseph Campbell

Surrogates are a viable option for intended parents (IPs) who are either unable to conceive or carry a child to term. Traditional surrogates conceive with their own eggs and sperm provided by the intended father or sperm donor, usually using intrauterine insemination (IUI) but sometimes in vitro fertilization (IVF). Traditional surrogacy is less expensive than gestational surrogacy and does not require the surrogate to undergo surgery. A gestational surrogate, also called a gestational carrier (GC), does not use her own ova and achieves pregnancy with IVF and embryo transfer. The GC carries the pregnancy to term for the intended parent(s). The gametes may be provided by both of the IPs, an egg donor and the intended father, donor sperm and the intended mother's oocytes, donated eggs and donated sperm, or donated embryos.

Traditional surrogacy is less frequently used than gestational surrogacy because of its potential for legal and emotional difficulties. A GC does not have to take the amount of gonadotropins necessary to stimulate oocyte production. Additionally, the attendant legal issues are more straightforward for GCs and the IPs because of the surrogate's lack of genetic connection to the resulting child.

MEDICAL BACKGROUND

Using a GC might resolve problems for patients who have had hysterectomies, irreparable uterine malformations, or absent uteri. Contracting with a GC is also appropriate for women who are suffering from severe medical illnesses incompatible with pregnancy, for example, autoimmune disorder; cardiac or renal disease; a history of chemotherapy or radiation therapy for cancer; Mayer-Rokitansky-Kuster-Hauser syndrome; repeated IVF failure, especially if problems with implantation are suggested; or recurrent miscarriages (Batzofin, Brisman, & Madsen, 2005; Brinsden, 2003; Brinsden et al., 2000; Corson, Kelly, Braverman, & English, 1998; Esfandiari, Claessens, O'Brien, Gotlieb, & Casper, 2004; Goldfarb et al., 2000; Meniru & Craft, 1997; Morton, 2005; Zinger, Liu, Husseinzadeh & Thomas, 2004).

PSYCHOSOCIAL LITERATURE

Although traditional surrogacy was mentioned in the Old Testament (in the story of Sarah and Abraham) and the first successful gestational surrogacy was reported in the mid-1980s (Utian, Sheean, Goldfarb, & Kiwi, 1985, pp. 1351), the psychological aspects have not been extensively studied. However, we have found that surrogates are motivated by altruism; empathy; financial gain; a sense of achievement; their desire for attention; improved self-esteem, self-worth, and self-confidence; as well as the wish to bestow the gift of parenthood on an infertile couple. Also, GCs have enjoyed prior pregnancies and are motivated to experience pregnancy again (Ciccarelli & Beckman, 2005; Hinman, n.d.; Jadva, Murray, Lycett, MacCallum, & Golombok, 2003; Ragone, 1994; van den Akker, 2007b).

GCs have been found to score within the normal range of the Minnesota Multiphasic Personality Inventory-2 (MMPI-2; Hathaway & McKinley, 1989) and are not significantly different from intended mothers (van den Akker, 2005, 2007a, 2007b). Furthermore, it has been suggested that surrogates usually adhere to traditional female roles, that is, they usually are homemakers with two or more children, belong to the middle or working class, and have graduated from high school (Ciccarelli & Beckman, 2005; Hinman, n.d.; Ragone, 1994).

The surrogate's satisfaction with her experience appears to be contingent on having a satisfactory relationship with the IP or IPs (Blyth, 1994), especially the intended mother (Ciccarelli & Beckman, 2005; Jadva et al., 2003; MacCallum, Lycett, Murray, Jadva, & Golombok, 2003; van den Akker, 2005, 2007b). Most feel positive about their surrogacy experiences (Circcarelli & Beckman, 2005; Jadva et al., 2003; Ragone, 1994), although some surrogates have occasionally reported dissatisfaction and/or regrets (Blyth, 1994; Ciccarelli & Beckman, 2005). Additionally, as our experience and our research have shown, surrogates occasionally experience some difficulties in the weeks following the presentation of the baby to his or her parents (Jadva et al., 2003).

Similarly, the majority of IPs perceived their relationship with the surrogates as harmonious (Jadva et al., 2003). The commissioning couples, especially the intended mothers, wanted to participate in a surrogacy arrangement because they believed a biogenetic link to their child was important (Ragone, 1994; van den Akker, 2005). Generally, the IPs are better educated (Baslington, 1996) and enjoy a higher socioeconomic status than surrogates (Blyth, 1994; van den Akker, 2000, 2007b).

Most IPs report that they received positive reactions from both maternal and paternal parents once they disclosed that GCs were going to assist them in the creation of their families (MacCallum, Lycett, Murray, Jadva, & Golombok, 2003). Additionally, differences in attitudes toward surrogacy have been found between genders and among various cultures (Chliaoutakis, 2002; Minai, Suzuki, Takeda, Hoshi, & Yamagata, 2007; Suzuki et al., 2006), which may necessitate specialized knowledge and disparate psychological counseling skills.

Mental health professionals have been urged to study and provide psychological counseling for surrogates prior to, during, and after their surrogacy commitment (Brinsden, 2003; Chliaoutakis, 2002; Goldfarb et al., 2000; Reilly, 2007; van den Akker, 2007a) and in some instances are required to do so by law. Although no rigorous psychological studies were found in the literature, a subject that sorely needs investigation is the impact of surrogacy on the GCs' already existing children. Most GCs, however, have self-reported that their children were positively affected by the experience (Jadva et al., 2003).

BIOETHICAL PERSPECTIVES

Some have argued that surrogacy redefines the term *motherhood* (Shuster, 1992; C. Snowden, 1994), and many have concluded that both traditional and gestational surrogacy should be used only when medically warranted (American College of Obstetricians and Gynecology Committee on Ethics, 2004; K. C. Chen & Ng, 2001; European Society of Human Reproduction and Embryology Task Force on Ethics and Law, 2005; Morton, 2005). This is, in fact, a legal requirement in several states.

The question has been raised whether either type of surrogate can provide truly informed consent because neither actually knows how she will feel until after she has relinquished the child she carries to the IP or IPs (Davis & Brown, 1984; Frenkel, 2001; Tangri & Kahn, 1993). This is especially important with regard to psychological attachment (Fischer & Gillman, 1991), which differentiates informed consent for surrogacy from that for research, surgery, or even abortion.

Once again, the issue of commodification has been raised regarding the exploitation and coercion of less advantaged women by wealthier, more highly educated individuals who contract for their services (Ber, 2000; Chang, 2004; M. Chen, 2003; Gould, 2004; McLachlan & Swales, 2000; Tangri & Kahn, 1993; Wilkinson, 2003), which also calls into question the ability of surrogates to give truly informed consent if monetary gain might be an undue influence. These arguments have been countered by those favoring surrogacy and reproductive liberty as well as a less paternalistic treatment of women (Brinsden et al., 2000; Bromham, 1995; Chliaoutakis, Koukouli, & Papadakaki, 2002; Soderstrom-Anttia et al., 2002). Although upper limits of compensation to surrogates have been suggested by American Society for Reproductive Medicine (ASRM) guidelines, Luk and Petrozza (2006) found that many clinics and agencies did not adhere to these guidelines. Consequently, some have called for federal legislation that would result in consistency among states and could therefore limit protracted legal battles (Batzofin et al., 2005; Mady, 1981; Maun, Williams, Graber, & Myers, 1994).

As mentioned in Chapter 5, family members and friends are frequently approached or volunteer to act as a GC. Should the IP(s) determine that the woman would be desirable to act as the GC, the mental health professional would adhere to the same protocol as followed with a known egg donor and her partner, should one exist.

EXISTING LAWS, POLICIES, AND LEGISLATION

The law with regard to surrogacy varies from state to state. Currently nearly half of the states have laws addressing surrogacy (Andrews & Elster, 2000). Some states, such as Illinois (750 Ill. Comp. Stat. Ann 47/10 *et seq.*, 2008), statutorily allow compensated gestational surrogacy arrangements, whereas other states, such as New York (NY CLS Dom. Rel. § 123, 2008), render such arrangements illegal. Some states may require that there be a medical need for the surrogacy, that at least one of the IPs is genetically related to the child (Va. Code Ann. § 20-160, 2008), that the parties undergo a mental health evaluation (750 Ill. Comp. Stat. Ann. 47/20, 2008), or that the IPs be married to one another (Fla. Stat. § 742.15, 2008). It is precisely this variability from state to state that makes it so important for individuals or couples seeking to build their families in this way to seek legal consultation in the process and consider a contractual arrangement. States where gestational surrogacy arrangements are legal, such as Illinois, actually require that the parties' agreement be set forth in a written contract (750 Ill. Comp. Stat.

Ann. 47/10, *et seq.*, 2008). However, in states where such contracts may not be required by law, they may still be a useful mechanism for the parties to clearly express their intent and delineate the anticipated boundaries of their relationship.

Case law that has evolved in the area of surrogacy has been as varied as the statutory law but has come to reflect the importance of intent in pursuing this family building option. One of the most highly publicized surrogacy cases to date is the New Jersey case of *In re: Baby* M (1988). Baby M involved a traditional surrogacy arrangement in which the surrogate, after giving birth to the child, changed her mind and wanted to parent the child. Although a contract existed between the surrogate and the intended father, the New Jersey court viewed the arrangement as being similar to an adoption arrangement and thus invalidated the contract as being against public policy. Despite the invalidation of the agreement, physical custody remained with the IPs, and the surrogate was granted visitation with the child.

Another significant case was *Johnson v. Calvert* (1993). This case involved a gestational surrogate who was gestating a child with both IPs' gametes and who changed her mind regarding relinquishment of the child. The court in this case found that both women actually had a claim to the child, one because of her genetic connection and the other because of her biological connection of gestation. Insofar as both had legitimate claims, the court believed that it was necessary to consider the intent of the parties to resolve the dispute and held that "she who intended to procreate the child—that is, she who intended to bring about the birth of a child that she intended to raise as her own—is the natural mother under California law" (*Johnson v Calvert*, 1993, p. 782). Fortunately, the parties had entered into a contract that served as the basis for determining their intent.

These cases serve as examples of the legal issues that may arise for those considering parenting through surrogacy, whether traditional or gestational. Even in arrangements with friends or family members, legal difficulties may ensue, and therefore it is important to consider the expectations of each participant before embarking on this path. The mental health professional can play a vital role in helping to clarify such expectations and prepare the participants for what they might encounter before, during, and after the birth of the child.

CLINICAL VIGNETTE

Michele, age 28, and Jonathan, age 31, had been unsuccessfully trying to have a child for 2 years. Michele, able to conceive, miscarried four times. Heartbroken but resolute, they took a 6-month hiatus from fertility treatment to regroup and decide among their available alternatives.

The couple decided to look for a gestational surrogate who, they hoped, would be able to carry a child conceived with Michele and Jonathan's gametes. They located a GC who was recruited by a reputable surrogacy agency. The couple's fertility clinic had medically treated other GCs provided by the same agency and found their personnel to be caring and helpful to both IPs and gestational surrogates alike.

Michele and Jonathan selected Staci, a 30-year-old married mother of two children, Paul, age 9, and Seth, age 7. Staci and her husband, Steven, had an easy time conceiving their own children, and she had enjoyed unremarkable pregnancies. Staci had never previously acted as a GC but wished to help others who could not have children without the assistance of a third party.

The fertility clinic provided its patients with a list of psychologists from whom they were to choose to conduct their psychoeducational session as well as their GC's psychological evaluation. Michele and Jonathan called two psychologists. Both had private practices within close proximity to their home as well as the home of their GC.

The first psychologist, Dr. Jill Adams, a member of the Mental Health Professional Group of the ASRM for the past 16 years, required one session for Michele and Jonathan, a second session with Staci and Steven, and a third joint session in which both couples would be present, for a total of three consecutive sessions. The second psychologist, Dr. Cliff Farrero, simply required one session during which he would distribute an MMPI-2 (Hathaway & McKinley, 1989) to each of the four individuals, followed by a meeting not to exceed 20 minutes. Thus, his fee was substantially less. Although Dr. Farrero was not a member of the ASRM and received neither formal or informal training nor supervision in the psychology of reproductive health, Michele and Jonathan appreciated the psychologist's respect for the participants' time and the money that they would save, especially after the expensive medical treatment they had already received.

Ethical Dilemmas in the Context of Professional Guidelines

The American Psychological Association's (APA's; 2002) "Ethical Principles of Psychologists and Code of Conduct" Standard 2.01, Boundaries of Competence, is breached in this vignette. On the basis of his education and training, Dr. Farrero is providing services in an area outside of his competence. By not availing himself of clinical supervision or attempting to obtain the required education necessary to become qualified as a mental health professional in reproductive medicine, he also violates ASRM standards.

Although he was aware of the various types of assisted reproductive technologies, Dr. Farrero would need to receive training in the medical aspects of infertility to competently practice in the field of fertility counseling. Such training would include the testing, diagnosis, and treatment of reproductive problems; the causes of female and male infertility; and of course, basic human reproductive physiology. His training in the psychology of infertility would need to include family building alternatives as well as the ethical and legal issues for the gamut of infertility treatments and pertinent psychological theories. Moreover, Dr. Farrero also should have experience in marital, family, grief, and sexual counseling.

According to the guidelines of the Committee on Infertility Counseling (1995), Dr. Farrero should have 1 year of experience providing infertility treatment under the supervision of or in consultation with a qualified and experienced infertility counselor. In violation of APA Ethics Code 2.03, Maintaining Competence, Dr. Farrero has not attended postgraduate courses relevant to fertility issues provided by ASRM or other accredited educational providers of continuing education.

Furthermore, Dr. Farrero may be in violation of APA Ethics Code Standard 3.04, Avoiding Harm. Because he is apparently unfamiliar with the pertinent issues, he cannot adequately prepare the four participants for this endeavor, and as a consequence, one or more may be harmed as a result of his lack of knowledge and expertise.

Additionally, even those in the field of fertility counseling cannot avoid problems with APA Ethics Code Standard 3.06, Conflict of Interest. All mental health professionals who consult with the IPs as well as the GC and her partner, if one exists, might be accused of such violation. However, during training in infertility counseling, Dr. Farrero would have been instructed to request each participant sign a conflict of interest waiver. Obtaining such a waiver is standard practice in this specialty and informs patients the mental health professional may find it necessary to provide advice to one couple that might contradict the other couple's wishes.

Moreover, as a result of Dr. Farrero's lack of experience in reproductive medicine, he would be unable to provide adequate information to any of the participants. Therefore, one or all of the individuals may be unable to provide truly informed consent for the procedures in which they would be participating, and accordingly, Dr. Farrero is in violation of APA Ethics Code Standard 3.10, Informed Consent.

Finally, Dr. Farrero is unaware that he should obtain a confidentiality form from Michele and Jonathan that would give him permission to speak with Staci and Steven (and vice versa), and that would authorize him to discuss topics disclosed in their separate couple's sessions. It is evident this psychologist does not know the standard of care within this field is to conduct a psychoeducational session for the IPs and an entirely different session that would include the psychological evaluation of the GC and her partner. Only through honest discourse and the sharing of information acquired in the couples' separate psychological interviews can a mental health professional ascertain whether each couple is capable of meeting the needs and expectations of the other couple. Possession of this information is crucial so the psychologist may determine whether both couples could sustain a successful relationship for a minimum of 12 months.

Balancing the Multiple Perspectives

The reports generated by Dr. Farrero are unlikely to contain adequate information, and therefore it is impossible to evaluate whether any conflicts exist or if issues of autonomy, access, and fairness come into play.

The Clinician or Fertility Clinic

A fertility clinic may believe its policies are professional and ethical because it refers its patients to licensed mental health professionals and adheres to ASRM guidelines. Furthermore, the clinic's referral list contains mental health professionals who have practices scattered around the city, thus enabling its patients to find a psychologist conveniently located to either their homes or places of employment. However, it may be more meaningful to compile a list of referrals of mental health professionals familiar with the recommendations of the ASRM.

Many patients already consider the fees for the medical procedures to be onerous. If they are satisfied with the fees for the psychological services, the physicians are less likely to receive complaints. Fertility specialists may naively believe by virtue of being licensed, a mental health professional would not practice outside of or accept patients whose issues did not fall within their areas of competency.

The Prospective Parents

Dr. Farrero did not ask Jonathan and Michele to provide him with a history of their fertility problems. Although testing is optional for IPs according to ASRM suggested guidelines, he did not provide any rationale, substantiation, or documentation as to why he believed this couple should be administered the MMPI-2 (Hathaway & McKinley, 1989). Although the MMPI-2 may provide Dr. Farrero with limited information about the couple's current level of functioning, the test does not reveal much about their relationship with each other or third parties prior to experiencing recurrent miscarriages.

One of the more difficult problems to broach with IPs is how they might respond to a negative pregnancy test, another miscarriage, or what they would wish to do should a physical anomaly be found during their GC's pregnancy. Dr. Farrero failed to explain to Jonathan and Michele that according to *Roe v. Wade* (1973), GCs have the option to refuse to have an amniocentesis, a chorionic villi sampling, or participate in an abortion or fetal reduction. Furthermore, Dr. Farrero neglected to discuss the options for embryo disposition (see Chapter 3, this volume). These omissions may create problems later in this pregnancy. These issues, however, can and should be discussed in any legal consultation and addressed in a contractual arrangement between the GC, her partner, and Jonathan and Michele.

Dr. Farrero did not ask Jonathan and Michele about their preferences for prenatal care, types and timing of communication during the pregnancy, for example, phone, e-mail, cards, and other concrete issues that could then be mediated during their joint session. Nor did he discuss the need to respect boundaries, the importance of not attempting to micromanage the GC's behavior, nor the frequency and types of communication they desired after completion of the surrogacy arrangement.

In addition, Dr. Farrero did not address how Jonathan and Michele intended to manage Staci and Steven's travel expenses (gasoline and tolls), lost wages, payment of additional health and life insurance, or should Staci be confined to bed rest, how they would provide for the GC's child care, additional medical expenses, housekeeping, and more. As a result of his lack of expertise in this field, this psychologist could not adequately discuss most of the issues relevant to the IPs. Consequently, Michele and Jonathan's well-being and relationship with their GC are jeopardized.

The Gestational Surrogate and Her Spouse

Being unfamiliar with medical protocols for infertility treatments, Dr. Farrero could not ascertain whether Staci and Steven could adhere to the demanding schedule required in this process, nor could he advise them about potential problems that they might encounter. Therefore, they could not provide informed consent. Moreover, their psychologist did not learn whether the promise of financial compensation had coerced Staci into becoming a GC.

During his 15 minutes with Staci and Steven, Dr. Farrero failed to address the impact Staci's pregnancy might have on her marriage, career, and children. Nor did he consider Staci's psychological history. Thus, he has no idea whether she had previously experienced loss or trauma, for example, rape, sexual abuse, death of a loved one, giving up a child for adoption, or whether she had ever received psychological therapy.

Similarly, Dr. Farrero did not discuss the possibility of a miscarriage, negative pregnancy result, bed rest, abortion, or fetal reduction. He did not inquire about the type of relationship Steven and Staci wished to have with the IPs during and after the child's birth. Incongruent expectations between the GC and the IPs may cause disappointment, which quite possibly could result in the GC's having regrets about her participation (Blyth, 1994; Ciccarelli & Beckman, 2005).

Dr. Farerro omitted any discussion of the necessity for separate legal representation to document the parties' contractual relationship. Additionally, he did not inquire how Steven and Staci would prefer to transfer the newborn to Jonathan and Michele or say goodbye at the hospital. Furthermore, he did not find out what could help them feel reassured about the commissioning couple's capacity for providing a loving, caring home for the child Staci would be carrying for them.

Lacking the joint session, Dr. Farrero was unable to mediate any of the more typical problems that may arise between the IPs and the GCs, that is, conflicts regarding prenatal care, travel, respect for boundaries and time, and other emotionally charged clashes. Moreover, Dr. Farrero did not establish a basis for an ongoing role during the course of the GC process and pregnancy.

The Potential Children

Although familiar with ASRM's position regarding disclosure to children conceived through assisted reproductive technologies, Dr. Farrero is unfamiliar with the research on how, when, and why disclosure should take place, and consequently he is unable to review these aspects with the IPs. He could not offer Michele and Jonathan a step-by-step template and suggestions for disclosure, leaving the IPs unsure of how to reveal this information to their child.

Additionally, Dr. Farrero did not obtain adequate information about Jonathan's and Michele's families. Consequently, he is unable to discuss whether those whom the couple may rely on for emotional, and perhaps financial, support would react negatively to their contracting with a GC.

Frequently ASRM members offer bibliotherapy to their patients, especially for issues surrounding disclosure. Members of the Mental Health Professional Group have compiled a thorough list of books appropriate for children of various ages. This list is available to Mental Health Professional Group members of the ASRM.

The Existing Children

Dr. Farrero did not take the time to find out if Staci and Steven's children were doing well, if their home life was serene or chaotic, or if their children were exhibiting any emotional or disciplinary problems. More important, the psychologist did not inquire whether Steven and Staci had any deceased children. If this was the case or had they experienced other severe losses, their two children might be placed in a situation that might traumatize them because they possibly will experience some degree of loss after the child their mother will be carrying is relinquished to Jonathan and Michele. Although there is a fairly simple and concrete method that mental health professionals teach GCs to use with children ages 3 to 8 and that explains their role in the IPs' gestation of a child (Horowitz, 1996), Dr. Farrero is unfamiliar with it and is not able to provide the information to Staci or Steven to help prepare their family for this pregnancy.

CONCLUSION

It is difficult to assess whether the potential risks are too great to permit these couples to proceed with IVF treatment and gestational surrogacy. Very little is known about these individuals. Dr. Farrero's report included an abbreviated section regarding their immediate and nuclear families and no information about their religiosity, cultural mores, values, et cetera. Consequently, it is difficult to gauge whether one or more of the individuals might be emotionally harmed as a result of their participation in a gestational surrogacy arrangement. However, a mental health professional, after thorough investigation, might find they are perfectly suited to enter this type of contract. The dearth of information provided by Dr. Farerro, however, renders it impossible to determine whether the risks might outweigh the benefits.

In conclusion, it is our goal that as a result of reading this book, and specifically this chapter, more mental health professionals will be motivated to explore the ethical practice of psychology within the field of reproductive medicine. We have emphasized the obligation to practice psychology in accordance with the APA's Ethics Code. Moreover, as illustrated by Dr. Farrero's limitations, we believe that psychologists are truly compelled to achieve and maintain competency in their professional practices, lest they do a great disservice to their clients, IVF clinics and physicians, the profession of psychology, and ultimately, themselves.

We hope that as more psychologists continue to conduct rigorous research with traditional surrogates, GCs, and IPs, additional practice guidelines will be generated. Furthermore, as demonstrated in this vignette, only those mental health professionals who keep themselves up to date with the current research and actively pursue instruction in this field are equipped to educate both surrogates and IPs so that their patients, in turn, can provide informed consent. Mental health professionals who belong to APA, ASRM, and/or the European Society of Human Reproduction and Embryology and regularly attend postgraduate workshops are uniquely positioned to assist GCs and IPs so that patients will be better equipped to cope with both the process and the possible outcomes of the pregnancies achieved with surrogacy.

8

OFFSPRING BORN OF COLLABORATIVE REPRODUCTIVE ARRANGEMENTS: ISSUES OF DISCLOSURE AND THIRD-PARTY IDENTIFICATION

Those who cannot remember the past are condemned to repeat it.
—George Santayana, *The Life of Reason*

At present, over 1% of babies born in the United States are conceived through assisted reproductive technology (ART; Wright, Chang, Jeng, & Macaluso, 2008). Historically, the focus of ART has been almost entirely on adults' access to technology to create a family, even when a collaborative reproductive arrangement has been used. Fueled by a renewed emphasis on the importance of genes, the victories of open adoption advocates, the open-identity movement, the voices of the offspring themselves affirming the importance of knowing their genetic heritage, and a human rights perspective, the needs of the offspring created are now coming sharply into focus. Several sperm banks have pioneered sperm donor identity disclosure programs using a double-track model (Pennings, 1997) that allows parents to choose whether they prefer an anonymous or identity-release donor. This change in priorities will likely present challenges to the field of reproductive medicine in the United States.

There are two major issues to be addressed with regard to the offspring of collaborative reproductive arrangements: disclosure and anonymity. Is it in offspring's best interest to be made aware of their donor origins through disclosure by their parents? If parents disclose to their offspring, what type of additional information do offspring want and/or need regarding their donors—no information, nonidentifying information, or identifying information? A primary ethical concern about the use of third-party reproduction arises when adults' rights to procreate clash with (potential) children's needs. Who trumps whom? In this chapter we focus on the offspring created through collaborative reproductive arrangements because it is expected that mental health professionals will increasingly be called on to consult with the offspring.

MEDICAL BACKGROUND

Donor gametes are often used to circumvent age-related infertility or to avert diseases or carrier status if there is a family history of severe heredity disease. Gamete donors undergo genetic screening prior to being allowed to donate their gametes, and consequently, rates of major birth defects in infants born after third-party reproduction appear similar to rates in the general public (Lansac et al., 1997; Reefhuis et al., 2009; Wiggins & Main, 2005). Nevertheless, although research has not looked specifically at pregnancies conceived with donor gametes, it is important to understand that the incidence of preterm deliveries, low birth weight, cerebral palsy, and small-for-gestational-age newborns is higher in ART singleton pregnancies than in spontaneous conceptions (Bower & Hansen, 2005; Hvidtjorn et al., 2006; Ludwig, Sutcliffe, Diedrich, & Ludwig, 2006; Schieve et al., 2002). The higher risks in multifetal pregnancies, also common in donor egg pregnancies, are reviewed in Chapter 4 of this volume. In addition, there is a growing body of literature suggesting an increased risk of major birth defects in in vitro fertilization (IVF) infants, including major malformations such as hypospadias (i.e., incomplete development of the urethra); cardiovascular, esophageal, and rectal defects; cleft lip and palate; and some rare imprinting disorders (i.e., when a gene inherited from one parent is not expressed as a result of differential DNA methylation) such as Beckwith–Wiedemann and Angelman syndromes (Ceelen, van Weissenbruch, Vermeiden, van Leeuwen, & Delemarre-van de Waal, 2008; Hansen, Bower, Milne, de Klerk, & Kurinczuk, 2005; Reefhuis et al., 2009). The use of intracytoplasmic sperm injection adds the further risk of passing on certain genetic problems and infertility to offspring (Dim, Bischoff, Lipschultz, & Lamb, 1999).

There is much that health care providers do not know as of yet about the effects of IVF treatment, particularly the long-term effects. It remains uncertain, as well, whether the increased risks reported previously are due to the treatment interventions infertile patients are undergoing, the infertility itself, potential ascertainment bias because children born after ART may be monitored more intensely, or methodological limitations of some of the studies (Allen, Wilson, & Cheung, 2006; Romundstad et al., 2008). Although much remains to be learned about the long-term safety of infertility treatment and despite the difficulty in trying to obtain informed consent from patients when information in the field is still evolving, prospective parents considering IVF, whether with or without donor gametes, should be made aware of the possible risks and benefits for children conceived with these treatments that have been suggested by congruent high-quality research findings to date. It is often useful for mental health professionals to reiterate risk–benefit information that physicians have already provided to patients, as patients sometimes forget, do not absorb the information, or are too intimidated to ask relevant questions of their doctors because of their fear of appearing ignorant.

PSYCHOSOCIAL CONCERNS

Many questions are raised by ART resulting in children and families created through the use of donor gametes and surrogacy arrangements. How do these atypical genetic and gestational relationships affect family relationships and the psychosocial development of the offspring?

Parent–Child Relationships and Child Development

Breaking ranks from adoption supporters, psychobiologists have argued that by sharing genes with their children, genetic parents are hardwired to care for them and protect them, whereas non-genetically-related parents would be less likely to do so (Cronin & Smith, 1991). Thus, it has been questioned whether the relationship between the nongenetic parent and child in a donor gamete pregnancy would be affected by the lack of a genetic tie. According to attachment theory, however, attachment is not a function of genetic relatedness but is developed through day-to-day interaction, companionship, connection, and shared experiences in a parent–child relationship (Bowlby, 1982; Goldstein, Freud, & Solnit, 1979).

Empirical studies have indicated that the parent–child relationship in collaborative reproductive arrangements (including donor egg, donor sperm, donor embryo, and surrogacy) is equal to or better than that in spontaneously conceiving families (Casey, Readings, Blake, Jadva, & Golombok, 2008; Golombok, MacCallum, Goodman, & Rutter, 2002; Golombok, MacCallum, Murray, Lycett, & Jadva, 2006; Murray, MacCallum, & Golombok, 2006). This includes the parent–child relationships in lesbian parent families (Bos, van Balen, & van den Boom, 2007; Chan, Raboy, & Patterson, 1998; Flaks, Ficher, Masterpasqua, & Joseph, 1995) and those families created by intent by single heterosexual women using third-party reproduction (MacCallum & Golombok, 2004; Murray & Golombok, 2005a). However, in the previously cited studies, the oldest of the donor-conceived children studied was 12, and most of the children had not yet been told of their genetic heritage. No research was found for gay male families or single heterosexual men using a surrogate and egg donor.

Most research conducted in Western societies has also revealed no significant differences between children created using collaborative reproductive arrangements and spontaneously conceived children through early adolescence in intelligence, psychomotor skills, or emotional and behavioral development (Golombok et al., 2002; Golombok, Murray, et al., 2006; MacCallum, Golombok, & Brinsden, 2007; Murray et al., 2006). Similar findings have been duplicated in planned lesbian families (Anderssen, Amlie, & Ytteroy, 2002; Bos et al., 2007; Flaks et al., 1995) and in families of single mothers by intent (Murray & Golombok, 2005b; Weissenberg, Landau, & Madgar, 2007) and, although investigated to a lesser extent, for young children born through surrogacy (Casey et al., 2008; Golombok, MacCallum, et al., 2006). Little information is available on the impact of surrogacy on the surrogate's own children, however. The majority of surrogates report that their own children reacted positively during the pregnancy and at the time the baby was relinquished, and none experienced major problems (Ciccarelli, 1997; Hohman & Hagan, 2001; Jadva, Murray, Lycett, MacCallum, & Golombok, 2003). However, because of negative societal reactions to surrogacy, it is possible that the surrogates felt a need to present themselves and their families in a positive light.

Disclosure

Erikson's (1963) theory of identity development suggests that determining one's identity (i.e., answering the question, Who am I?) is a primary focus of concern during adolescence. This implies that accidentally discovering one's donor gamete origins or even experiencing a planned disclosure by one's parents during adolescence or later in life could have significant psychological ramifications. Although being told as a child of one's donor gamete origins may be more easily integrated into the developing child's self-concept, being told as an adolescent or later may require that the individual reappraise his or her sense of self, a more complex task. One could hypothesize that the fact of one's donor gamete conception may assume a larger role within the individual's life as a result of later disclosure and lack of information about one's gamete progenitor(s) because it may complicate the adolescent process of identity formation, although at present, empirical verification is lacking. In addition, accidental and/or traumatic discovery later in life may have significant implications for the bond of trust previously created within the parent–offspring relationship.

Because the vast majority of heterosexual couples using donor sperm have not shared this information with their children, do not intend to, or are unsure if they will disclose this information (Golombok, Murray, et al., 2006; Leeb-Lundberg, Kjellberg, & Sydsjo, 2006; Lycett, Daniels, Curson, & Golombok, 2005), most donor-conceived individuals raised in two-parent heterosexual families are not aware of their genetic heritage. Although initially a large percentage of couples using ovum recipiency planned to disclose this information to their offspring (Greenfeld & Klock, 2004; Hahn & Craft-Rosenberg, 2002; Murray et al., 2006), many parents later changed their minds (Durna, Bebe, Steigrad, Leader, & Garrett, 1997; Klock, 1997) despite having usually told at least one other friend or family member (Klock & Greenfeld, 2004; Lycett et al., 2005; Murray et al., 2006). Clinical experience confirms this reluctance on the part of heterosexual couples to disclose, primarily because of the intended parents' desire to appear to be a "normal" family, wanting to protect the nongenetic parent's relationship with the child, and/or wishing to consider their children's need for privacy.

In contrast, lesbian parents almost universally disclose the fact of their child's being conceived with donor sperm (Jacob, Klock, & Maier, 1999; Scheib, Riordan, & Rubin, 2005; Vanfraussen, Ponjaert-Kristoffersen, & Brewaeys, 2001); single mothers by intent report a greater intention to disclose compared with two-parent heterosexual families using donor insemination (DI; Klock, Jacob, & Maier, 1996; Leiblum, Palmer, & Spector, 1995; Murray & Golombok, 2005a); and the majority of couples using a surrogacy arrangement to gestate their child plan to disclose this to their child, whether the intended mother's own egg was or was not used (Casey et al., 2008; Golombok, Murray, et al., 2006; van den Akker, 2000). With the increasing use of genetic testing in medicine, however, the risk that donor offspring may find out about their genetic origins from medical professionals, a biology teacher requesting cheek squabs for an experiment on DNA, or someone else other than their parents always looms.

What impact does disclosure versus nondisclosure have on the offspring created through third-party reproduction and their families? Secrets can create asymmetry in family relationships between those who know versus those who do not know the secret, tend to be revealed at inappropriate times, or can create barriers to open communication (Baran & Pannor, 1993; Bok, 1978, Papp, 1993; Turner & Coyle, 2000). In addition, disclosure of this information could disrupt family life and identity formation. Without explicit updated information about a donor, those parents who choose to disclose may have limited information to share with their child. Although no different than is often the case in adoption, how might this impact the donor offspring's quest for identity formation?

Much of what is predicted regarding the impact of secrecy on families has been abstracted from the adoption and family therapy literature, which suggests that children benefit from having the circumstances of their birth disclosed as well as from being told this information at an early age because this makes it easier for children to integrate this information into their self-concept (Hajal & Rosenberg, 1991; Hoopes, 1990). However, there are significant differences between the experiences of adoption and third-party reproduction, and thus it may be unwarranted to generalize from research on adopted offspring to offspring conceived by donor gametes. Nevertheless, initial research suggests that when children born of DI are informed of their origins in gradual stages prior to adolescence, they appear to be accepting of this information, comfortable with their conception origins, and positive in their reactions to disclosure (Hewitt, 2002; Jadva, Freeman, Kramer, & Golombok, 2009).

The majority of offspring who are aware of their genetic origins appear comfortable sharing this information with people close to them, as well, including relatives and friends (Hewitt, 2002; Scheib, Riordan, & Rubin, 2005). Reactions of others were reported to be generally positive, with offspring in single-parent families receiving more positive reactions to sharing this information than those raised in two-parent lesbian or heterosexual families (Scheib et al., 2005).

Offspring in single-mother or lesbian families and those whose parents chose an identity-release donor, wherein identifying information about the sperm donor is made available to the offspring at age 18 upon their request, were more likely to be told of their donor origins at a younger age (Jadva et al., 2009; Scheib et al., 2003). Early awareness does not appear to negatively impact family relationships and, instead, has either a neutral or positive effect on the offspring's relationship with his or her parents (Scheib et al., 2005; Vanfraussen, Ponjaert-Kristoffersen, & Brewaeys, 2003). Parents, too, report being more at ease with early disclosure to their offspring and that planned disclosure to a child with whom they have a strong and close emotional bond has a positive or neutral outcome (MacDougall, Becker, Scheib, & Nachtigall, 2007). In research available to date, no parents reported regretting disclosure, and some stated that they felt relieved after disclosure (Lindblad, Gottlieb, & Lalos, 2000; Lycett et al., 2005; MacDougall et al., 2007). However, it must be kept in mind that children who have not been disclosed to also seem to have positive family relationships and to be developing normally (Brewaeys, Ponjaert, van Hall, & Golombok, 1997; Golombok et al., 2002; Lycett, Daniels, Curson, & Golombok, 2004; MacCallum et al., 2007; Murray et al., 2006; Nachtigall, Tschann, Quiroga, Pitcher, & Becker, 1997; Shenfield & Steele, 1997), although most children empirically studied are still relatively young.

Physical resemblance to others may in and of itself play a role in identity formation because knowing who one looks and acts like can contribute to a coherent sense of self (Hoopes, 1990) as it represents relatedness and family continuity (Daniels & Meadows, 2006). Because family resemblances and inheritance of characteristics are such a frequent topic of discussion in social discourse, these references may raise discomfort for parents of donor gamete children, especially for those who have not disclosed this to their children (Becker, Butler, & Nachtigall, 2005; M. Karpel, 1980).

Also, children may sense when information is being withheld from them because of topic avoidance or subtle signals sent by and between their parents when taboo topics, such as physical resemblance, are raised (DePaulo, 1992; Papp, 1993; Paul & Berger, 2007), and because of their normal egocentrism, they often believe that they are to blame for family discomfort (Hetherington & Stanley-Hagan, 1999). A secret of this import is likely to become increasingly difficult to maintain as a child becomes an adolescent and adult, as well.

How do those individuals who learn of their third-party conception during adolescence or adulthood fare? Information about this is derived primarily from the personal accounts of the individuals conceived by donor insemination, many of whom learned this fact accidentally or under less than ideal circumstances. These offspring often report feeling angry, not about their means of conception but about being deceived by their parents and the medical profession. They feel frustrated and disadvantaged at not being able to obtain any information about their donor, both for themselves and for their own children, as well as relieved at having their suspicions of being "different" confirmed by this late disclosure (Baran & Pannor, 1993; Donor Conception Support Group of Australia, Inc., 1997; Hewitt, 2002; Jadva et al., 2009; Kirkman, 2004; Mahlstedt, LaBounty, & Kennedy, 2008; McWhinnie, 2001; Morrissette, 2006; Orenstein, 1995; Turner & Coyle, 2000). Typically, the offspring wish they were told earlier and feel mistrust toward their parents and some loss of their sense of identity. It is important for mental health professionals to consider that the lack of trust that these offspring report may impact their future relationships, including the psychotherapeutic relationship, as well.

Adults who were told at an early age expressed less anger about their conception than those told after the age of 18 (Jadva et al., 2009). Although these samples were often obtained from donor offspring support networks and may be biased in terms of offspring who have negative feelings to air about the secrecy surrounding their conception, ignoring the voices of the offspring themselves would be a mistake because they provide a powerful reminder that fertility treatment has significant long-term implications for individuals and families.

In conclusion, the currently available literature suggests that DI offspring who know about their donor conception before puberty can incorporate this information into their developing sense of self rather than needing to adjust their already established self-identity. Parents report satisfaction with having disclosed to their young children, most of whom respond with either curiosity or disinterest, and despite worries that their children may become too interested in the donor in the future, no reports were found of parents regretting having told their offspring. Yet, no data at present unequivocally demonstrate that family problems arise as a result of nondisclosure of collaborative reproductive conception to offspring, and the majority of parents still do not plan to disclose or are uncertain whether and how to disclose. Nevertheless, mental health professionals generally agree that it is in the best interests of families for children to grow up knowing about their genetic heritage, and many support early parental disclosure so that no information regarding a child's identity will be withheld from him or her, need to be changed at a later time in the child's development, or have the potential to undermine trust in the parent–child relationship (Shehab et al., 2008). This has resulted in general support within the profession for the establishment of a donor registry (Corson & Mechanick-Braverman, 1998) and has contributed to the development of an American Society for Reproductive Medicine (ASRM) Ethics Committee recommendation to inform offspring of their conception by gamete donation (Ethics Committee of the ASRM, 2004f).

Sharing information with intended parents about the health needs and natural curiosity of offspring regarding their donors may result in parents' greater likelihood to disclose to their children. Nevertheless, it is the parents' right to decide in their role as arbiter for the children and within the cultural, social, and religious context in which they will raise their child whether it is in the best interest of their child or their best interest to disclose this information. Optimally, psychological consultation will be offered in advance of participation in third-party reproduction and will continue to be made available to offspring, parents, and donors and subsequent offspring as families grow and mature.

Third-Party Identification

Most currently available studies involve offspring created with donor sperm. Initially, offspring often react to disclosure with curiosity and wish to know what the donor is like, whether he is similar to them, whether they resemble the donor, and whether they can have a photograph (MacDougall et al., 2007; Rumball & Adair, 1999; Scheib et al., 2005). As they get older, offspring report wanting information about the donor's current circumstances, his reasons for donating, feelings about being contacted, and his health and family history (Jadva, Freeman, Kramer, & Golombok, 2009; Lindblad et al., 2000; Lycett et al., 2005; Scheib et al., 2005).

Recipient parents and donor-conceived offspring often appear to have diverging perspectives on the importance of genes versus relationships in the family narrative, however, and there is a good deal of variation among individuals and even within the same individual across time as the offspring mature (Kirkman, 2004). Although there are few donor-conceived individuals to inform health care providers' clinical practices, denying the significance of genes conflicts with the voices of offspring from whom these providers have heard thus far. Furthermore, donor-conceived individuals are reminded of the importance of their genetic background every time they are asked for their medical history.

The majority of offspring created from identity-release donor sperm reportedly planned to request donor information, although only 30% of those ages 18 and 25 actually requested the donor's identity (Scheib, Ruby, & Benward, 2008). Those most likely to request this information were women raised in single-mother or lesbian-headed families (Scheib et al., 2005, 2008). Once informed of their donor conception, the vast majority of offspring do not wish to establish a parent–child relationship with their identifiable donor, although many do attempt to search for and find their donors and/or genetic half siblings, reporting this as a positive experience and generally maintaining regular contact with them (Hewitt, 2002; Jadva et al., 2007; Mahlstedt et al., 2008; Scheib et al., 2008). Reasons given for searching for one's donor were curiosity as well as wanting to make a genetic connection, to determine if there are similarities between the donor and oneself, and to satisfy a desire to know a "missing part of themselves" (Jadva et al., 2007; Scheib et al., 2005, Turner & Coyle, 2000; Vanfraussen et al., 2003). Adolescent offspring expressed a surprising respect for the donor's privacy, however, not wishing to intrude on him (Scheib et al., 2005).

If offspring do wish to contact their donor and are unable to do so, might they experience frustration and, if they are considered selfish or ungrateful by others for wanting this contact, feel a disenfranchised grief, that is, unrecognized or unsupported grief (McWhinnie, 2006), as well? This may create a psychological burden of guilt when offspring wish to satisfy their curiosity about their genetic progenitor. Quite telling is that some adult offspring of donor conception in the United States, although feeling neutral to positive about their means of conception, believe that only identity-release sperm donation should be practiced (Mahlstedt et al., 2008). Further empirical research is sorely needed.

Yet, not all DI offspring with whom parents have disclosed their genetic origin are interested in learning additional information about their donor progenitor, and the desire to know more about the donor or the absence of such desire seems to be unrelated to self-esteem, emotional adjustment, or to the quality of the parent–child relationship. Instead, it may be a reflection of a basic human need to have knowledge of one's genetic forebears (Vanfraussen et al., 2003). Despite the increasing popularity of a donor sibling registry in the United States, it is unclear at present if nonidentifying information will adequately satisfy donor offspring's curiosity and desire for medical information or whether an open-identity donor program would be preferable in meeting these needs. It is also possible that offspring may experience a loyalty bind about requesting any further information about their donors when raised in a two-parent family, as over 50% of offspring in a study of lesbian couple families did not want to know the donor's identity, primarily out of loyalty to their social mother (Vanfraussen et al., 2001), and many offspring raised in heterosexual families reported that they would have been satisfied with nonidentifying information (Hewitt, 2002). Further research is needed to answer this question.

Because studies reviewed previously are of DI offspring, it is possible that the issues for donor oocyte offspring many differ because of having been gestated by their social mother. Those conceived with donor embryos in which both the sperm and the egg were from donors are likely to have more complex emotional needs in sorting through identity issues. Although many parents through embryo donation did not plan to disclose to their offspring, the more information they were given about their donors, even if nonidentifying, the more likely they were to disclose (MacCallum, 2009). This finding is similar to the finding for parents through donor insemination (Scheib et al., 2003) and fathers of children created through ovum donation (Klock & Greenfeld, 2004). Further research both on donor oocyte and donor embryo offspring is needed as well as studies differentiating the impact of disclosure or lack thereof by parents on offspring of collaborative reproductive arrangements.

Being ethically bound to try to protect the welfare of all parties in a collaborative reproductive arrangement, mental health professionals who consult with donors and intended parents prior to treatment should inform them that laws and guidelines could change over time and discuss the potential impact on all parties providing informed consent. During the initial meeting(s) with the donor, the mental health professional should also discuss the pros and cons of disclosure to her present and potential future family as well as suggest methods to help her to accomplish this if she chooses to disclose. A similar discussion should take place with the intended parents (see Chapter 5, this volume).

Studies addressing the effect of parental expectations on children conceived through collaborative reproductive arrangements can help to answer questions about whether children encounter problems as a result of parental attempts at genetic enhancement. Through parental selection of specific characteristics in the donors, despite the difficulty in actually influencing outcome because of random genetic assortment in uniting an egg with a sperm and the influence of environment as well, we believe that if parents have certain expectations of their child that differ from those of parents spontaneously conceiving, this may impinge on the donor-conceived child's right to an open future (Feinberg, 1980).

Unfortunately, there is very little research thus far to help guide mental health professionals in charting this new area of counseling with individuals conceived through gamete donation (Human Fertilisation and Embryology

Authority Register Counselling Project Steering Group, 2003; Pettle, 2003). Pettle (2003) proposed an initial model of the process of assisting donor-conceived offspring from revelation to integration of this new information on the basis of her exploratory research. She suggested six stages that donor-conceived offspring may go through: (a) the initial crisis; (b) reflection on the deception and concealment; (c) deconstruction and reconstruction of existing relationships in light of the new information; (d) reevaluation of earlier experiences, creating explanations, and giving meaning to the experiences; (e) efforts to complete the narrative by accessing more details and possibly meeting genetic relatives; and (f) explanations for secret keeping and revelation. Because each individual's needs are unique, counseling with offspring and families of third-party reproduction will need to vary depending, in all likelihood, on the age and method of disclosure, the degree of upset that the offspring or family demonstrates, and the amount of information available to the parents and their willingness to share this with their child(ren). Some donor-conceived offspring will simply need help in integrating this new information, whereas others may need therapeutic intervention.

Despite the need for empirical validation of counseling models and for additional research to inform clinical practice from the literature that has emerged thus far as well as from our clinical experience, we expect that mental health professionals with an expertise in reproductive medicine will be called on to play a role in counseling clients coping with issues that may have been created by these collaborative reproductive arrangements. Peer consultation, supervision, and/or posting a general question without any identifying information on the listserv of the Mental Health Professionals Group of ASRM can be helpful if the professional is in doubt as to how to proceed in this uncharted counseling territory.

BIOETHICAL PERSPECTIVES

Successful collaborative reproductive arrangements result in the birth of children. Although these children have no rights before birth, these most vulnerable parties to collaborative reproductive arrangements do have both rights and needs after birth. However, these may conflict with the privacy rights of their parents as well as with the rights of the donor and the donor's family.

Welfare of the Child

There are several concerns regarding child welfare and the professional obligation to do no harm in collaborative reproductive arrangements. Is it ethical to deliberately bring a child into the world who will not know half or all (in the case of embryo donation) of his or her genetic provenance if the parents do not intend to disclose the nature of the conception to their offspring? As many parents do not plan to disclose this information to their children, should children have a right to truthful information about their genetic origins? Do parents have an ethical and moral responsibility to build a relationship of trust through honesty with their children with regard to information that is relevant to their child's identity? The timing and circumstances of disclosure may also either benefit or harm the offspring. In addition, are individuals without access to up-to-date information about their donor's and their donor's family's medical history in a disadvantaged position relative to most of the rest of the population? When compared with adopted offspring? Although counter to the opinion of most mental health professionals, might these offspring be better off if never informed? And, with respect to surrogacy, is it harmful to the surrogate's own children to witness this process?

For the welfare of the child created through third-party reproduction, should those working in the field of reproductive medicine advocate for parental disclosure? If parents do disclose, some information is likely to be available to the offspring that may be important to him or her for medical, psychological, or social reasons. In addition, should a national registry be made available to offspring in the United States on their reaching the age of majority? Should this registry offer relevant updated nonidentifying information about donors or should identifying information be made available as well?

Some researchers have concluded that there is insufficient evidence regarding the consequences of openness versus secrecy to encourage reproductive endocrinologists to attempt to convince parents to disclose to their offspring (Shenfield & Steele, 1997). One can imagine some circumstances, societies, or cultures in which a breach of the family bloodline and/or lineage could result in extreme social sanctions and/or stigma such that concealment of the nature of the child's conception may actually be in the best interests of the child. And, in all societies, parents are left with the responsibility to decide whether they wish to disclose this information to their child.

Strong opinions about the ethics of the practice of anonymous donation exist as well in light of the possibility that it can cause distressing lifelong psychological consequences to the offspring (Frith, 2007; Johnston, 2002; McWhinnie, 2001). Although a good deal of information about a donor offspring's genetic heritage may be available without making the donors identifiable, is it appropriate for society to become complicit in intentionally depriving children of the ability to access identifying information about their donor if they so choose? On the other hand, it may be more difficult to recruit donors if their guaranteed privacy is not at least an option (Brett, Sacranie, Thomas, & Rajkhowa, 2008; Janssens, Simons, van Kooij, Blokzijl, & Dunselman, 2006). Having fewer gamete donors would result in having fewer family-building options (Fortescue, 2003), and subsequently donor gamete offspring may not be born at all. If anonymity is abolished, although a large number of sperm donors will be lost, research suggests that some will be replaced with a different type of sperm donor, one who is older, who has children of his own, who donates primarily for altruistic reasons, and who believes that offspring have a right to access complete information regarding their genetics (Daniels, Blyth, Crawshaw, & Curson, 2005).

Giving the (assumed) needs of donor gamete offspring primacy, as well as offering them the option to determine for themselves the importance of contact with their genetic progenitors, has resulted in several countries banning donor anonymity (e.g., Sweden, the United Kingdom, the Netherlands, Switzerland, Austria, and parts of Australia). In addition, Article 7 of the U.N. Convention on the Rights of the Child (1989) states that a child has the right to "know and be cared for by his/ her parents."

To meet the needs of donor offspring for accurate, updated information would appear, from a practical standpoint, to require the creation of a national donor registry within the United States. However, a registry could be implemented without divulging the identities of the donors, for example, they could be given identifying numbers different from their social security numbers and the offspring could access this information in an ongoing manner without learning the donor's identity. This would not ensure that donor-conceived offspring are informed of their means of conception by their parents, however, as disclosure cannot be realistically mandated in a democratic society. If not informed, offspring would have no knowledge of their need to access such a registry.

There is also concern about the impact that donor gamete conception might have on the relationship between siblings within a family. What if one sibling is spontaneously conceived or adopted, for example, whereas the other is conceived with donated gametes? What might occur in the situation wherein one child is conceived using only one gamete donor and another is conceived using two, as is sometimes the case with older single mothers by intent? Will it make a difference if siblings have been created with the same or different gamete donors? What if one sibling got the smarter, prettier, taller, or more talented donor? If a parent used a different donor for a second child, might the older child feel hurt or insulted and think the parent was not satisfied with the first born and how he or she developed? What if there are inequalities in the type or quantity of information available to siblings about their different donors? What if one sibling makes contact with multiple genetic half siblings and the other is either uninterested or unable to make these contacts? How might this impact on sibling relationships, rivalry, and competition? Should only mental health professionals familiar with the issues in third-party reproduction be permitted to counsel these offspring prior to and after their contacts with donor sibling registries, genetic half siblings, and their own donors in the event that any issues or problems arise that the offspring choose to address?

Potential inadvertent consanguinity is also a concern to donor gamete offspring reaching adulthood. Both lack of disclosure to offspring and creating large numbers of offspring from a single donor increase this bioethical concern because accidental incest and mating between those who are closely genetically related raises the risk of major recessive genetic disorders in subsequent offspring.

Another bioethical concern involves the terminology used for third-party reproduction because language, too, can have an impact on the offspring and their family. Referring to spontaneous conception as *natural* can imply that third-party conception is unnatural. Also, although clinical experience suggests that single women or lesbians may often refer to the gamete provider as the offspring's *father*, this may confuse the child and make it difficult for him or her to differentiate between a provider of reproductive material and a parent. The terminology used may create expectations of a relationship on the part of the child (and the parent) that will likely never be met as this is not what typically was previously agreed on by the gamete donor.

Welfare of the Donor and His or Her Family

If anonymity is not offered, donors may worry about any responsibilities they may eventually have, both emotionally as well as financially, to offspring created with their gametes. If they are foresighted, they may also worry about the impact of the existence of these offspring on their own future children, especially as early research has suggested that donor recipient parents and their offspring may be more curious about genetic half siblings than the donor him- or herself (Freeman, Jadva, Kramer, & Golombok, 2009). To be able to give informed consent, donors should be encouraged to think about their potential responsibilities to offspring in advance of consenting to donate their gametes, particularly in light of potentially changing laws.

If gamete donors contracted to remain anonymous, what responsibility do physicians, clinic staff, and mental health professionals have to them? What would be the impact of the unexpected introduction of an offspring conceived from one's donated gametes on the donor and the family of the donor, particularly if the donor has not disclosed to his or her family that he or she had donated gametes to infertile individuals many years ago? How would this information about genetic half siblings be integrated by the donor's own children, not to mention his or her spouse? Given that donors must be protected from financial and/or other obligations to the donor-conceived offspring, what does the mental health professional need to do to insulate and safeguard donors?

Commodification

Intended parents are often given the opportunity to select a gamete donor from among lists of prospective donors, giving them some degree of (attempted) control over the genetic characteristics of their children. Despite the probabilistic nature of genes; the sheer complexity of most personal and psychological characteristics, traits, and abilities; and the nature of gene–environmental interactions, this may, nevertheless, result in the commodification of the children who are so created, particularly if parents are deselecting some characteristics that they themselves possess and are dissatisfied with and selecting others to enhance their child (Cameron, 2005). Will this impact on the child's self-concept?

Existing Laws, Policies, and Legislation

One of the most interesting and unresolved legal conundrums raised by collaborative reproductive arrangements is whether children created in this way should have a right to information about their origins, and if so, how access should be accomplished. It has been argued, as discussed previously, that eliminating donor anonymity is one way to be sure that children can learn what they want about donors when they want. Several countries do prohibit anonymous gamete donation (see Appendix B).

Eliminating donor anonymity, however, in no way guarantees that a child, even on reaching adulthood, will learn the information he or she needs or wants because no laws currently require disclosure to offspring of their origins. The ASRM does encourage disclosure (Ethics Committee of the ASRM, 2004f). However, this recommendation is unlikely ever to be codified or adopted as law in any state given that the law in the United States recognizes parents as having the fundamental right to the care, control, and upbringing of their children (Meyer v. Nebraska, 1923; Troxel v. Granville, 2000). Presently, no law mandates that parents disclose to a child that he or she was adopted, and thus it would be unlikely that parents conceiving through collaborative reproductive arrangements would be legally compelled to disclose to their children the origin of their conception. Another factor militating against disclosure to children is that in the medical process of conception, the child is not the patient, so it is unclear if physicians might be found to have a duty to disclose information to offspring.

Although the law may not require disclosure and may not prohibit anonymity, laws do exist in some jurisdictions that mandate record collection and maintenance and this too is something that the ASRM has recommended. Furthermore, the ASRM published Practice Committee Guidelines in 2008 asserting that "a mechanism must exist to maintain [the] records as a future medical resource for any offspring produced" (Practice Committee of the

ASRM and the Practice Committee of the Society for Assisted Reproductive Technology, 2008, p. S42).

Some states do, in fact, have requirements for record retention. It is unclear, however, whether the intent is to maintain a future medical resource for offspring. New York (10 New York Codes, Rules and Regulations sec. 52-8.9, 2009), for example, has rules requiring that each reproductive tissue bank shall maintain certain donor records, which include (a) for donors, pertinent family history of any genetic disorders; (b) documentation of donor and client-depositor written informed consent; and (c) for semen donors, outcome of any prior artificial insemination or other assisted reproductive procedures, if known. If no live birth results, the records need only be maintained for 7 years, but in the event of a known live birth, the records must be maintained for 25 years (10 New York Codes, Rules and Regulations Sec. 52-8.9, 2009).

Another state, Ohio, requires that upon request of the recipient, the physician provide (a) the medical history of the donor, including, but not limited to, any available genetic history of the donor and persons related to him by consanguinity, the blood type of the donor, and whether he has an RH factor; (b) the race, eye and hair color, age, height, and weight of the donor; (c) the educational attainment and talents of the donor; (d) the religious background of the donor; and (e) any other information that the donor has indicated may be disclosed (Ohio Revised Code Ann. Sec. 3111.93, 2008).

The Ohio law is reflective of the interest in preserving information but also in maintaining anonymity. The state requires that the informed consent process include a

> statement that the donor shall not be advised by the physician or another person performing the artificial insemination as to the identity of the recipient or, if married, her husband and that the recipient and, if married, her husband, shall not be advised by the physician or another person performing the artificial insemination as to the identity of the donor. (Ohio Revised Code Ann. Sec. 311.93, 2008)

Although preserving anonymity continues to be the norm in the United States, as recently as 2007, one state, Virginia, did consider legislation that would have prohibited the use of anonymous donated gametes (Va. H.B. 2123, 2007). This bill, however, was indefinitely passed on and has not been reintroduced.

The law continues to evolve as methods of family formation change and increase in complexity. Jurisprudence tends to be reactive rather than proactive. The rights of many are involved in gamete donation including those of the recipients, the donors, and the children who are born. Seeking to balance the legal interests of such diverse interests is no easy task. Laws may continue to be enacted requiring collection, maintenance, and access to nonidentifying information about such arrangements, but it is unlikely that state or federal law will require disclosure to offspring of their donor origins because this might be considered a violation of a fundamental right to privacy.

CLINICAL VIGNETTE

Dara is a 16-year-old high school junior whose mother recently learned that she has breast cancer. Overhearing her parents arguing, she stopped outside of their closed bedroom door to listen to the thrust of the disagreement. Dara was surprised to hear her father beseeching her mother with requests to tell Dara and her 13-year-old sister "the truth." Her father went on to say that they had kept their secret too long and that the girls had the right to know their means of conception, if only so they would not have to worry that they too may be prone to cancer because their maternal grandmother had also died of breast cancer when Dara was 10. Using money she had saved from her summer job, Dara came to a psychologist's psychotherapy office after having found a therapist on the Internet and determined that individual specialized in infertility.

Dara's intensity was palpable. She had put two and two together and realized that she and her sister must have been conceived with donor eggs. This revelation, although shocking, made sense to her because she had often wondered why she and her sister seemed so different from their mother in terms of looks, interests, and temperament. The conflict in her emotions was obvious as she expressed anger and a sense of betrayal that her parents had never shared this important information with her but also concern for her mother's health.

Dara was plagued by many questions: Should she confront her parents and let them know what she overheard? Should she disclose this information to her younger sister? Dara wants information about her donor, particularly medical information, but wonders if she can obtain this information and whether she should try to search for her donor. Wouldn't that break her mother's heart? What if the donor wanted nothing to do with her? Dara turns to the psychologist and asks what she should do.

Ethical Dilemmas in the Context of Professional Guidelines

The American Psychological Association's (APA's; 2002) "Ethical Principles of Psychologists and Code of Conduct" indicates that psychologists have the ethical obligation to strive to benefit those with whom they work and attempt to do no harm (Principle A, Beneficence and Nonmaleficence). Dara has come to a psychologist of her own volition with concerns about the means of her conception, her genetic heritage, and the impact that acknowledgement of her awareness of this information would have on her parents and her sibling. Minors (considered below age 18 in most states) generally cannot consent to mental health treatment but rather require a parent or guardian to consent on their behalf. However, state laws vary considerably, and some states do allow minors to consent to mental health treatment without parental consent. Thus, mental health professionals must be familiar with minor consent laws as well as parents' legal rights in the state in which they practice. In addition, they must understand how their state law interacts with the Health Insurance Portability and Accountability Act (HIPAA) Privacy Rule (U.S. Department of Health and Human Services, 2003) regarding disclosure of confidential information.

If an individual makes an appointment with a psychologist in a state requiring parental consent and that individual's status as a minor is unknown to the mental health professional, the therapist may discuss with the adolescent the need and rationale to obtain parental consent. If parental consent is required, it may be a good idea to create a written agreement regarding the limits of confidentiality and the circumstances under which information would be disclosed to the parents (APA Ethics Code Standard 10.01, Informed Consent to Therapy) that is signed by both the adolescent and parent(s) to build trust in the therapeutic relationship, stress the importance of confidentiality to the parent(s) for treatment to be successful, and determine those parents who may be unwilling to limit their access to information regarding their adolescent's therapy so that the psychologist can decide whether to accept the adolescent as a client (APA, 2005).

If parental consent is not required, and the adolescent is deemed by the mental health professional to be mature enough to make health care decisions and provide informed consent, this should be documented in the medical record (APA Ethics Code Standard 6.01, Documentation of Professional and Scientific Work and Maintenance of Records). The adolescent may still be encouraged to involve his or her parent(s) as appropriate. If parental consent is not required, information could not be disclosed to the adolescent's parents without his or her consent according to the HIPAA Privacy Rule, except in situations in which the adolescent is determined to be at risk of harming him- or herself or others. If in doubt, the mental health professional should consult the risk management services of his or her malpractice carrier or obtain legal advice.

Autonomy in the field of mental health implies that it is a competent patient's right to choose a course of action on the basis of his or her own risk–benefit analysis (APA Ethics Code Principle E, Respect for People's Rights and Dignity, and Standards 3.10, Informed Consent, and 10.01, Informed Consent to Therapy). Prior to conception, a potential offspring, obviously, is unable to give informed consent to the use of a collaborative reproductive arrangement, although in this situation, Dara's parents and her donor provided what they believed to be informed consent to an anonymous oocyte donation. Although her parents' privacy rights may be infringed on by Dara's confronting them with what she overheard during their argument and by her discussing her genetic heritage with others, the psychologist's obligation would be to support his or her patient, Dara, but also remain sensitive to her family's needs and be cognizant of inflicting the least harm to her family system as was possible (APA Ethics Code Principles A, Beneficence and Nonmaleficence, and E, Respect for People's Rights and Dignity).

Mental health professionals working in the field of reproductive medicine and third-party reproduction also have an obligation to remain current in their knowledge of research on both disclosure versus nondisclosure and the use of anonymous versus open-identity donors (APA Ethical Standard 2.04, Bases for Scientific and Professional Judgments) so that they practice within their areas of competence if they accept a client such as Dara (APA Ethics Code Standard 2.01, Boundaries of Competence).

Documentation of contacts and concerns and the creation of a flexible treatment plan in light of the many questions that are unanswered thus far by empirical research are also required (APA Ethics Code Standards 2.04, Bases for Scientific and Professional Judgments, and 6.01, Documentation of Professional and Scientific Work and Maintenance of Records).

Although nondisclosure to offspring of conception by gamete donation protects the privacy of recipient parents, it may undermine the interests of offspring regarding their medical history and ancestral heritage. Thus, in their statement titled "Informing Offspring of Their Conception by Gamete Donation," the Ethics Committee of the ASRM (2004f) encouraged disclosure of the fact of donor conception to offspring as well as characteristics of the donor if available, while recognizing that the ultimate choice is that of recipient parents. These are guidelines only, however, and even if mandated by law, there is no way to enforce them and compel parents to inform their offspring of the truth of their method of conception.

In "Interests, Obligations, and Rights of the Donor in Gamete Donation" (Ethics Committee of the ASRM, 2009b), the ASRM created a recommendation for donor information disclosure, suggesting four possible levels of information sharing that a donor and intended parents may agree on prior to consenting to undergo a collaborative reproductive arrangement. According to these levels, the donor would agree to (a) provide nonidentifying information; (b) be contacted by the program for medical updates and further updates, if requested, while maintaining anonymity; (c) have nonidentifying contact when the child reaches a certain age and both the donor and offspring agree to the disclosure; or (d) have identifying information shared with the offspring when the offspring reaches the age of maturity and both agree to the disclosure. These recommendations, of course, do not ensure parental disclosure and were not in practice at the time of Dara's conception.

The European Society for Human Reproduction and Embryology (2002) has recommended a double-track system to best balance the autonomy and privacy rights of parents, the privacy rights of the donor, and the right of the offspring to know of his or her origins and have access to all information that the donor has provided, either identifying or nonidentifying, depending on the choice of the recipient parent(s) and the donor, while maintaining that donors should be traceable should there be a genetic problem in the offspring. Thus, both ASRM and the European Society of Human Reproduction and Embryology appear to be directing the field of reproductive medicine toward greater openness in collaborative reproductive arrangements within the United States and Europe.

Although the Food and Drug Administration requires that donor records be kept for a minimum of 10 years (U.S. Department of Health and Human Services, Food and Drug Administration, Center for Biologics Evaluation and Research, 2009), the Practice Committee of the ASRM and the Practice Committee of the SART (2008), in "Guidelines for Gamete and Embryo Donation," recommended that a record of each donor's initial selection process and subsequent follow-up evaluations be permanently maintained so as to be available as a medical resource to any offspring produced. This does not include identifying information, however.

Practical Considerations

The primary practical consideration in this scenario is the limited availability of counselors who are knowledgeable about the emotional issues involved for people conceived through collaborative reproductive arrangements. Knowledge specific to this experience is deemed vital for these individuals to feel fully understood by the mental health professional with whom they consult. In addition, Dara may have difficulty locating her donor, if this is her wish. The IVF clinic her parents used, if still in existence, may be unwilling or unable to contact Dara's donor to ask about her willingness to update her medical and personal information or to become an open-identity donor because (a) Dara is under age (following the European model of making information available to the offspring on reaching the age of majority) or (b) the original promise of anonymity.

In addition, Dara's family will be confronting the mother's cancer diagnosis and treatment decisions. This is obviously a hard time for any family, and it may be especially difficult to have the medical crisis compounded by Dara's discovery of her conception history. Nevertheless, loving families can traverse tough times and remain intact.

Balancing Multiple Perspectives

The primary concern in donor gamete conception has been to provide a child for an infertile couple or individual. Thus, the future needs of the offspring created have typically not been considered. In light of the information that mental health care providers have about adopted individuals' desire to have access to information about their birth parents, however, society may likely be confronted in the future with numerous donor gamete offspring demanding similar information about their donors, and policies may need to be changed. Mental health professionals may wish to advocate for these changes, but until that occurs, they must adhere to present laws and practice guidelines.

There are various ways to approach the multiple perspectives of the stakeholders involved in this clinical vignette. One is to view them as having competing rights. Another is to determine both the individual interests of each stakeholder and the obligations each has to the others involved in a collaborative reproductive arrangement. We prefer the latter approach in trying to ensure that the needs and rights of all relevant parties are respected.

The Clinician or Fertility Clinic

The primary focus of most reproductive endocrinologists is to help fulfill the desires of the infertile couple or individual to create a child while protecting the health of recipients, donors, and offspring. Most IVF clinics do not have protocols to determine the welfare of the children produced, however, because once a pregnancy is established, the clinics typically transfer the pregnant patient to an obstetrician. The expectant parent and her partner, if there is one, are responsible for determining the best interests of the child after his or her birth. However, IVF clinics and physicians should be aware that providing as much information as possible regarding the donor, even if nonidentifying, to recipients during treatment may promote later disclosure to offspring (Klock & Greenfeld, 2004; MacCallum, 2009; Scheib et al., 2003). The ASRM does have guidelines recommending maintaining permanent records of each donation (Practice Committee of the ASRM and the Practice Committee of the SART, 2008), and it does appear to be the norm at present that most IVF programs offer nonidentifying information about the donors to intended recipient parents. However, although they may maintain donor records, most do not have a protocol to update donor records or transmit relevant information to offspring of collaborative reproductive arrangements.

In this vignette, the IVF clinic is also expected to protect the donor, who is actually a patient of the program, whereas donor-conceived individuals are not. The clinic is expected to honor the informed consent form that it had the donor sign prior to undergoing an oocyte donation cycle by maintaining her future anonymity if that was a part of the agreement. If it does not, this may be violating not only the terms of the consent but also state and/or federal privacy laws, even if such disclosure was not made until Dara came of age. However, having recently become more aware of the expressed needs of the offspring, the clinic or egg donor agency may be willing to try to contact Dara's donor to see if she would now be willing to (a) provide updated medical and other germane information to offspring created with her oocytes and (b) continue to update her medical information on a regular basis with any information pertinent to the health of the offspring. If the donor had originally agreed to consider being contacted by the offspring on reaching maturity, the clinic or egg donor agency may also ask if she would be willing to be contacted by an offspring who is voicing interest in this, as many donors, once they mature and become aware of the needs and interests of offspring, have voiced a willingness for this contact. Realistically, however, clinics and egg donor agencies may not have the administrative resources necessary to participate in this labor-intensive process. It must be noted that no similar requirement has been suggested for adoption agencies, however.

Existing Children

Offspring created through collaborative reproductive arrangements have an interest in being healthy, knowing who their genetic progenitors are, and knowing what their health risks are so as to pursue preventive or protective measures if they choose. Like donor offspring before her, particularly those accidentally learning of their donor gamete conception under unfortunate circumstances, Dara is expressing interest in her genetic heritage and exploring whether she should search for the oocyte donor to whom she is genetically related. With the information she inadvertently overheard from her parents, she is also feeling betrayed in having been led to believe that she is the genetic offspring of her mother. To protect minors, as stated earlier, the mental health professional would need to determine prior to working with Dara whether she has the right to consent to treatment or whether her parents would need to provide such consent in the state in which she lives and presumably would be treated.

Dara may need help in developing a strategy to approach her parents both to obtain their consent for treatment, if necessary by state law or deemed useful by the therapist and client, and to make them aware of the information she overheard so that she could ask them for the information that they (may) have about the donor in a manner that would be minimally disruptive to her family at this critical time (her mother having been diagnosed with breast cancer; APA Ethics Code Principle E). Her curiosity about the donor needs to be normalized, although Dara may need to recognize that she may not be able to obtain identifying information about her donor and she may need help in coping with her feelings about this. Although having expressed concern about whether she should inform her younger sister about her conception, as a typical impulsive teenager, angry about the information she has just learned, it may be difficult for her to restrain from blurting out this information to her sister. The sister, too, may need assistance in resolving her feelings about this new information, and both sisters may need help in reappraising their identities with the potential unavailability of further information about the oocyte donor.

Once Dara begins to process this new information about herself, she may also wonder whether anybody else knows the truth of her conception, whether her parents sought specific qualities in her oocyte donor (e.g., high IQ, high Scholastic Assessment Test scores, "model" looks), and whether she has disappointed her parents because she considers herself an average student of average looks. This would reflect critics' concerns that collaborative reproductive arrangements may result in commodification of the individuals created. Dara will need her parents' support to come to terms with this and to realize that her parents love her for who she is not for any predetermined template of who she was supposed to become.

The Parents

Dara's parents, having the right to reproductive autonomy in the United States, chose to use an anonymous oocyte donor to create her and to use the same donor to create their second child. They went to great lengths to maintain a genetic link to one parent (her father) and a gestational link to the other (her mother). While experiencing infertility, prospective parents are usually more focused on their own pain, not that of their future children, and often have difficulty thinking about a potential child as they attempt to protect themselves against disappointment should the ART procedure not work for them. Although not legally mandated to disclose donor conception to their children in the United States, parents, in general, have a responsibility to foster a loving and honest relationship with their children, promoting the interests and rights of their children on a long-term basis (Goldstein et al., 1979). To many, this would imply that parents using collaborative reproductive arrangements should inform their child of his or her genetic origins as well as provide accurate medical information. Some parents, however, often fearing damage to family relationships, may believe it is in their child's best interest not to be informed of his or her donor gamete origins. In the United States, and universally for that matter, parents are allowed to determine if and when to reveal their method of conception to their child or to keep it undisclosed if they believe this is necessary to maintain the integrity of their family or is in their child's best interest. It would be important to determine the reasons these parents chose not to disclose information about their daughters' conception to them. Advice they received; their social, family, and religious context at the time of their conception; fear of rejection by their child; and fear of community rejection of themselves and/or their children may all have been taken into consideration when making their decision.

Dara's parents are likely to be confronted by their daughter about their choice of secrecy and what may be perceived by Dara as deception. It may be particularly disruptive to the parent–child relationship if Dara's parents refuse to provide consent for her to see a mental health professional. Unfortunately, in this scenario, there will be little opportunity for the needs and feelings of the parents to be recognized and processed before they are confronted by their daughter. This unfortunate circumstance may make it more difficult for them to focus on their daughters and explain their decisions, and they may need instead to pursue damage control in this situation. Being provided with information by the mental health professional regarding typical adolescent curiosity regarding the donor and donor half siblings may help these parents, particularly Dara's mother, understand the relevance of the donor to their children even if she seems less significant to them. If Dara has not already informed her younger sister, the available literature suggests that it probably would be in the younger sister's best interest to be told of her conception with both parents together (Paul & Berger, 2007) explaining how Dara had learned and then including Dara in the family discussion. Experienced professionals in the field of reproductive health and medicine have suggested placing an emphasis on how the nontraditional family was created rather than solely focusing on the collaborative arrangement used to create the child (Daniels & Thorn, 2001).

Even at this late stage, disclosure will not be a one-time event, however, as their daughters' needs will change as they mature and continue to assess the meaning of being members of a family that was created through oocyte donation. Open family communication has been found to be more relevant in predicting adjustment in adopted children than the actual availability of information about the birth parent(s) (Brodzinsky, 2007) and has been associated with more positive family functioning in DI families (Paul & Berger, 2007), as well. Therefore, if these parents encourage their children to express their feelings and thoughts and remain available to them to answer their questions and provide some of the information they likely do have available to them about the donor even if their donor had been anonymous, they will demonstrate their support. Furthermore, this will likely assist in rebuilding trust between the parents and their daughters. Success in rebuilding their daughter's trust in them may also help these parents rebuild confidence in their own parenting skills.

Additional support and empathy may be needed if the parents had told others about their daughters' conception because Dara or her sister may directly ask this question of their parents and have feelings about others knowing about this when they were uninformed. Dara and her sister also may now wish to share this information with others, and the family may encounter social condemnation if they belong to a community that opposes the use of donor gametes. The parents will need to sensitively assist their daughters in deciding with whom they wish to share this information so that they are least likely to be harmed by a negative community reaction.

The Donor

The oocyte donor in the present case may have been promised anonymity by the IVF clinic or donor egg agency, and thus her expectation is that she would remain unknown to the recipient parents and the offspring she helped to create. She may not have been told of the possibility that offspring may be able to identify her as a genetic progenitor some day as a result of changing laws and technology (i.e., the Internet and easy availability of DNA analysis), changes that probably were not anticipated 17 years ago when Dara was conceived. Some donors who anonymously provided gametes, however, have recently demonstrated their willingness to allow their identities to be revealed to their donor offspring (Dyer, 2008). If the reproductive endocrinologist and mental health professional originally involved in this collaborative arrangement had not explained to the donor that laws regarding donor anonymity may change in the future, her informed consent may not have been truly informed. However, her feelings about anonymity may have changed over time as she matured and, possibly, had a family of her own. If so, she may be willing to provide relevant, yet nonidentifying, updated information about herself to the IVF clinic or egg donor agency, or she may be willing to become an open-identity donor and be directly contacted by Dara when she reaches the age of majority. If she agrees to become an identifiable donor and she has not informed her husband, children, or parents of her oocyte donation, she may have concerns about how they will react to this information, and may need some guidance as to how to inform them and anticipate their potential questions or concerns. In addition, she may benefit from assistance in coping with the possibility of multiple genetically related offspring attempting to make contact with her, as many ovum donors have not been notified of the number of pregnancies and births that result from their donations.

The donor certainly should not be coerced into disclosing additional information or be manipulated into becoming an open-identity donor. She may experience anger at the clinic for violating her contract and contacting her now after the original agreement for anonymity, or she may feel guilty toward the donor-conceived offspring if she is unwilling to become an identified donor.

Unlike organ or blood donation, gamete donation is life creating rather than life sustaining, and thus we believe that it is in the best interest of gamete donors to consider their long-term moral obligations to their genetically related offspring as part of providing informed consent. This includes initially providing accurate information about themselves and their family to the IVF clinic (both in terms of health and social histories), informing recipients and offspring through the IVF clinic of any medical diseases that surface subsequent to their donation, and regularly updating their medical histories. A corollary clinic or agency obligation would be to notify donors of information that might be learned through the child if the donor and recipient parents had agreed to this when providing informed consent. Donors do not have parental or financial obligations to these offspring, however, and appropriate legal measures need to be in place to ensure this. Prior to their donation, donors must also be encouraged to consider the potential long-term psychological impact of their gamete donation on themselves and their family of origin as well as on their future family (i.e., children and spouse). Unfortunately, mental health professionals have scant research available to them elucidating the long-term psychological implications of gamete donation on which to base their counseling with donors.

Donors also owe respect to the integrity of the family of their genetic offspring and to the child's security within this stable family group. Therefore, donors should not intrude uninvited into the offspring's life.

As the field of reproductive medicine begins to integrate lessons learned from the history of adoption in the United States, it is likely that donors will be asked to provide information so that offspring may access nonidentifying information, including medical updates, or to agree to authorize the release of identifying information and to agree to personal contact once the offspring reaches the age of maturity.

CONCLUSION

The technology of third-party reproduction has again outpaced health care providers' ability to predict, understand, and deal with the implications of scientific achievements in ART, particularly the implications for the offspring created. Health and identity issues for those born through collaborative reproductive arrangements are challenging those in the field of reproductive medicine as well as policymakers to clarify and protect the rights of the offspring in this process.

The value of openness and honesty with children of third-party reproduction needs to be introduced by medical professionals and mental health professionals alike because both play an influential role in parents' decision making (Gurmankin, Baron, Hershey, & Ubel, 2002; Shehab et al., 2008), as does the availability of updated information about the donor. As demonstrated in the clinical vignette, mental health professionals are likely to be called on by offspring and parents when disclosure is made late in the offspring's development or occurs unexpectedly, accidentally, or traumatically (Daniels & Meadows, 2006).

Dara has contacted a psychologist experienced in the field of infertility and third-party reproduction because she was overwhelmed by feelings triggered by her overhearing her parents indicate that she was conceived from a donor oocyte. Although she had no choice in being the product of donor gamete conception, Dara does have considerable choice in how she comes to terms with being donor conceived. In this regard, acknowledging and accepting Dara's feelings and offering her therapeutic tools to help her reframe this experience and find meaning in it can be empowering for her. If the mental health professional is legally allowed to accept Dara's consent to mental health treatment, he or she must determine what the present issues are for Dara because donor offspring are diverse in their reactions and needs, how to assist her process of emotional expression, and what resources are available to help her in this process.

The psychologist also needs to keep in mind the importance of supporting the family, which is undergoing this disclosure process, and the donor's (assumed) original wish to remain anonymous. Involvement of Dara's parents in the treatment process, while recognizing the health crisis that Dara's mother is currently facing, should be considered and discussed, even if their consent to Dara's treatment was not required per state statutes, because obtaining validation and having opportunities for further discussion with at least one parent is usually advantageous to donor offspring. The psychologist should also inform Dara that she may be unable to locate her donor or obtain any additional information because currently there is no registry in the United States and help her reconcile this possibility. Acknowledgement of the frustration and/or sadness that Dara may feel if she is unable to obtain further information regarding her donor will be necessary.

Because of Dara's concern for her mother's feelings, she would be introduced to the concept of empathic assertion, that is, the direct expression of one's needs and feelings while also considering the needs and intentions of the recipient party. She could incorporate this approach with her parents regarding disclosure of what she overheard and subsequently ask for the information from them that she wishes to obtain.

If it is within the professional expertise of the mental health professional, with Dara's consent, counseling with the parents or referral to another mental health professional if more appropriate, may be offered, as well, which may assist them with disclosure to their younger daughter or with any disagreements that may continue. Family counseling, too, may be suggested to help them process the many issues that this unplanned disclosure of donor gamete conception may present to this family, particularly in rebuilding trust between the children and their parents. In addition, Dara's parents may benefit from participation in a network composed of other parents with donor offspring (Daniels, Thorn, & Westerbrooke, 2007) and referral to such a support system, if available, would be made.

Adolescents, most of whom are quite savvy about computer technology, quickly learn of the existence of a donor sibling registry if disclosure has taken place. It might be important to explore the implications of conducting a search for genetic half siblings to herself and her sister, including the possibility of finding multiple half siblings, and their potential relationships with one another. Again, Dara would be assisted in confronting the realistic expectation that such contacts may not be available to her or that even if such contacts may be made, other offspring or their parents, some of whom may not have disclosed to their offspring, may not wish to be available to meet or offer any further information. The potential challenges of forming and redefining family are limitless. The mental health professional's continued availability for ongoing counseling, support, and information would be beneficial to Dara.

Although the birth of a healthy baby may conclude medical treatment for the parents using collaborative reproductive arrangements, it is only the beginning of life for the offspring. Giving future offspring the right to obtain genetic information has intuitive appeal, and it seems unreasonable to deprive them of preventive or disease-delaying medical options. One advantage of disclosure demonstrated in the present case is that Dara can now avoid unnecessary worry about developing breast cancer or unneeded preventive measures because she now knows she is not prone to the same heritable diseases as her mother.

Establishing guidelines for the provision of counseling services to these offspring, both before and after obtaining donor information, will be essential. Many mental health professionals will need additional training to gain competency in the counseling issues that donor-conceived offspring and the offspring of the donor and surrogates will present.

We believe that mental health professionals working in the field of reproductive medicine have a professional obligation to (a) contribute to creating a social climate that reduces the stigma associated with infertility to make it easier for recipient parents to be open about their use of collaborative reproductive arrangements and forthright with their offspring; and (b) advocate for accurate record keeping on donors, which may entail the creation of a donor registry to collect, maintain, and update donor information so that donor-conceived individuals can easily access this information on reaching the age of majority. We believe that offspring are entitled to this choice. We hope that their parents, donors, and the medical establishment will agree.

9

NEW FRONTIERS IN REPRODUCTIVE TECHNOLOGY AND ETHICS FOR PSYCHOLOGISTS

We shall not cease from exploration
And the end of all our exploring
Will be to arrive where we started
And know the place for the first time.

—T. S. Eliot, *Little Gidding*

In the ever-evolving field of reproductive medicine, new and promising technologies will continue to be developed, often at remarkable speed, leaving psychosocial research, law, policies, ethics, and professional guidelines struggling to keep pace. Although public anxiety about the uncertainty of medical science is not restricted to the assisted reproductive technologies (ART), it may be uniquely aroused because of anxiety regarding embryo technology, the very personal nature of reproduction, and the importance of genetics and the family. What do mental health professionals foresee in the future?

One common goal of reproductive medicine is to increase pregnancy rates while lowering the rate of multiple births. Better ways of assessing embryo quality and the likelihood of embryo implantation would appear to be just around the corner and will likely augment both physician and patient enthusiasm for single-embryo transfer. Although techniques already exist to assess for specific genetic mutations or chromosomal rearrangements prior to embryo transfer in at-risk patients (i.e., preimplantation genetic diagnosis) or to screen patients with no known genetic risks for chromosomal abnormalities (i.e., preimplantation genetic screening), additional applications of preimplantation genetic diagnosis are likely as the knowledge of the human genome increases and more gene-disease correlates are found.

Comparative genome hybridization already shows promise, as it can simultaneously analyze all chromosomes in an embryo and possibly in an oocyte as well and may improve pregnancy rates. Karyomapping, a new experimental technology that delineates all of the embryo's chromosomes, offers the possibility to detect any inherited disease other than those arising from spontaneous random mutations using a single test that can be completed within a matter of weeks (British Broadcasting Corporation News, 2008). If costs and the discomfort of procedures can be minimized and availability of insurance coverage increased, the use of these techniques to reduce disease and disease proneness is likely to increase. However, concerns have been expressed that this technology could be used to screen for positive traits such as height, intelligence, thinness, or temperament, as well (Watt, 2004).

These possibilities are both exciting and present potential ethical minefields (Klipstein, 2005; Robertson, 2003), raising concerns related to what constitutes a disease, the destruction of normal embryos, whether it is appropriate to enhance normal function, and potential harm to the child (e.g., physical harm, commodification). Who will be left to make these determinations as to when preimplantation genetic diagnosis is ethically acceptable or not? Preimplantation genetic assessment also raises the specter of eugenics, namely, credit card eugenics (McGee, 2000), because its high cost and availability primarily to the affluent may result in genetic disorders becoming diseases of the disadvantaged and a widening of class and social disparities in the population. It may also potentially affect the disabled community and may impact the parent–child relationship by normalizing the notion that a child's genetic makeup falls within the purview of parental reproductive choice (President's Council on Bioethics, Reproduction and Responsibility, 2004). However, no technology will provide 100% certainty of freedom from disease and/or defect, and the multifactorial nature of most traits makes it unlikely that one will be able to select desired traits through embryo assessment.

In an effort to make fertility treatment safer, simpler, and less expensive, the new frontier in reproductive medicine is likely to include development of in vitro maturation, an experimental procedure, at present, in which a reproductive endocrinologist extracts immature, unstimulated oocytes through fine needle aspiration. These eggs are allowed to mature in a petri dish, fertilized through intracytoplasmic sperm injection, and then transferred to a woman's uterus 3 to 5 days later. In vitro maturation could also be used to obtain donor oocytes. Minimal ovulation-inducing hormone drugs or none at all would be used, reducing the cost and eliminating potential side effects of high dosages of these medications.

Efforts to maintain and extend fertility are likely to include increased awareness by young people of their fertility potential (e.g., measures to predict ovarian reserve) and those limitations imposed by aging. Improved methods of oocyte freezing will raise the issue of whether delaying reproduction solely for social reasons is ethical, especially if it increases the risk that a woman might miss the opportunity to use her own eggs because she relied on using her cryopreserved eggs, which may not successfully fertilize or implant when she attempts to use them. Even the possibility that adult females may harbor primitive cells in their ovaries that can become new eggs and produce offspring has been raised after these cells were obtained from adult mice (Wade, 2009).

In the future, scientists may create artificial gametes that could be used, for example, by postmenopausal women, sterile men, those prone to primary ovarian insufficiency, and homosexual couples, thus offering the possibility of genetic reproduction in same-sex relationships. If adult cells can be reprogrammed into embryonic stem-cell-like tissue and induced to become different specialized tissue, the need to use embryos for regenerative medicine may be dramatically reduced, providing cells for new therapies in both reproductive and general medicine while diminishing the potential ethical roadblocks.

Other advances may include improved fertility preservation for those children and adults of childbearing age undergoing treatment for cancer and safe uterine transplantation for women born absent a uterus or with a malformed uterus or who have had a hysterectomy. Additionally, increased awareness and elimination of environmental contaminants that reduce fertility may result in a cleaner biosphere.

Thus far, researchers in the field of epigenetics (the study of interactions of genes and environment, i.e., heritable changes that turn on or off the expression of a particular gene without changing the DNA) have found that in animals, prenatal diet, behavior, or surroundings (possibly including those of the womb or some aspect of IVF) can induce these changes, and these changes in gene expression can be passed on from one generation to the next (Arnaud & Feil, 2005; Paolini-Giacobino, 2007; Waterland & Jirtle, 2003). Although this may suggest a risk to children being created through ART, it may also offer women who use donor oocytes the comfort of knowing that they too may genetically impact the child they gestate and their future grandchildren while at the same time suggesting that gestational carriers may also genetically impact on the fetus of intended parents.

Regarding third-party reproduction, unfortunately, the same mistakes that were previously made concerning adoption, that is, secrecy, shame, and the lack of provision of information, have been repeated. A growing number of adolescents and adults are looking for information regarding their donors, asking questions such as, Where do I come from, What is my medical history, and Who do I look like? As American culture becomes less secretive, with increased comfort in talking about all sorts of topics (e.g., erectile dysfunction, contraception, breast cancer), less shame and stigma will be attached to infertility and third-party reproduction. As a result, the offspring may ask more questions and demand more information, which psychologists in the field of reproductive medicine and health are uniquely qualified to provide. We predict this will result in the creation of a donor registry in the United States to meet these demands. However, complex issues such as the purpose and types of information to be collected, kept, and made available by the registry; where and for how long this information will be stored; how it will be protected; and who will maintain and pay for the registry will all require some time to resolve. With the increase in information available through genetic analysis, both donors and intended parents will probably be asked to complete forms indicating how much medical information they desire and whether they want notification if a heritable disease is discovered.

It is likely that the role of the mental health professional will expand in years to come, focusing more on the families and the offspring who have already been born through collaborative reproductive arrangements. Psychologists will continue to allay parental anxiety, build confidence, and help parents understand the normal needs and curiosity of their donor offspring (e.g., need for information for identity formation) as well as prepare them for potential reactions to disclosure, including what to expect from their children at different developmental stages. Parents, through gamete donation, may also benefit from networks consisting of similarly created families. Mental health professionals' involvement with donor offspring is likely to continue well beyond childhood because identity development continues well beyond age 18. Psychologists will likely be called on to assist offspring who intend to meet their donors and genetic half siblings, attempting to avoid mismatched expectations between the offspring, genetic half siblings, and their identity-release donors. Gamete donors, too, are likely to need help to prepare for these meetings and to learn developmentally appropriate ways to share this information with their own children. Additional resource materials need to be developed for parents as well as for offspring and gamete donors.

Mental health professionals have an ethical obligation, both before and after treatment, to donors, recipients, and offspring who are created through third-party reproduction. Thus, psychologists must take the lead in raising the questions and issues that need to be addressed and provide information and feedback to the physicians and clinics involved. Mental health professionals will need to strive to engage all stakeholders in discussions to best determine their needs so that standards that balance the needs of all stakeholders are developed. If those in the field of reproductive medicine do not recognize the present and potential future needs of the children they help to create regarding their genetic background, however, it is likely that the field will be legislated by others outside of the profession.

The need to protect the rights of deceased individuals regarding posthumous reproduction (which has begun to be addressed by a small handful of states over the past 2 decades) will probably necessitate additional legal guidance. Psychologists will be called on to intervene and assist those patients considering this controversial alternative to family building.

Cross-border reproductive care (formerly referred to as reproductive tourism), international oocyte donation, and outsourcing of surrogacy are likely to continue as long as differential costs, restrictive legislation and policies, and limited access to treatment occur worldwide. Lack of regulation raises concerns about exploitation of the underprivileged residing in poorer countries as well as the impact of this issue and possible donor misinformation having been provided on the children conceived. The use of gestational surrogates from other countries, in particular, creates questions about whether this is financial exploitation and industrial outsourcing pushed to the extreme or a way that abjectly poor women in developing countries can gain a measure of empowerment as long as they are provided with quality medical care and voluntarily consent to participate. Familiarity with international law, including the transfer of custody, and sensitivity to diverse cultures is required.

We foresee an increasing awareness of the psychological aspects of infertility and its treatment, including the development of an empathic approach to multifetal pregnancy reduction by those involved in reproductive medicine as it is a very significant decision for those who have struggled so long to have a child. Furthermore, we believe that high-quality research to disentangle the pre- and postnatal effects of ART treatment from those of infertility on women and children is necessary. Additionally, longitudinal research on the physical and psychosocial ramifications of ART on children, women, men, and the families being created is vitally needed in this field.

Mental health professionals working in the field of reproductive medicine have an ethical responsibility to care about the moral complexities arising from the medical–technical innovations in the field, to take seriously the outcome of their conduct, to respect the autonomy of those involved and capable of providing informed consent, and to protect those unable to give informed consent. Psychologists continually confront whether the constitutional right of procreative autonomy of the intended parents or the best interest of the potential child should take precedence when their interests conflict. Although discomfort in the pit of one's stomach or sleepless nights can often be an initial indication of an ethical dilemma, clinical situations in reproductive medicine are often quite nuanced, and the use of a problem-solving format can assist in analyzing the benefits and risks of proposed options as they are examined in the context of the interests of all stakeholders involved.

There are no absolute answers to the ethical dilemmas mental health professionals face. However, we have concluded that we neither wish to have the United States medical establishment straitjacketed by the influence of political ideology or religion because this undermines the quality of health care in a free, pluralistic society nor do we necessarily want the implementation of laws that would be inflexible in the face of the rapid changes that occur in reproductive medicine. Even after an ethical issue is dissected, the available research evaluated, and the issues fully considered, one is still likely to be left with a range of options. These are enormously difficult issues to resolve, and as there would appear to be no universally right or wrong resolution, each case needs to be decided on the basis of its own facts and circumstances.

Psychologists and other mental health professionals are on most defensible ground in their work with those experiencing fertility issues by attempting to follow the American Psychological Association's (2002) "Ethical Principles of Psychologists and Code of Conduct" as well as ethical and professional guidelines recommended by the American Society for Reproductive Medicine. Yet, ethical guidelines generally are lofty in their aspirational nature, that is, the ceiling to which mental health professionals aspire, whereas standards are the floor below which psychologists do not go (Behnke, 2006). For everything in between, mental health professionals need to rely on available data as well as professional judgment while they attempt to balance the multiple perspectives and needs of all stakeholders involved, including the prospective parents, donor and surrogate, potential child, existing child(ren), and the policies and obligations of the physician(s) and fertility center. Consideration must be given to society at large as well as practical concerns (e.g., feasibility, cost, access).

It is our hope that mental health professionals working in the field of reproductive medicine can use the format we have suggested to perform an ethical analysis when confronting dilemmas in reproductive medicine, present and future. Respecting autonomy, avoiding paternalism, and providing quality medical and emotional care while protecting the interests of the children being created require a uniquely delicate balance, making reproductive medicine both a challenging and fascinating field of work for mental health professionals.

APPENDIX A: SAMPLE OF RELIGIOUS APPROACHES TO ASSISTED REPRODUCTIVE TECHNOLOGIES (ART)

	Religion					
			Jewish[c,d]			
Approach	Catholic[a]	Protestant[b]	Orthodox	Conservative	Reform	Muslim[e,f]
ART		X	X	X	X	
Single participants				X	X	
Masturbation for ART		X	Specific methods	X	X	
Donor sperm recipiency		X	Special retrieval and non-Jewish donor	non-Jewish donor	X	
Donor oocyte recipiency		X	non-Jewish donor	non-Jewish donor	X	
Gamete donation		X		Oocytes only	X	
Embryo donation		X		X		
Surrogacy	X	X	non-Jewish donor	Unmarried surrogate	Unmarried surrogate	
Multifetal reduction				X	X	X
Embryo research		X	X	X	X	X

Note. Xs indicate that a particular approach is allowed. This table is based on information contained in the sources listed here.

[a]Magesterium of the Catholic Church. (1987, February 22). *Instruction on the respect for human life in its origin and on the dignity of procreation: Replies to certain questions of the day.* Retrieved from www.catholic.com/library/

[b]Whitney, E. (2005, February 24). *Assisted reproduction—A Christian clinician's view.* The American Surrogacy Center. Retrieved from http://www.surrogacy.com/Articles/news_view.asp?ID=83

[c]Grazi, R. V., & Wolowelsky, J. B. (1992). Donor gametes for assisted reproduction in contemporary Jewish law and ethics. *Assisted Reproduction Reviews, 2,* 154–160.

[d]Schenker, J. G. (1997). Infertility evaluation and treatment according to Jewish law. *European Journal of Obstetrics, Gynecology, and Reproductive Biology, 71,* 113–121.

[e]Dickens, B. M. (2001, September). Ethical issues arising from the use of assisted reproductive technologies. In E. Rowe & D. Griffin (Eds.), *Current practices and controversies in assisted reproduction: Ethical aspects of infertility and art.* Report of the World Health Organization Meeting of Medical, Ethical, and Social Aspects of ART, Geneva, Switzerland.

[f]Serour, G. I. (2005). Religious perspectives of ethical issues in ART. Islamic perspectives of ethical issues in ART. *Middle East Fertility Society Journal, 10,* 185–190.

APPENDIX B: SAMPLE OF INTERNATIONAL APPROACHES TO ASSISTED REPRODUCTIVE TECHNOLOGIES

Issue	Country				
	United Kingdom	Italy	Sweden	Israel	Japan
When is an embryo considered to be a person?	Unclear if 14 days after fertilization or at birth of live child	On contact of sperm with oocyte	14 days after fertilization	40 days after fertilization	14 days after fertilization
Number of embryos transferred	1–2	Only 3 embryos allowed to be created; every embryo created must be transferred	1 recommended unless patient has poor prognosis (e.g., older age, many previous IVF failures, very poor quality embryos)	Not specified	Generally 3, more than 3 depends on embryo quality and stage of development, maternal age, and other conditions
Cryopreservation of					
Sperm	Yes	Yes	Yes	Yes	Yes
Embryo	Yes	No	Yes	Yes	Yes
Ovarian tissue	Yes	Not mentioned	Yes	Yes	Yes
Minimum storage period for frozen gametes, embryos	10 years with 5-year extension option (longer if stored for medical reasons)	NA	5 years	10 years[a]	Until the end of the individual's reproductive life
Gamete donation					
Sperm	Yes	No	Yes	Yes	No with IVF, yes with non-IVF
Oocyte	Yes	No	Yes[b]	Yes, only through egg sharing	No
Embryo	Yes	No	No[b]	No[a]	Yes, but not with donor gametes

Financial compensation of gamete donors	No	NA	Yes, minimally[a]	Minimal for sperm, not for oocyte[b]	Yes for sperm,[c] NA for oocytes
Donor anonymity	Banned	NA	Banned	Required	Yes[c]
Identity release	At age 18, donor offspring conceived after 2005 have right to access donor identity	NA	At maturity, offspring have access to donor identity	Information released from central registry to donor offspring only in dire circumstances or to avoid consanguinity (only with donor permission)	Under discussion at present
IVF surrogacy;gestational carrier	Yes. Surrogate and her partner are listed on child's original birth register.	No	No	Yes. Traditional surrogacy not allowed.[a]	No
Treatment given to					
Single women	Yes	No	No[b]	Yes	No
Lesbian couples	Yes	No	Yes[b]	Yes	No
Upper age limit for women	Less than 41 for own oocytes, 45 for recipients of donor oocytes	50	Yes for both IVF with own or donor oocytes, age limits differ at different clinics[b]	Less than 45 for IVF with own oocytes, less than 52 to receive donor oocytes	50

(continues)

	Country				
Issue	United Kingdom	Italy	Sweden	Israel	Japan
Multifetal pregnancy reduction	Yes	No	Yes	Yes	Yes if needed to protect life of woman or child
Experimentation on embryos	Yes up to 14 days after fertilization	No	Yes	No	Yes
Welfare of the child considered	Yes. Clinics should assess prospective parents for previous convictions related to harming children, contact with social services over care of existing children, serious violence or discord within the family		Traceability of donors and possibility of their being asked for medical history in case of genetically related child health problems		

Note. IVF = in vitro fertilization; NA = not applicable. This table is based on information from "IffS Surveillance 07," by H. W. Jones, Jr., J. Cohen, I. Cooke, and R. Kempers. Copyright 2007 by the American Society for Reproductive Medicine. Reprinted by permission from the American Society for Reproductive Medicine (*Fertility and Sterility,* 2007, Vol. No 87, Suppl. 1, S1–S67). [a]V. Samuels (personal communication, June 23, 2008). [b]A. Lalos (personal communications, May 9, 2008, and July 4, 2008). [c]O. Yoshino (personal communications, June 23, 2008, and July 7, 2008). [d]"Statute of Limitions'" Redeemed by Cyberspace" [Reply to letter to the editor], by H. W. Jones, Jr., J. Cohen, I. Cooke, and R. Kempers, 2007, *Fertility and Sterility, 88,* 1479.

REFERENCES

Abdallah, R. T., & Muasher, S. J. (2006). Surviving cancer, saving fertility: The promise of cryopreservation. *Sexuality, Reproduction, & Menopause, 4*, 7–12.

Abma, J. C., Chandra, A., Mosher, W. D., Peterson, L. S., & Piccino, L. J. (1997). Fertility, family planning, and women's health: New data from the 1995 National Survey of Family Growth. *Vital Health Statistics, 23*, 1–114.

Ackerman, N. W. (1958). *Psychodynamics of family life: Diagnosis and treatment of family relationships*. New York, NY: Basic Books.

Adair, V. A., & Purdie, A. (1996). Donor insemination programmes with personal donors: Issue of secrecy. *Human Reproduction, 11*, 2558–2563.

Adler-Levy, Y., Lunenfeld, E., & Levy, A. (2007). Obstetric outcome of twin pregnancies conceived by in vitro fertilization and ovulation induction compared with those conceived spontaneously. *European Journal of Obstetrics and Gynaecology and Reproductive Biology, 133*, 173–178.

Adsuar, N., Pritts, E., Olive, D. L., & Lindheim, S. R. (2003). Assessment of attitudes regarding directives of oocyte and embryo management among ovum donors in an egg donation program. *Fertility and Sterility, 80*(Suppl. 3), S87.

Adsuar, N., Zweifel, J. E., Pritts, E. A., Davidson, M. A., Olive, D. L., & Lindheim, S. R. (2005). Assessment of wishes regarding disposition of oocytes and embryo management among ovum donors in an anonymous egg donation program. *Fertility and Sterility, 84*, 1513–1516.

Ahuja, K. K., Mostyn, B. J., & Simons, E. G. (1997). Egg sharing and egg donation: Attitudes of British egg donors and recipients. *Human Reproduction, 12*, 2845–2852.

Ahuja, K. K., & Simons, E. G. (1996). Anonymous egg donation and dignity. *Human Reproduction, 11*, 1151–1154.

Ahuja, K. K., Simons, E. G., & Edwards, R. G. (1999). Money, morals and medical risks: Conflicting notions underlying the recruitment of egg donors. *Human Reproduction, 14*, 279–284.

Ainsworth, M. (1985). Patterns of infant–mother attachments: Antecedents and effects on development. *Bulletin of the NY Academy of Medicine, 66*, 771–790.

Alexander, J. M., Hammon, K. R., & Steinkampf, M. P. (1995). Multifetal reduction of high-order multiple pregnancy: Comparison of obstetrical outcome with nonreduced twin gestations. *Fertility and Sterility, 64*, 1201–1203.

Al-Inany, H., Aboulghar, M. A., Mansour, R. T., & Serour, G. I. (2005). Ovulation induction in the new millennium: Recombinant follicle stimulating hormone versus human menopausal gonadotropin. *Gynecological Endocrinology, 20*, 161–169.

Aliyu, M. H., Salihu, H. M., Blankson, M. L., Alexander, G. R., & Keith, L. (2004). Risks in triplet pregnancy: Advanced maternal age, premature rupture of membranes and risk estimates of mortality. *Journal of Reproductive Medicine, 49*, 721–726.

Allen, V. M., Wilson, R. D., & Cheung, A. (2006). Pregnancy outcomes after assisted reproductive technology. *Journal of Obstetrics and Gynaecology Canada, 28*, 220–250.

Almashat, S., Ayotte, B., Edelstein, B., & Margrett, J. (2008). Framing effect debiasing in medical decision making. *Patient Education and Counseling, 71*, 102–107.

American Academy of Pediatrics. (2003). Family pediatrics: Report of the task force on the family. *Pediatrics, 111*, 1541–1571.

American College of Obstetricians and Gynecologists Committee on Ethics. (2004). *Surrogate motherhood: Ethics in Obstetrics and Gynecology* (2nd ed.). Washington, DC: American College of Obstetricians and Gynecologists.

American Fertility Association. (2003, Spring). Why you should care. *InFocus: The American Fertility Association Quarterly Magazine*. Retrieved from http://www.theafa.org

American Medical Association House of Delegates. (2004). Resolution: 443. Retrieved from http://www.amaassn.org/ama1/pub/upload/mm/15/res_hod443_a04.doc

American Psychological Association. (2002). Ethical principles of psychologists and code of conduct. *American Psychologist, 57*, 1060–1073. Retrieved from http://www.apa.org/ethics/code2002.html

American Psychological Association. (2005). *A matter of law: Privacy rights of minor patients*. Retrieved from http://www.apapractic.org/insider/practice/pracmanage/legal/minor.html

American Society for Reproductive Medicine. (2003). *Challenges of parenting multiples* [Patient fact sheet]. Retrieved from http://www.asrm.org/Patients/FactSheets/challenges.pdf

American Society for Reproductive Medicine. (2006). *Third party reproduction: A guide for patients* [Patient information booklet]. Retrieved from http://www.asrm.org/Patients/patientbooklets/thirdparty.pdf

American Society for Reproductive Medicine. (2008a). *Complications and problems associated with multiple births* [Patient fact sheet]. Retrieved from http://www.asrm.org/Patients/FactSheets/complications_multiplebirths.pdf

American Society for Reproductive Medicine. (2008b). *Fertility drugs and the risk of multiple births* [Patient fact sheet]. Retrieved September 27, 2008, from http://www.asrm.org/Patients/FactSheets/fertilitydrugs_multiplebirths.pdf

Americans With Disabilities Act of 1990, 42 U.S.C.A. § 12101 *et seq.* (2008).

Anderson, C. A., & Hammen, C. L. (1993). Psychosocial outcomes of children of unipolar depressed, bipolar, medically ill, and normal women: A longitudinal study. *Journal of Consulting and Clinical Psychology, 61*, 448–454.

Anderssen, N., Amlie, C., & Ytteroy, E. A. (2002). Outcomes for children with lesbian or gay parents: A review of studies from 1978 to 2000. *Scandinavian Journal of Psychology, 43*, 335–351.

Andrews, L. B., & Elster, N. (2000). Regulating reproductive technologies. *Journal of Legal Medicine, 21*, 55–65.

Antsaklis, A., Souka, A. P., Daskalakis, G., Papantoniou, N., Koutra, P., Klavalakis, Y., & Mesogitis, S. (2004). Embryo reduction versus expectant management in triplet pregnancies. *Journal of Maternal Fetal Neonatal Medicine, 16*, 219–222.

Applegarth, L. D. (2006). Embryo donation: Counseling donors and recipients. In S. N. Covington & L. H. Burns (Eds.), *Infertility counseling: A comprehensive handbook for clinicians* (2nd ed., pp. 356–369). New York, NY: Cambridge University Press.

Arnaud, P., & Feil, R. (2005). Epigenetic deregulation of genomic imprinting in human disorders and following assisted reproduction. *Birth Defects Research, Part C, Embryo Today, 75*(2), 81–97.

Azar, S. T., & Rohrbeck, C. A. (1986). Child abuse and unrealistic expectations: Further validation of the Parent Opinion Questionnaire. *Journal of Consulting and Clinical Psychology, 54*, 867–868.

Baetens, P., & Brewaeys, A. (2001). Lesbian couples requesting donor insemination: An update of the knowledge with regard to lesbian mother families. *Human Reproduction Update, 7*, 512–519.

Baetens, P., Camus, M., & Devroey, P. (2003). Counselling lesbian couples: Requests for donor insemination on social grounds. *Reproductive Biomedicine Online, 6*, 75–83. Retrieved from http://www.rbmonline.com/4DCGI/Issue/Detail

Baetens, P., Devroey, P., Camus, M., Van Steirteghem, A. C., & Ponjaert-Kristoffersen, I. (2000). Counselling couples and donors for oocyte donation: The decision to use either known or anonymous oocytes. *Human Reproduction, 15*, 476–484.

Bahadur, G., Ling, K. L., Hart, R., Ralph, D., Riley, V., Wafa, R., et al. (2002). Semen quality and cryopreservation in adolescent cancer patients. *Human Reproduction, 17*, 3157–3161.

Balaban, B., Urman, B., Isiklar, A., Altas, C., Aksoy, S., Mercan, R., & Nuhoglu, A. (2001). The effect of pronuclear morphology on embryo quality parameters and blastocyst transfer outcome. *Human Reproduction, 16*, 2357–2361.

Bangsboll, S., Pinborg, A., Yding, A. C., & Nyboe, A. A. (2004). Patients' attitudes towards donation of surplus cryopreserved embryos for treatment or research. *Human Reproduction, 19*, 2415–2419.

Bankowski, B. J., Lyerly, A. D., Faden, R. R., & Wallach, E. E. (2005). The social implications of embryo cryopreservation. *Fertility and Sterility, 84*, 823–832.

Baor, L., Bar-David, J., & Blickstein, I. (2004). Psychosocial resource depletion of parents of twins after assisted versus spontaneous reproduction. *International Journal of Fertility and Women's Medicine, 49*, 13–18.

Baran, A., & Pannor, R. (1993). *Lethal secrets: The psychology of donor insemination. Problems and solutions* (2nd ed.). New York, NY: Amistad Press.

Barratt, C., Englert, Y., Gottlieb, C., & Jouannet, P. (1998). Gamete donation guidelines. The Corsendonl consent document for the European Union. *Human Reproduction, 13*, 500–501.

Baslington, H. (1996). Anxiety overflow. *Women's Studies International Forum, 19*, 675–684.

Batzofin, J., Brisman, M., & Madsen, P. (2005). Gestational surrogacy: Consistent laws are necessary to provide effective treatment. *Sterility and Fertility, 84*(Suppl. 1), S355–S356.

Becker, G., Butler, A., & Nachtigall, R. D. (2005). Resemblance talk: A challenge for parents whose children were conceived with donor gametes in the US. *Social Science and Medicine, 61*, 1300–1309.

Behnke, S. (2006). APA's Ethical Principles of Psychologists and Code of Conduct: An ethics code for all psychologists . . . ? *Monitor on Psychology, 37*, 66–67.

Belsky, J. (1993). Etiology of child maltreatment: A developmental–ecological analysis. *Psychological Bulletin, 114*, 413–434.

Benatar, D. (2006). Reproductive freedom and risk. *Human Reproduction, 21*, 2491–2493.

Benjet, C., Azar, S. T., & Kuersten-Hogan, R. (2003). Evaluating the parental fitness of psychiatrically diagnosed individuals advocating a functional-contextual analysis of parenting. *Journal of Family Psychology, 17*, 238–251.

Ben-Shlomo, I., Geslevich, J., & Shalev, E. (2001). Can we abandon routine evaluation of serum estradiol levels during controlled ovarian hyperstimulation for assisted reproduction? *Fertility and Sterility, 76*, 300–303.

Ber, R. (2000). Ethical issues in gestational surrogacy. *Theoretical Medicine and Bioethics, 21*, 153–169.

Berg, J. W. (2001). Risky business: Evaluating oocyte donation. *American Journal of Bioethics, 1*, 18–19.

Berg, J. W., Appelbaum, P. S., Lidz, C. W., & Parker, L. S. (2001). *Informed consent: Legal theory and clinical practice* (2nd ed.). New York, NY: Oxford University Press.

Berger, D. M. (1980). Couples' reactions to male infertility and donor insemination. *American Journal of Psychiatry, 137*, 1047–1049.

Berger, D. M., Eisen, H., Shuber, J., & Doody, K. F. (1986). Psychological patterns in donor insemination couples. *Canadian Journal of Psychiatry, 31*, 818–823.

Bergh, C., Moller, A., Nilsson, L., & Wikland, M. (1999). Obstetric outcome and psychological follow-up of pregnancies after embryo reduction. *Human Reproduction, 14*, 2170–2175.

Bitler, M., & Schmidt, L. (2006). Health disparities and infertility: Impact of state-level insurance mandates. *Fertility and Sterility, 85*, 858–865.

Blascovich, J., Mendes, W. B., Hunter, S. B., & Lickel, B. (2000). The social psychology of stigma. In T. Heatherton, R. Kleck, M. R. Hebl, & J. G. Hull (Eds.), *Stigma* (pp. 307–333). New York, NY: Guilford Press.

Blaser, A., Maloigne-Katz, B., & Gigon, U. (1988). Effect of artificial insemination with donor semen on the psyche of the husband. *Psychotherapy and Psychosomatics, 49*, 17–21.

Blau, P. (1994). *Structured contexts of opportunities*. Chicago, IL: University of Chicago Press.

Blennborn, M., Nilsson, S., Hillervik, C., & Hellberg, D. (2005). The couple's decision-making in IVF: One or two embryos at transfer? *Human Reproduction, 20*, 1292–1297.

Blickstein, I., & Keith, L. G. (2000). *Iatrogenic multiple pregnancy: Clinical implications*. New York, NY: Parthenon.

Blois, J. de, & O'Rourke, K. D. (1995). Healthcare and social responsibility. *Health Progress, 76*(4), 1–7. Retrieved from http://www.chausa.org/Pub/MainNav/News/HP/Archive/1995

Blyth, E. (1994). "I wanted to be interesting. I wanted to be able to say 'I've done something interesting with my life'": Interviews with surrogate mothers in Britain. *Journal of Reproductive and Infant Psychology, 13*, 185–196.

Blyth, E. (2002). Subsidized IVF: The development of 'egg sharing' in the United Kingdom. *Human Reproduction, 17*, 3254–3259.

Blyth, E. D., Firth, L., & Farrand, A. (2005). Is it possible to recruit gamete donors who are both altruistic and identifiable? *Fertility and Sterility, 84* (Suppl. 7), S21.

Boisen, A. (1936). *The exploration of the inner world*. New York, NY: Harper.

Boivin, J., Rice, F., Hay, D., Harold, G., Lewis, A., & van den Bree, M. M., & Thapar, A. (2009). Associations between maternal older age, family environment and parent and child wellbeing in families using assisted reproductive technologies to conceive. *Social Sciences and Medicine, 68*, 1948–1955.

Boivin, J., Scanlan, L. C., & Walker, S. M. (1999). Why are infertile patients not using psychosocial counselling? *Human Reproduction, 14*, 1384–1391.

Bok, S. (1978). *Lying: Moral choice in public and private life*. New York, NY: Vintage Books.

Borrero, C. (2001). Gamete and embryo donation. In E. Vayena, P. Rowe, & D.Griffin (Eds.), *Medical, ethical and social aspects of assisted reproduction* (p.166–176). Geneva, Switzerland: World Health Organization.

Bos, H. M. W., van Balen, F., & van den Boom, D. C. (2007). Child adjustment and parenting in planned lesbian-parent families. *American Journal of Orthopsychiatry, 77*, 38–48.

Boss, P. (1999). *Ambiguous loss: Learning to live with unresolved grief*. Cambridge, MA: Harvard University Press.

Boulet, S. L., Schieve, L. A., Nannini, A., Ferre, C., Devine, O., Cohen, B., et al. (2008). Perinatal outcomes of twin births conceived using assisted reproduction technology: A population-based study. *Human Reproduction, 23*, 1941–1948.

Boulot, P., Vigna, J., Vergnes, C., Dechaud, H., Faure, J. M., & Hedon, B. (2000). Multifetal reduction of triplets to twins: A prospective comparison of pregnancy outcome. *Human Reproduction, 15*, 1619–1623.

Bowen, M. (1966). The use of family theory in clinical practice. *Comprehensive Psychiatry, 7*, 345–374.

Bower, C., & Hansen, M. (2005). Assisted reproductive technologies and birth outcomes: Overview of recent systematic reviews. *Reproduction, Fertility and Development, 17*, 329–333.

Bowlby, J. (1961). Processes of mourning. *International Journal of Psychoanalysis, 42*, 317–339.

Bowlby, J. (1982). *Attachment* (2nd ed., Vol. 1). New York, NY: Basic Books.

Bragdon v. Abbott, 524 U.S. 624 (1998).

Brakman, S.-V. (2005). *Embryo adoption.* Retrieved from http://www.lahey.org/NewsPubs/Publications/Ethics/JournalSpring2005/Journal_Spring2005_feature.asp

Brandes, B. M., & Mesrobian, T. G. (2005). Evaluation and management of genetic anomalies in two patients with Klinefelter's syndrome and review of the literature. *Urology, 65*, 976–977.

Braverman, A. M. (2001). Exploring ovum donors' motivations and needs. *American Journal of Bioethics, 1*, 16–17.

Braverman, A. M., Benward, J. M., & Scheib, J. E. (2002). Views and practices about record keeping and dissemination in donor conception. *Fertility and Sterility, 78*(Suppl. 1), S29–S30.

Breakwell, G. M. (1987). *Coping with threatened identities.* London, England: Routledge.

Breakwell, G. M. (1998). Identity processes and social changes. In G. M. Breakwell & E. Lyons (Eds.), *Changing European identities: Social psychological analyses of social change* (pp. 13–30). Oxford, England: Taylor Francis.

Brett, S., Sacranie, R. R., Thomas, G. E., & Rajkhowa, R. (2008). Can we improve recruitment of oocyte donors with loss of donor anonymity? A hospital-based survey. *Human Fertility, 11*, 101–107.

Brewaeys, A., de Bruyn, J. K., Louwe, L. A., & Helmerhorst, F. M. (2005). Anonymous or identity registered sperm donors? A study of Dutch recipients' choices. *Human Reproduction, 20*, 820–824.

Brewaeys, A., Devroey, P., Helmerhorst, F. M., Van Hall, E. V., & Ponjaert, I. (1995). Lesbian mothers who conceived after donor insemination: A follow-up study. *Human Reproduction, 10*, 2731–2735.

Brewaeys, A., Ponjaert, I., Van Hall, E., & Golombok, S. (1997). Donor insemination: Child development and family functioning in lesbian mother families. *Human Reproduction, 12*, 1349–1359.

Brewaeys, A., Ponjaert-Kristoffersen, I., Van Steirteghem, A. C., & Devroey, P. (1993). Children from anonymous donors: An inquiry into homosexual and heterosexual parents' attitudes. *Journal of Psychosomatic Obstetrics and Gynaecology, 14*(Suppl.), 23–35.

Brinsden, P. R. (2003). Gestational surrogacy. *Human Reproduction Update, 9*, 483–491.

Brinsden, P. R., Appleton, T. C., Murray, E., Hussein, M., Akagbosu, F., & Marcus, S. F. (2000). Treatment by in vitro fertilisation with surrogacy: Experience of one British centre. *BMJ, 320*, 924–929.

British Andrology Association. (1999). British andrology society guidelines for the screening of semen donors for donor insemination. *Human Reproduction, 14*, 1823–1826.

British Broadcasting Corporation News. (2008). *'One-stop' embryo test unveiled.* Retrieved from http://news.bbc.co.uk/go/fr/1/health/7688299.stm

Britt, D. W., Risinger, S. T., Mans, M., & Evans, M. I. (2003). Anxiety among women who have undergone fertility therapy and who are considering multifetal pregnancy reduction: Trends and implications. *Journal of Maternal Fetal Neonatal Medicine, 13*, 271–278.

Broderick, P., & Walker, I. (2001). Donor gametes and embryos: Who wants to know what about whom, and why? *Politics and Life Sciences, 20*, 29–42.

Broderick, P. C., & Blewitt, P. (2005). *The life span: Human development for helping professionals* (2nd ed.). Englewood Cliffs, NJ: Prentice Hall.

Brodzinsky, D. (2007). Family structural openness and communication openness as predictors in the adjustment of adopted children. *Adoption Quarterly, 9*, 1–18.

Bromham, D. R. (1995). Surrogacy: Ethical, legal, and social aspects. *Journal of Assisted Reproduction and Genetics, 12*, 509–516.

Browne, A., & Finkelhor, D. (1986). Impact of child sexual abuse: A review of the research. *Psychological Bulletin, 99*, 66–77.

Budd, K. S. (2001). Assessing parenting competence in child protection cases: A clinical practice model. *Clinical Child and Family Psychology Review, 4*, 1–18.

Bujan, L., Sergerie, M., Kiffer, N., Moinard, N., Seguela, G., Mercadier, et al. (2007). Good efficiency of intrauterine insemination programme for serodiscordant couples with HIV-1 infected male partner: A retrospective comparative study. *European Journal of Obstetrics and Gynaecology and Reproductive Biology, 135*, 76–82.

Buster, J. E., Bustillo, M., Thorneycroft, I. H., Simon, J. A., Boyers, S. P., Marshall, J. R., et al. (1983, July 23). Nonsurgical transfer of an in vivo fertilized donated ova to five infertile women: Report of two pregnancies [Letter to the editor]. *The Lancet, 2*, 223–224.

Bustillo, M., Buster, J. E., Cohen, S. W., Thorneycroft, I. H., Simon, J. A., Boyers, S. P., et al. (1984). Nonsurgical ovum transfer as a treatment in infertile women: Preliminary experience. *Journal of the American Medical Association, 251*, 1171–1173.

California Cryobank. (2007). *About California cryobank sperm donors.* Retrieved from http://www.spermbank.com/newdonors/index.cfm?ID=4

Callahan, T. L., Hall, J. E., Ettner, S. L., Christiansen, C. L., Greene, M. F., & Crowley, W. F., Jr. (1994). The economic impact of multiple-gestation pregnancies and the contribution of assisted-reproduction techniques to their incidence. *New England Journal of Medicine, 331*, 244–249.

Cameron, N. M. (2005). Pandora's progeny: Ethical issues in assisted human reproduction. *Family Law Quarterly, 39*, 745–749.

Caplan, G. (1964). *Principles of preventative psychiatry*. New York, NY: Basic Books.

Cardno, A. G., Marshall, E. J., Coid, B., Macdonald, A. M., Ribchesger, T. R., Davies, N. J., et al. (1999). Heritability estimates for psychotic disorders: The Maudsley twin psychosis series. *Archives of General Psychiatry, 56*, 162–168.

Carr, E. K., Friedman, T., Lannon, B., & Sharp, P. C. (1990). The study of psychological factors in couples receiving artificial insemination by donor: A discussion of methodological difficulties. *Journal of Advanced Nursing, 15*, 906–910.

Carson, S. A., Casson, P. R., & Shuman, D. J. (1999). *The American Society for Reproductive Medicine complete guide to fertility*. Chicago, IL: Contemporary Books.

Casey, P., Readings, J., Blake, L., Jadva, V., & Golombok, S. (2008). Child development and parent–child relationships in surrogacy, egg donation and donor insemination families at age 7 [Abstract]. *Human Reproduction, 23*(Suppl. i6). Retrieved from http://humrep.oxfordjournals.org/cgi/reprint/23/suppl_1/i4?etoc

Ceelen, M., van Weissenbruch, M. M., Vermeiden, J. P. W., van Leeuwen, F. E., & Delemarre-van de Waal, H. A. (2008). Growth and development of children born after in vitro fertilization. *Fertility and Sterility, 90*, 1662–1673.

Chaffin, M., Kelleher, K., & Hollenberg, J. (1996). Onset of physical abuse and neglect: Psychiatric, substance abuse, and social risk factors from prospective community data. *Child Abuse and Neglect, 20*, 191–203.

Chambers v. Melmed, 141 Fed. Appx. 718 (10 Cir. 2005).

Chan, R., Raboy, B., & Patterson, C. (1998). Psychosocial adjustment among children conceived via donor insemination by lesbian and heterosexual mothers. *Child Development, 69*, 443–457.

Chang, C. L. (2004). Surrogate motherhood. *Formosan Journal of Medical Humanities, 5*, 48–62. Abstract retrieved from http://www.ncbi.nlm.nih.gov/pubmed/15460596

Charlesworth, M. (1992). Oocyte donation: Ethical perspectives. *Reproduction, Fertility and Development, 4*, 605–609.

Cheang, C.-U., Huang, L.-S., Lee, T.-H., Liu, C.-H., Shih, Y.-T., & Lee, M.-S. (2007). A comparison of the outcomes between twin and reduced twin pregnancies produced through assisted reproduction. *Fertility and Sterility, 88*, 47–52.

Check, J. H., Fox, F., Deperro, D., Davies, E., & Krotec, J. W. (2003). Efficacy of sharing oocytes from compensated donors between two recipients. *Clinical Obstetrics & Gynecology, 30*, 199–200.

Chen, J. L., Phillips, K. A., Kanouse, D. E., Collins, R. L., & Miu, A. (2001). Fertility desires and intentions of HIV-positive men and women. *Family Planning Perspectives, 33*, 144–152.

Chen, K. C., & Ng, H. T. (2001). Legal and ethical considerations of assisted reproductive technology and surrogate motherhood in AOFOG (Asia & Oceania

Federation of Obstetrics and Gynecology) countries. *Journal of Gynaecological Research, 27,* 89–95.

Chen, M. (2003). Wombs for rent: An examination of prohibitory and regulatory approaches to governing preconception arrangements. *Heath Law of Canada, 23,* 33–50.

Chervenak, F. A., & McCullough, L. B. (2000). Ethical considerations. In I. Blickstein & L. G. Keith (Eds.), *Iatrogenic multiple pregnancy: Clinical implications* (pp. 263–270). New York, NY: Parthenon.

Chervenak, F. A., & McCullough, L. B. (2008). How physicians and scientists can respond responsibly and effectively to religiously based opposition to human embryonic stem cell research. *Fertility and Sterility, 90,* 2056–2059.

Chesler, P. (1972). *Women and madness.* New York, NY: Doubleday.

Children of older fathers at risk for bipolar disorder. (2008, September 9). *Bio-Medicine.* Retrieved from http://www.bio-medicine.org/medicine-news-1/Children-of-Older-Fathers-at-Risk-for-BipolarDisorder-25956-1/-1

Childress-Beatty, L. (2009, February). Ethical practice in a reproductive medicine setting: Psychologists' work in this area involves an abundance of roles, clients, and different settings. *Monitor on Psychology, 40,* 66–67.

Chliaoutakis, J. E. (2002). A relationship between traditionally motivated patterns and gamete donation and surrogacy in urban areas of Greece. *Human Reproduction, 17,* 2187–2191.

Chliaoutakis, J. E., Koukouli, S., & Papadakaki, M. (2002). Using attitudinal indicators to explain the public's intention to have recourse to gamete donation and surrogacy. *Human Reproduction, 17,* 2995–3002.

Chodorow, N. I. (1978). *The reproduction of mothering: Psychoanalysis and the sociology of gender.* Los Angeles: University of California Press.

Choi, Y., Bishai, D., & Minkovitz, C. S. (2009). Multiple births are a risk factor for postpartum maternal depressive symptoms. *Pediatrics, 123,* 1147–1154.

Ciccarelli, J. C. (1997). *The surrogate mother: A post-birth follow-up study.* Unpublished doctoral dissertation, California School of Professional Psychology, Los Angeles.

Ciccarelli, J. C., & Beckman, L. J. (2005). Navigating rough waters: An overview of psychological aspects of surrogacy. *Journal of Social Issues, 61,* 21–43.

Clarke, R. N., Klock, S. C., Geighegan, A., & Travassos, D. E. (1999). Relationship between psychological stress and semen quality among in-vitro fertilization patients. *Human Reproduction, 14,* 753–758.

Coffler, M. S., Kol, S., Drugan, A., & Itskovitz-Eldor, J. (1999). Early transvaginal embryo aspiration: A safer method for selective reduction in high order multiple gestations. *Human Reproduction, 14,* 1875–1888.

Cohen, C. B. (2001). The interests of egg donors: Who is deceiving whom? *American Journal of Bioethics, 1,* 20–21.

Cohen, J. (1995). Oocyte donation. *Journal of Assisted Reproduction and Genetics, 12*, 232–233.

Cohen, J. (2003). A short review of ovarian stimulation in assisted reproductive techniques. *Reproductive Biomedicine Online, 6*, 361–366. Retrieved from http://www.rbmonline.com/4DCGI/Issue/Detail

Collins, W. A., Maccoby, E. E., Steinberg, L., Hetherington, E. M., & Bornstein, M. H. (2000). Contemporary research on parenting: The case for nature and nurture. *American Psychologist, 55*, 218–232.

Colliton, W. F. (2004). In-vitro fertilization and the wisdom of the Roman Catholic Church. Retrieved from http://www.hli.org/commentaries_william_colliton_invitro_fertilization.pdf

Committee on Infertility Counseling (1995). Qualification guidelines for mental health professionals in reproductive medicine. In L. H. Burns & S. N. Covington (Eds.), *Infertility counseling: A comprehensive handbook for clinicians* (pp. 529–530). New York, NY: Parthenon.

Conaway, L. P., & Hansen, D. J. (1989). Social behavior of physically abused and neglected children: A critical review. *Clinical Psychology Review, 9*, 627–652.

Conger, J. J. (1975). Proceedings of the American Psychological Association, Incorporated, for the year 1974: Minutes of the annual meeting of the Council of Representatives. *American Psychologist, 30*, 620–651.

Conn. Gen. Stat. § 19a-32d(d)(3) (2008).

Cook, K. (1990). Linking actors and structures: An exchange network prospective. In C. Calhoun, M. Meyer, & R. Scott (Eds.), *Structures of power and constraint* (pp. 115–116). Cambridge, England: Cambridge University Press.

Cook, M. (Ed.). (2003, February 14). Reproductive tourism flourishing. *Australiasian Bioethics Information, 63*. Retrieved from http://www.australiaasianbioethics.org/newsletters/063-2003-02-14.html

Cook, R., & Golombok, S. (1995). Ethics and society: A survey of semen donation: Phase II—The view of the donors. *Human Reproduction, 10*, 951–959.

Cooper-Hilbert, B. (1998). *Infertility and involuntary childlessness: Helping couples cope.* New York, NY: Norton.

Corea, G. (1985). *The mother machine: Reproductive technologies from artificial insemination to artificial wombs.* New York, NY: Harper & Row.

Corson, S. L., Kelly, M., Braverman, A. M., & English, M. E. (1998). Gestational carrier pregnancy. *Fertility and Sterility, 69*, 670–674.

Corson, S. L., & Mechanick-Braverman, A. (1998). Why we believe there should be a gamete registry. *Fertility and Sterility, 69*, 809–811.

Craft, I. (1997). An ethical dilemma: Should egg donors be paid? *BMJ, 314*, 1400.

Crawford, I., McLeod, A., Zamboni, B. D., & Jordan, M. B. (1999). Psychologists' attitudes toward gay and lesbian parenting. *Professional Psychology: Research and Practice, 30*, 394–401.

Crawshaw, M. A., Blyth, E. D., & Daniels, K. R. (2007). Past semen donors' view about the use of a voluntary contact register. *Reproductive Biomedicine Online*, *14*, 411–417. Retrieved from http://www.rbmonline.com/4DCGI/Issue/Detail

Criniti, A., Thyer, A., Chow, G., Lin, P., Klein, N., & Soules, M. (2005). Elective single blastocyst transfer reduces twin rates without compromising pregnancy rates. *Fertility and Sterility*, *84*, 1613–1619.

Crisostomo, L., & Molina, V. V. (2002). Pregnancy outcomes among farming households of Neuva Ecija with conventional pesticide use versus integrated pest management. *International Journal of Occupational & Environmental Health*, *8*, 232–242.

Cronin, H., & Smith, J. M. (1991). *The ant and the peacock: Altruism and sexual selection from Darwin to today*. Cambridge, England: Cambridge University Press.

Curie-Cohen, M. (1980). The frequency of consanguineous matings due to multiple use of donors in artificial insemination. *American Journal of Human Genetics*, *32*, 589–600.

Daar, J. F. (2001). Regulating the fiction of informed consent in ART medicine. *American Journal of Bioethics*, *1*, 19–20.

Daniels, K. R. (1987). Semen donors in New Zealand: Their characteristics and attitudes. *Clinical Reproductive Fertility*, *5*, 177–190.

Daniels, K. R. (1994). Adoption and donor insemination: Factors influencing couples' choices. *Child Welfare*, *73*, 5–14.

Daniels, K. R. (2000). To give or sell human gametes—The interplay between pragmatics, policy, and ethics. *Journal of Medical Ethics*, *26*, 206–211.

Daniels, K. R. (2004). *Building a family with the assistance of donor insemination*. Palmerston North, New Zealand: Dunmore Press.

Daniels, K. R. (2005). Is blood really thicker than water? Assisted reproduction and its impact on our thinking about family. *Journal of Psychosomatic Obstetrics & Gynecology*, *26*, 265–270.

Daniels, K. R. (2007). Anonymity and openness and the recruitment of gamete donors. Part I: Semen donors. *Human Fertility*, *10*, 151–158.

Daniels, K. R., Blyth, E., Crawshaw, M., & Curson, R. (2005). Short communication: Previous semen donors and their views regarding the sharing of information with offspring. *Human Reproduction*, *20*, 1670–1675.

Daniels, K. R., Curson, R., & Lewis, G. M. (1996). Semen donor recruitment: A study of donors in two clinics. *Human Reproduction*, *11*, 746–751.

Daniels, K. R., Lalos, A., Gottlieb, C., & Lalos, O. (2005). Semen providers and their three families [Abstract]. *Journal of Psychosomatic Obstetrics and Gynaecology*, *26*, 15–22.

Daniels, K. R., Lewis, G., & Gillet, W. (1996). Telling donor insemination offspring about their conception: The nature of couples' decision making. *Social Science and Medicine*, *40*, 1213–1220.

Daniels, K., & Meadows, L. (2006). Sharing information with adults conceived as a result of donor insemination. *Human Fertility, 9*, 93–99.

Daniels, K. R., & Taylor, K. (1993). Secrecy and openness in donor insemination. *Politics and the Life Sciences, 12*, 155–170.

Daniels, K. R., & Thorn, P. (2001). Sharing information with donor insemination offspring. A child-conception versus a family-building approach. *Human Reproduction, 16*, 1792–1796.

Daniels, K. R., Thorn, P., & Westerbrooke, R. (2007). Confidence in the use of donor insemination: An evaluation of the impact of participating in a group preparation programme. *Human Fertility, 10*, 13–20.

Daniluk, J. C. (1988). Infertility: Intrapersonal and interpersonal impact. *Fertility and Sterility, 49*, 982–990.

Daskalakis, G., Anastasakis, E., Papantoniou, N., Mesogitis, S., & Antsaklis, A. (2009). Second trimester amniocentesis in assisted conception versus spontaneously conceived twins. *Fertility and Sterility, 91*, 2572–2577.

Davis v. Davis, 842 S.W.2d 588 (Tenn. 1992).

Davis, J. H., & Brown, D. W. (1984). Artificial insemination by donor (AID) and the use of surrogate mothers. *Western Journal of Medicine, 141*, 127–130.

Day, M. C., Barton, J. R., O'Brien, J. M., Istwan, N. B., & Sibai, B. M. (2005). The effect of fetal number on the development of hypertensive conditions of pregnancy. *Obstetrics and Gynecology, 106*, 927–931.

de Boer, A., Oosterwijk, J. C., & Rigters-Aris, C. A. (1995). Determination of maximum number of artificial inseminations by donor children per sperm donor. *Fertility and Sterility, 63*, 419–421.

De Croo, I., Van der Elst, J., Everaert, K., de Sutter, P., & Dhont, M. (2000). Fertilization, pregnancy and embryo implantation rates after ICSI in cases of obstructive and non-obstructive azoospermia. *Human Reproduction, 15*, 1383–1388.

DeForge, D., Blackmer, J., Garritty, C., Yazdi, F., Cronin, V., Barrowman, N., et al. (2005). Fertility following spinal cord injury: A systematic review. *Spinal Cord, 43*, 693–703.

de Lacey, S. (2005). Parent identity and 'virtual' children: Why patients discard rather than donate unused embryos. *Human Reproduction, 20*, 1661–1669.

de Lacey, S. (2007). Patients' attitudes to their embryos and their destiny: Social conditioning? *Best Practice and Research in Clinical Obstetrics and Gynecology, 21*, 101–112.

de Lacey, S., Davies, M., Homan, G., Briggs, N., & Norman, R. J. (2007). Factors and perceptions that influence women's decisions to have a single embryo transferred. *Reproductive Biomedicine Online, 15*, 526–531. Retrieved from http://www.rbonline.com/4DCGI/Issue?Data/

Del Zio v. Presbyterian Hospital, 1978 U.S. Dist. LEXIS 14450 (S.D.N.Y. 1978).

de Neubourg, D., Gerris, J., Mangelschots, K., Van Royen, E., Vercruyssen, M., Steylemans, A., & Elseviers, M. (2006). The obstetrical and neonatal outcome of babies born after single-embryo transfer in IVF/ICSI compares favourably to spontaneously conceived babies. *Human Reproduction, 21,* 1041–1046.

de Neubourg, D., Mangelschots, K., Van Royen, E., Vercruyssen, M., Ryckaert, G., Valkenburg, M., et al. (2002). Impact of patients' choice for single embryo transfer of a top quality embryo versus double embryo transfer in the first IVF/ICSI cycle. *Human Reproduction, 17,* 2621–2625.

Deneux-Tharaux, C., Carmona, E., Bouvier-Colle, M. H., & Breart, G. (2006). Postpartum maternal mortality and cesarean delivery. *Obstetrics and Gynecology, 108,* 541–549.

Denschlag, D., Tempfer, C., Kunze, M., Wolff, G., & Keck, C. (2004). Assisted reproductive techniques in patients with Klinefelter syndrome: A critical review. *Fertility and Sterility, 82,* 775–779.

DePaulo, B. M. (1992). Nonverbal behavior and self-presentation. *Psychological Bulletin, 111,* 203–243.

Diamond, R., Kezur, D., Meyers, M., Scharf, C. N., & Weinshel, M. (1999). *Couples therapy for infertility.* New York, NY: Guilford Press.

Dickens, B. M. (2001, September). Ethical issues arising from the use of assisted reproductive technologies. In E. Rowe & D. Griffin (Eds.), *Current practices and controversies in assisted reproduction: Ethical aspects of infertility and art.* Report of the World Health Organization Meeting of Medical, Ethical, and Social Aspects of ART, Geneva, Switzerland.

Dickenson, D. (2002). Commodification of human tissue: Implications for feminists and development ethics. *Developing World Bioethics, 2,* 55–63.

Dim, E. D., Bischoff, F. Z., Lipschultz, L. I., & Lamb., D. J. (1999). Genetic concerns for the subfertile male in the era of ICSI. *Prenatal Diagnosis, 18,* 1349–1365.

Dodd, J., & Crowther, C. (2004). Multifetal pregnancy reduction of triplet and higher-order multiple pregnancies to twins. *Fertility and Sterility, 81,* 1420–1422.

Donor Conception Support Group of Australia Inc. (1997). *Let the offspring speak: Discussions on donor conception.* New South Wales, Australia: Author.

Douglas, W. O. (1942). 1942 Skinner v. Oklahoma ex rel. Wiliamson, 316. 535.

Dowdney, L., & Skuse, D. (1993). Parenting provided by adults with mental retardation. *Journal of Child Psychology and Psychiatry, 34,* 25–47.

Downey, G., & Coyne, J. C. (1990). Children of depressed parents: An integrative review. *Psychological Bulletin, 108,* 50–76.

Dresser, R. (2001). Donation, disclosure, and deception. *American Journal of Bioethics, 1,* 15–16.

Dubowitz, H., Black, M. M., Kerr, M. A., Hussey, J. M., Morrel, T. M., Everson, M. D., & Starr, R. H., Jr. (2001). Type and timing of mothers' victimization: Effects on mothers and children. *Pediatrics, 107,* 728–735.

Duke, S. R., Anda, R. F., Felitti, V. J., Croft, J. B., Edwards, V. J., & Giles, W. H. (2001). Growing up with parental alcohol abuse: Exposure to childhood abuse, neglect, and household dysfunction. *Child Abuse and Neglect, 25,* 1627–1640.

Durna, E. M., Bebe, J., Steigrad, S. J., Leader, L. R., & Garrett, D. G. (1997). Donor insemination: Attitudes of parents towards disclosure. *Medical Journal of Australia, 167,* 256–259.

Dyer, C. (2008). More than 100 sperm and egg donors prove ready to reveal identity to offspring. *BMJ, 337,* 2110a. Extract retrieved from http://www.bmj.com/cgi/content/extract/337/oct16_1/a2110

Ehlers, C. L., Frank, E., & Kupfer, D. J. (1988). Social zeitgebers and biological rhythms. A unified approach to understanding the etiology of depression. *Archives of General Psychiatry, 45,* 948–952.

Ehrensaft, D. (2005). *Mommies, daddies, donors, surrogates.* New York, NY: Guilford Press.

Eliot, T. S. (1944). *Little Gidding.* Boston, MA: Houghton Mifflin Harcourt.

Ellison, M. A., & Hall, J. E. (2003). Social stigma and compounded losses: Quality-of-life issues for multiple-birth families. *Fertility and Sterility, 80,* 405–414.

Elster, N., & the Institute for Science, Law, and Technology Working Group on Reproductive Technology. (2000). Less is more: The risks of multiple births. *Fertility and Sterility, 74,* 617–623.

Empire State Stem Cell Board. (2009). *Resolution of the funding committee regarding recommended standards for the compensation of women donating oocytes solely for research purposes.* Retrieved from http://stemcell.ny.gov/docs/Compensation ofGameteDonorsresolutionoffundingcomm.pdf

Engelhardt, H. (2006). *Being Christian in a post-Christian world.* Retrieved from http://www.saintpeterorthodox.com/portals/2/speakers/engelhardt/engelhardt1.pdf

Erikson, E. (1963). *Childhood and society* (2nd ed.). New York, NY: Norton.

Esfandiari, N., Claessens, E. A., O'Brien, A., Gotlieb, L., & Casper, R. F. (2004). Gestational carrier is an optimal method for pregnancy in patients with vaginal agenesis (Rokitansky syndrome). *International Journal of Fertility and Women's Medicine, 49,* 79–82.

Etaugh, C. A., & Bridges, J. S. (2005). *Women's lives: A topical approach.* Boston, MA: Allyn & Bacon.

Ethics Committee of the American College of Obstetrics and Gynecology. (1994). Preembryo research, history, scientific background and ethical considerations. *International Journal of Gynecology and Obstetrics, 45,* 291–301.

Ethics Committee of the American Society for Reproductive Medicine. (2004a). Child-rearing ability and the provision of fertility services. *Fertility and Sterility, 82*(Suppl. 1), S208–S211.

Ethics Committee of the American Society for Reproductive Medicine. (2004b). Disposition of abandoned embryos. *Fertility and Sterility, 82*(Suppl. 1), S253.

Ethics Committee of the American Society for Reproductive Medicine. (2004c). Family members as gamete donors and surrogates. *Fertility and Sterility, 82*(Suppl. 1), S217–S223.

Ethics Committee of the American Society for Reproductive Medicine. (2004d). Financial incentives in recruitment of oocyte donors. *Fertility and Sterility, 82* (Suppl. 1), S240–S244.

Ethics Committee of the American Society for Reproductive Medicine. (2004e). Human immunodeficiency virus and infertility treatment. *Fertility and Sterility,* 82(Suppl. 1), S228–S231.

Ethics Committee of the American Society for Reproductive Medicine. (2004f). Informing offspring of their conception by gamete donation. *Fertility and Sterility,* 82(Suppl. 1), S212–S216.

Ethics Committee of the American Society for Reproductive Medicine. (2007). Financial compensation of oocyte donors. *Fertility and Sterility, 88,* 305–309.

Ethics Committee of the American Society for Reproductive Medicine. (2009). Interests, obligations, and rights of the donor in gamete donation. *Fertility and Sterility, 91,* 22–27.

European Society of Human Reproduction and Embryology Task Force on Ethics and Law. (2002). Part III: Gamete and embryo donation. *Human Reproduction, 17,* 1407–1408.

European Society of Human Reproduction and Embryology Task Force on Ethics and Law. (2003). ESHRE Task Force 6: Ethical issues related to multiple pregnancies in medically assisted procreation. *Human Reproduction, 18,* 1976–1979.

European Society of Human Reproduction and Embryology Task Force on Ethics and Law. (2005). ESHRE Task Force 10: Surrogacy. *Human Reproduction, 20,* 2705–2707.

Evans, M. I., Dommergues, M., Wapner, R. J., Goldberg, J. D., Lynch, L., Zador, I. E., et al. (1996). International collaborative experience of 1789 patients having multifetal pregnancy reduction: A plateauing of risks and outcomes. *Journal of the Society for Gynecologic Investigation, 3,* 23–26.

Faraone, S. V., Perlis, R. H., Doyle, A. E., Smoller, J. W., Goralnick, J. J., Holmgren, M. A., & Sklar, P. (2005). Molecular genetics of attention-deficit/hyperactivity disorder. *Biological Psychiatry, 57,* 1313–1323.

FDA Suitability determination for donors of human cellular and tissue-based products. Proposed rule. (1999). 64 Fed. Reg. 52696–52723.

Feinberg, J. (1980). On the child's right to an open future. In W. Aiken & H. LaFollette (Eds.), *Whose child? Children's rights, parental authority, and state power* (pp.124–153). Totowa, NJ: Rowman & Littlefield.

Feldman, L. (2007, February 17). Father's over 35 risk having autistic or schizophrenic kids. *Huliq News.* Retrieved from http://www.huliq.com/17846/fathers-35-risk-having-autistic-or-schizophrenic-kids

Ferguson v. McKiernan, 940 A. 2d 1236 (Pa. 2007).

Fertility Cryobank. (2007). Sperm donation-benefits, compensation, and procedures. Retrieved from http://www.spermdonorweb.com/sd_process

Fiddelers, A. A. A., van Montfoort, A. P. A., Dirksen, C. D., Dumoulin, J. C. M., Land, J. A., Dunselman, G. A. J., et al. (2006). Single versus double embryo transfer: Cost effectiveness analysis alongside a randomized clinical trial. *Human Reproduction, 21,* 2090–2097.

Fielding, P., Handley, S., Duqueno, L., Weaver, S., & Lui, S. (1998). Motivation, attitudes, and experiences of donation: A follow-up of women donating eggs in assisted conception treatment. *Journal of Community and Applied Social Psychology, 8,* 273–287.

Fischer, S., & Gillman, I. (1991). Surrogate motherhood: Attachment, attitudes, and social support. *Psychiatry, 54,* 13–20.

Fitzgerald, H. (1994). *The mourning handbook.* New York, NY: Simon & Schuster.

Fla. Stat. § 742.14 (2008).

Fla. Stat. § 742.15 (2008).

Flaks, D. K., Ficher, I., Masterpasqua, F. R., & Joseph, G. (1995). Lesbians choosing motherhood: A comparative study of lesbian and heterosexual parents and their children. *Developmental Psychology, 31,* 105–114.

Ford, W. C. L., North, K., Taylor, H., Farrow, A., Hull, M. G. R., Golding, G., & the ALSPAC Study Team. (2000). Increasing paternal age is associated with delayed conception in a large population of fertile couples: Evidence for declining fecundity in older men. *Human Reproduction, 15,* 1703–1708.

Fortescue, E. (2003). Gamete donation–Where is the evidence that there are benefits in removing the anonymity of donors? A patient's viewpoint. *Reproductive Biomedicine Online, 7,* 139–144.

Frable, D. E., Platt, L., & Hoey, S. (1998). Concealable stigmas and positive perceptions: Feeling better around similar others. *Journal of Personality and Social Psychology, 74,* 909–922.

Freeman, T., Jadva, V., Kramer, W., & Golombok, S. (2009). Gamete donation in parents' experiences of searching for their child's donor siblings and donors. *Human Reproduction, 1,* 1–12.

Frenkel, D. A. (2001). Legal regulation of surrogate motherhood in Israel. *Journal of Medicine and Law, 20,* 605–612.

Friedler, S., Raziel, A., Schachter, M., Straussburger, D., Bern, O., & Ron-El, R. (2002). Outcome of first and repeated testicular sperm extraction and ICSI in patients with non-obstructive azoospermia. *Human Reproduction, 17,* 2356–2361.

Friedman, S. (1980). Artificial insemination with donor semen mixed with semen of the infertile husband. *Fertility and Sterility, 33,* 125–128.

Frith, L. (2007). Gamete donation, identity, and the offspring's right to know. *Virtual Mentor, 9,* 644–647. Retrieved from http://virtualmentor.ama-assn.org/2007/09/oped1-0709.html

Fumento, M. (2005, May 19). Sperm donation: A matter of health, not rights. *Scripps Howard News Service.* Retrieved from http://www.fumento.com/disease/sperm-donor.html

Fuscaldo, G., Russell, S., & Gillam, L. (2007). How to facilitate decisions about surplus embryos: Patients' views. *Human Reproduction, 22,* 3129–3138.

Fuscaldo, G., & Savulescu, J. (2005). Spare embryos: 3000 reasons to rethink the significance of genetic relatedness. *Reproductive Biomedicine Online, 10,* 164–168. Retrieved from http://www.rbmonline.com/4DCGI/Issue/Detail

Gabrielsen, A., Fedder, J., & Agerholm, I. (2006). Parameters predicting implantation rate of thawed IVF/ICSI embryos: A retrospective study. *Reproductive Biomedicine Online, 12,* 70–76. Retrieved from http://www.rbmonline.com/4DCGI/Issue/Detail

Garceau, L., Henderson, J., Davis, L. J., Petrou, S., Henderson, L. R., McVeigh, E., et al. (2002). Economic implications of assisted reproductive techniques: A systematic review. *Human Reproduction, 17,* 3090–3109.

Garel, M., & Blondel, B. (1992). Assessment at 1 year of the psychological consequences of having triplets. *Human Reproduction, 7,* 729–732.

Garel, M., Stark, C., Blondel, B., Lefebvre, G., Vauthier-Brouzes, D., & Zorn, J. R. (1997). Psychological reactions after multifetal pregnancy reduction: A 2-year follow-up study. *Human Reproduction, 12,* 617–622.

Gates, G. J., & Ost, J. (2004). *Gay and lesbian atlas.* Washington, DC: Urban Institute Press.

Gestational Carrier Task Force, Mental Health Professional Group of the American Society for Reproductive Medicine. (2000). (Proposed) Psychological guidelines for evaluation and counseling of gestational carriers and intended parents. In S. N. Covington & L. H. Burns (Eds.), *Infertility counseling. A comprehensive handbook for clinicians* (2nd ed., pp. 574–578). New York, NY: Cambridge University Press.

Gilligan, C. (1993). *In a different voice: Psychological theory and women's development* (Reissued ed.). Cambridge, MA: Harvard University Press.

Glazebrook, C., Sheard, C., Cox, S., Oates, M., & Ndukwe, G. (2004). Parenting stress of first-time mothers of twins and triplets conceived after in vitro fertilization. *Fertility and Sterility, 81,* 505–511.

Glazer, E. S., & Sterling, E. W. (2005). *Having your baby through egg donation.* Indianapolis, IN: Perspectives Press.

Gleicher, N., & Barad, D. (2006). The relative myth of elective single embryo transfer. *Human Reproduction, 21,* 1337–1344.

Gleicher, N., Campbell, D. P., Chan, C. L., Karande, V., Rao, R., Balin, M., & Pratt, D. (1995). The desire for multiple births in couples with infertility problems contradicts present practice patterns. *Human Reproduction, 10,* 1079–1084.

Glinianaia, S. V., Rankin, J., & Wright, C. (2008). Congenital anomalies in twins: A register-based study. *Human Reproduction, 23,* 1306–1311.

Goffman, E. (1963). *Stigma: Notes on the management of spoiled identity.* Englewood Cliffs, NJ: Prentice-Hall.

Goldfarb, J. M. (2006). Solutions to the problem of multiple pregnancy with IVF [Letter to the editor]. *Fertility and Sterility, 86,* 773–774.

Goldfarb, J. M., Austin, C., Peskin, B., Lisbona, H., Desai, N., & Loret de Mola, J. R. (2000). Fifteen years experience with an in-vitro fertilization surrogate gestational pregnancy programme. *Human Reproduction, 15*, 1075–1078.

Goldstein, J., Freud, A., & Solnit, A. J. (1979). *Beyond the best interests of the child.* New York, NY: Collier Macmillan.

Goldstein, M. (2004, Summer). Beginning treatment: Evaluation and treatment of the infertile male. *InFocus: The American Fertility Association Quarterly Magazine,* 6–8.

Golombok, S., MacCallum, F., Goodman, E., & Rutter, M. (2002). Families with children conceived by donor insemination: A follow-up at age 12. *Child Development, 73,* 952–968.

Golombok, S., MacCallum, F., Murray, C., Lycett, E., & Jadva, V. (2006). Surrogacy families: Parental functioning, parent–child relationships and children's psychological development at age 2. *Journal of Child Psychology and Psychiatry, 47,* 213–222.

Golombok, S., Murray, C., Jadva, V., Lycett, E., MacCallum, F., & Rust, J. (2006). Non-genetic and non-gestational parenthood: Consequences for parent–child relationships and the psychological well-being of mothers, fathers and children at age 3. *Human Reproduction, 21,* 1918–1924.

Golombok, S., Olivennes, F., Ramogida, C., Rust, J., Freeman, T., & The Follow-Up Team. (2007). Parenting and the psychological development of a representative sample of triplets conceived by assisted reproduction. *Human Reproduction, 22,* 2896–2902.

Gould, I. (2004). Surrogacy: Is there a case for legal prohibition? *Journal of Medicine and Law, 12,* 205–216.

Grace, V. M., & Daniels, K. R. (2007). The (ir)relevance of genetics: Engendering parallel worlds of procreation and reproduction. *Sociology of Health and Illness, 29,* 1–19.

Grady, D. (2006, May 19). Sperm donor seen as source of disease in 5 children. *The New York Times,* p. A16.

Grazi, R. V., & Wolowelsky, J. B. (1992). Donor gametes for assisted reproduction in contemporary Jewish law and ethics. *Assisted Reproduction Reviews, 2,* 154–160.

Greenfeld, D. A., & Klock, S. C. (2004). Disclosure decisions among known and anonymous oocyte donation recipients. *Fertility and Sterility, 81,* 1565–1571.

Grisso, T., & Applebaum, P. S. (1998). *MacArthur Competence Assessment Tool for Treatment (MACCAT-T).* Sarasota, FL: Professional Resource Press.

Grobman, W. A., Milad, M. P., Stout, J., & Klock, S. C. (2001). Patient perceptions of multiple gestations: An assessment of knowledge and risk aversion. *American Journal of Obstetrics and Gynecology, 185,* 920–924.

Gurmankin, A. D. (2001). Risk information provided to prospective oocyte donors in a preliminary phone call. *American Journal of Bioethics, 1,* 3–13.

Gurmankin, A. D., Baron, J., Hershey, J. C., & Ubel, P. A. (2002). The role of physicians' recommendations in medical treatment decisions. *Medical Decision Making, 22*, 262–271.

Gurmankin, A. D., Caplan, A. C., & Braverman, A. M. (2005). Screening practices and beliefs of assisted reproductive technology programs. *Fertility and Sterility, 83*, 61–67.

Gurmankin, A. D., Sisti, D., & Caplan, A. L. (2004). Embryo disposal practices in IVF clinics in the United States. *Politics and the Life Sciences, 22*, 2–6.

Hahn, S. J., & Craft-Rosenberg, M. (2002). The disclosure decisions of parents who conceive children using donor eggs. *Journal of Obstetrical and Gynecological Neonatal Nursing, 31*, 283–293.

Hajal, F., & Rosenberg, E. G. (1991). The family life cycle in adopted families. *American Journal of Orthopsychiatry, 61*, 78–85.

Hammarberg, K., & Tinney, L. (2006). Deciding the fate of supernumerary frozen embryos. A survey of couples' decisions and the factors influencing their choice. *Fertility and Sterility, 86*, 86–91.

Hansen, M., Bower, C., Milne, E., de Klerk, N., & Kurinczuk, J. J. (2005). Assisted reproductive technologies and the risk of birth defects—A systematic review. *Human Reproduction, 20*, 328–338.

Hansen, M., Colvin, L., Petterson, B., Kurinczuk, J. J., de Klerk, N., & Bower, C. (2009). Twins born following assisted reproductive technology: Perinatal outcome and admission to hospital. *Human Reproduction, 24*, 2321–2331. doi:10.1093/humrep/dep173

Hart, V. A. (2002). Infertility and the role of psychotherapy. *Issues in Mental Health Nursing, 23*, 31–41.

Haskett, M. E., Smith Scott, S., Grant, R., Ward, C. S., & Robinson, C. (2003). Child-related cognitions and affective functioning of physically abusive and comparison parents. *Child Abuse and Neglect, 27*, 663–686.

Hathaway, S. R., & McKinley, J. C. (1989). *Minnesota Multiphasic Personality Inventory—2*. Minneapolis: University of Minnesota Press.

Hay, D. A., MacIndoe, R., & O'Brien, P. J. (1988). The older sibling of twins. *Australian Journal of Early Childhood, 13*, 25–28.

Heidenreich, A., Altmann, P., & Engelmann, U. H. (2000). Microsurgical vasovasostomy versus microsurgical epididymal sperm aspiration/testicular extraction of sperm combined with intracytoplasmic sperm injection. *European Urology, 37*, 609–614.

Helmerhorst, F. M., Perquin, D. A., Donker, D., & Keirse, M. J. (2004, January 31). Perinatal outcome of singletons and twins after assisted conception: A systematic review of controlled studies. *BMJ, 328*, 261. Retrieved from http://www.bmj.com/cgi/content/full/328/7434/261

Heng, B. C. (2006). Donation of surplus frozen embryos for stem cell research or fertility treatment—Should medical professionals and healthcare institutions be allowed to exercise undue influence on the informed decision of their former patients? *Journal of Assisted Reproduction and Genetics, 23*, 381–382.

Hernandez-Diaz, S., Werler, M. M., & Mitchell, A. A. (2007). Gestational hypertension in pregnancies supported by infertility treatments: Role of infertility, treatments, and multiple gestations. *Fertility and Sterility, 88*, 438–445.

Herslag, A., Schiff, S. F., & DeCherney, A. H. (1991). Retrograde ejaculation. *Human Reproduction, 6*, 255–258.

Hetherington, E. M., & Stanley-Hagan, M. (1999). The adjustment of children with divorced parents: A risk and resiliency perspective. *Journal of Child Psychology and Psychiatry, 40*, 129–140.

Hewitt, G. (2002). Missing links: Identity issues of donor conceived people. *British Journal of Fertility Counselling, 9*, 14–20.

Hinman, L. M. (n.d.). *Reproductive technology and surrogacy: An introduction to the issues.* Retrieved from http://ethics.sandiego.edu/Applied/Bioethics/index.asp

Hodapp, R. M., & Krasner, D. V. (1995). Families of children with disabilities: Findings from a national sample of eighth-grade students. *Exceptionality, 5*, 71–81.

Hoffman, D. I., Zellman, G. L., Fair, C. C., Mayer, J. F., Zeitz, J. G., Gibbons, W. E., & Turner, T. G. (2003). Cryopreserved embryos in the United States and their availability for research. *Fertility and Sterility, 79*, 1063–1069.

Hohman, M. M., & Hagan, C. B. (2001). Satisfaction with surrogate mothering: A relational model. *Journal of Human Behavior in the Social Environment, 4*, 61–84.

Hojgaard, A., Ottosen, L. D. M., Kesmodel, U., & Ingerslev, H. J. (2007). Patient attitudes towards twin pregnancies and single embryo transfer—A questionnaire study. *Human Reproduction, 22*, 2673–2678.

Holm, S. (2007). The decision-making role of fathers in assisted reproduction. *Reproductive Biomedicine Online, 14*(Suppl.1), 81–85. Retrieved from http://www.rbmonline.com/4DCGI/Issue/Detail

Homans, G. (1961). *Social behavior.* New York, NY: Harcourt, Brace & World.

Hoopes, J. L. (1990). Adoption and identity formation. In D. M. Brodzinsky & M. D. Schechter (Eds.), *The psychology of adoption* (pp. 144–166). Oxford, England: Oxford University Press.

Hope, T., Lockwood, G., & Lockwood, M. (1995, June 3). An ethical debate: Should older women be offered in vitro fertilisation? The interests of the potential child. *BMJ, 310*, 1455–1456.

Horowitz, J. E. (1996). *Explaining gestational surrogacy to children.* Unpublished manuscript.

Hovav, Y., Almagor, M., & Yaffe, H. (2002). Comparison of semen quality obtained by electroejaculation and spontaneous ejaculation in men suffering from ejaculation disorder. *Human Reproduction, 17*, 3170–3172.

Huang, C.-T., Au, H.-K., Chien, L.-W., Chang, C.-W., Chien, Y.-Y., & Tzeng, C.-R. (2006). Twin pregnancy outcome among cases of spontaneous conception, intrauterine insemination, and in vitro fertilization/intracytoplasmic sperm injection. *Fertility and Sterility, 86,* 1017–1019.

Human Fertilisation and Embryology Authority. (2006). *Donating eggs for research: Safeguarding donors.* Retrieved from www.hfea.gov.uk/consultations

Human Fertilisation and Embryology Authority Register Counselling Project Steering Group (2003). *Opening the record: Planning the provision of counseling to people applying for information from the HFEA Register.* Retrieved from http://www.bica.net/files/opening_the_record_0.pdf

Hvidtjorn, D., Grove, J., Schendel, D. E., Vaeth, M., Ernst, E., Nielsen, L. F., & Thorsen, P. (2006). Cerebral palsy among children born after in vitro fertilization: The role of preterm delivery-a population-based, cohort study. *Pediatrics, 118,* 475–482.

Ind. Code Ann. § 16-41-14-5 (2007).

Inhorn, M. C., & Patrizio, P. (2009). Rethinking reproductive "tourism" as reproductive exile. *Fertility & Sterility, 92,* 904–906.

In re Baby M., 537 A.2d 1227 (N.J. 1988).

In re Parentage of J.M.K., 119 P.3d 840 (Wash. 2005).

International Committee for Monitoring Assisted Reproductive Technology. (2006). World collaborative report on in vitro fertilization, 2000. *Fertility and Sterility, 85,* 1586–1622.

In the Interest of H.C.S., 219 S.W.3d 33 (Tex. App. 2006).

In the Interest of K.M.H., 169 P.3d 1025 (Kan. 2007).

Jacob, M. C., Klock, S. C., & Maier, D. (1999). Lesbian couples as therapeutic donor insemination recipients: Do they differ from other patients? *Journal of Psychosomatic Obstetrics and Gynecology, 20,* 203–215.

Jadva, V., Freeman, T., Golombok, S., & Kramer, W. (2007, October). *Searching for donor relationships: The experiences of donor conception offspring, parents, and donors.* Abstract presented at the annual meeting of the American Society for Reproductive Medicine, Washington, DC.

Jadva, V., Freeman, T., Kramer, W., & Golombok, S. (2009). The experiences of adolescents and adults conceived by sperm donation: Comparisons by age of disclosure and family type. *Human Reproduction, 24,* 1909–1919. doi: 10.1093/humanrep/dep110

Jadva, V., Murray, C., Lycett, E., MacCallum, F., & Golombok, S. (2003). Surrogacy: The experiences of surrogate mothers. *Human Reproduction, 18,* 2196–2204.

Jain, A., Lin, J. P., Robins, J. C., Williams, D. B., Eckert, J., & Thomas, M. A. (2005). The effect of multiple cycles in oocyte donors [Abstract]. *Fertility and Sterility, 84*(Suppl. 1), S171.

Jain, T., Harlow, B. L., & Hornstein, M. D. (2002). Insurance coverage and outcomes of in vitro fertilization. *New England Journal of Medicine, 347,* 661–666.

Jain, T., & Missmer, S. A. (2008). Support for embryonic stem cell research among infertility patients. *Fertility and Sterility, 90,* 506–512.

Janssens, P. M. W., Simons, A. H. M., van Kooij, R. J., Blokzijl, E., & Dunselman, G. A. J. (2006). A new Dutch law regulating provision of identifying information of donors to offspring: Background, content and impact. *Human Reproduction, 21*, 852–856.

Jimenez, D. (2005, February 2). Sperm donation harder than you think. *Golden Gate [E]Press.* Retrieved from http://xpress.sfsu.edu/archives/life/002639.html

Johnson, M. H. (1999). The medical ethics of paid egg sharing in the U.K.: Opinion. *Human Reproduction, 14*, 1912–1918.

Johnson v. Calvert, 851 P.2d 776 (Cal. 1993).

Johnson v. Superior Court, 80 Cal. App. 4th 1050, (2d Dist. 2000).

Johnston, J. (2002). Mum's the word: Donor anonymity in assisted reproduction. *Health Law Review, 11*, 51–55. Retrieved from http://www.noveltechethics/ca/pictures/File/publications/2002/Johnston_Mums_word_2002.pdf

Jones, H. W., Jr., Cohen, J., Cooke, I., & Kempers, R. (2007). IFFS Surveillance 07. *Fertility and Sterility, 87*(Suppl. 1), S1–S67.

Jones, H. W., Jr., & Veeck, L. (2002). What is an embryo? *Fertility and Sterility, 77*, 658–659.

Jordan, C. B., Belar, C. D., & Williams, R. S. (2004). Anonymous oocyte donation: A follow-up of donors' experiences. *Journal of Psychosomatics Obstetrics and Gynaecology, 25*, 145–151.

Jouriles, E. N., Barling, J., & O'Leary, K. D. (1987). Predicting child behavior problems in maritally violent families. *Journal of Abnormal Child Psychology, 15*, 165–173.

Jun, S. H., Racowski, C., Fox, J. H., & Hornstein, M. P. (2001). The role of preparatory cycles in ovum recipients: A retrospective study [Abstract]. *Fertility and Sterility, 76*(Suppl. 3), S252.

Kahn, R. S., Brandt, D., & Whitaker, R. C. (2004). Combined effect of mothers' and fathers' mental health symptoms on children's behavioral and emotional well-being. *Archives of Pediatric and Adolescent Medicine, 158*, 721–729.

Kalfoglou, A. L. (2001). Navigating conflict of interest in oocyte donation. *American Journal of Bioethics, 1*, 1–2.

Kalfoglou, A. L., & Geller, G. (2000). A follow-up study with oocyte donors exploring their experiences, knowledge, and attitudes about the use of the oocytes and the outcome of the donation. *Fertility and Sterility, 74*, 660–667.

Kalfoglou, A. L., & Gittelsohn, J. A. (2000). A qualitative follow-up study of women's experiences with oocyte donation. *Human Reproduction, 15*, 798–805.

Kanhai, H. H., deHaan, M. J., van Zanten, L. A., Geerinck-Vercammen, C., van der Ploeg, H. M., & Gravenhorst, J. B. (1994). Follow-up of pregnancies, infants, and families after multifetal pregnancy reduction. *Fertility and Sterility, 62*, 955–959.

Kant, I. (1981). *Grounding for the metaphysics of morals.* J. W. Ellington (Trans.). Indianapolis, IN: Hacket. (Original work published 1785)

Karpel, L., Flis-Treves, M., Blanchet, V., Olivennes, F., & Frydman, R. (2005). Oocyte donation Parent's secrets and lies. *Journal of Gynecology, Obstetrics, and Biological Reproduction, 34*, 557–567.

Karpel, M. (1980). Family secrets. *Family Process, 19*, 295–306.

Kass v. Kass, 673 N.Y.S. 2d 350 (1998).

Kaufman, J., & Zigler, E. (1987). Do abused children become abusive parents? *American Journal of Orthopsychiatry, 57*, 186–192.

Keller, H. (2007). *Optimism.* Stilwell, KS: Digireads.com. (Original work published 1903)

Kendler, K. S., Karkowski, L. M., Corey, L. A., Prescott, C. A., & Neale, M. C. (1999). Genetic and environmental risk factors in the aetiology of drug initiation and subsequent misuse in women. *British Journal of Psychiatry, 175*, 351–358.

Kendler, K. S., Pedersen, N. L., Neale, M. C., & Mathé, A. A. (1995). A pilot Swedish twin study of affective illness including hospital- and population-ascertained subsamples: Results of model fitting. *Behavioral Genetics, 25*, 217–232.

Kendler, K. S., & Prescott, C. A. (1999). A population-based twin study of lifetime major depression in men and women. *Archives of General Psychiatry, 5*, 39–44.

Kennedy, R. (2005). Risks and complications of assisted conception. *British Fertility Society Fact Sheet.* Retrieved from http://www.britishfertilitysociety.org.UK/public/factsheets/conceptionrisks.html

Kennedy, R. F. (1974). *Times to remember: An autobiography.* New York, NY: Doubleday.

Kidd, S. A., Eskenazia, B., & Wyrobek, A. J. (2001). Effects of male age on semen quality and fertility: A review of the literature. *Fertility and Sterility, 75*, 237–238.

Kiely, J. L., & Kiely, M. (2001). Epidemiologic trends in multiple births in the United States, 1971–1998. *Twin Research, 4*, 131–133.

Kim, S. S. (2006). Fertility preservation in female cancer patients: Current developments and future directions. *Fertility and Sterility, 85*, 1–11.

Kingsberg, S. A., Applegarth, L. D., & Janata, J. (2000). Embryo donation programs and policies in North America: Survey results and implications for health and mental health professionals. *Fertility and Sterility, 73*, 215–220.

Kirkman, M. (2004). Genetic connection and relationships in narratives of donor-assisted conception. *Australian Journal of Emerging Technologies and Society, 2*, 1–20.

Kirshbaum, M., & Olkin, R. (2002). Parents with physical, systemic or visual disabilities. *Sexuality and Disability, 20*, 65–80.

Klass, D., Silverman, P. R., & Nickman, S. L. (1996). *Continuing bonds: New understandings of grief.* Washington, DC: Taylor & Francis.

Kleck, R. (1968). Physical stigma and nonverbal cues emitted in face-to-face interaction. *Human Relations, 21*, 19–28.

Klein, J., & Sauer, M. V. (2002). Oocyte donation: Best practice and research. *Clinical Obstetrics and Gynecology, 16*, 277–283.

Kliman, H. J., Copperman, A. B., Honig, S., Walls, D., & McSweet, J. C. (2005). Optimization of endometrial preparation results in a Normal Endometrial Function Test® (EFT®) and good reproductive outcome in donor ovum recipients. *Fertility and Sterility, 84*(Suppl. 1), S271–S272.

Klipstein, S. (2005). Preimplantation genetic diagnosis: Technological promise and ethical perils. *Fertility and Sterility, 83*, 1347–1353.

Klock, S. C. (1997). The controversy surrounding privacy or disclosure among donor gamete recipients. *Journal of Assisted Reproduction and Genetics, 14*, 378–380.

Klock, S. C., Braverman, A. M., & Rausch, D. T. (1998). Predicting anonymous egg donor satisfaction: A preliminary study. *Journal of Women's Health, 7*, 229–237.

Klock, S. C., & Greenfeld, D. A. (2004). Parents' knowledge about the donors and their attitudes toward disclosure in oocyte donation. *Human Reproduction, 19*, 1575–1579.

Klock, S. C, Jacob, M. C., & Maier, D. (1996). A comparison of single and married recipients of donor insemination. *Human Reproduction, 11*, 2554–2557.

Klock, S. C., & Maier, D. (1991). Psychological factors related to donor insemination. *Fertility and Sterility, 56*, 489–495.

Klock, S. C., Sheinin, S., & Kazer, R. R. (2001a). Couples' attitudes regarding embryo disposition after in vitro fertilization (IVF). *Fertility and Sterility, 76*(Suppl. 1), S25.

Klock, S. C., Sheinin, S., & Kazer, R. R. (2001b). The disposition of unused frozen embryos. *New England Journal of Medicine, 345*, 69–70.

Klock, S. C., Stout, J. E., & Davidson, M. (2002). Post-donation psychological status of anonymous ooctye donors. *Fertility and Sterility, 78*(Suppl. 1), S29.

Knoppers, B. M., & LeBris, S. (1991). Recent advances in medically assisted conception: Legal, ethical, and social issues. *American Journal of Law and Medicine, 17*, 329–361.

Kolettis, P. N. (2002). The evaluation and management of the azoospermic patient. *Journal of Andrology, 23*, 293–305.

Kübler-Ross, E. (1970). *On death and dying.* New York, NY: Simon & Schuster.

Kuller, J. A., Meyer, W. R., Traynor, K. D., & Hartmann, K. E. (2001). Disposition of sperm donors with resultant abnormal pregnancies. *Human Reproduction, 16*, 1553–1555.

Kump, L., Licciardi, F., Krey, L., Noyes, N., Grifo, J., & Berkeley, A. S. (2003). An oocyte donor's willingness to donate—Does the recipient's lifestyle make a difference? *Fertility and Sterility, 80*(Suppl. 3), S140.

Lalos, A., Daniels, K., Gottlieb, C., & Lalos, O. (2003). Recruitment and motivation of semen providers in Sweden. *Human Reproduction, 18*, 212–216.

Lalos, A., Lalos, O., Jacobsson, L., & von Shoultz, B. (1986). Depression, guilt, and isolation among infertile women and their partners. *Journal of Psychosomatic Obstetrics and Gynaecology, 5*, 197–206.

Langeveld, N. E., Grootenhuis, M. A., Voute, P. A., de Haan, R. J., & van den Bos, C. (2004). Quality of life, self-esteem and worries in young adult survivors of childhood cancer. *Psychooncology, 13*, 867–881.

Lansac, J., Thepot, F., Mayaux, M. J., Czyglick, F., Wack, T., Selva, J., & Jalbert, P. (1997). Pregnancy outcome after artificial insemination or IVF with frozen semen donor: A collaborative study of the French CECOS federation on 21,597 pregnancies. *European Journal of Obstetrics and Gynecology and Reproductive Biology, 74*, 223–228.

Larsen, W. J. (1997). *Human embryology* (2nd ed.). New York, NY: Churchill Livingstone.

Laruelle, C., & Englert, Y. (1995). Psychological study of in vitro fertilization-embryo transfer participants' attitudes toward the destiny of their supernumerary embryos. *Fertility and Sterility, 63*, 1047–1050.

Lazarus, R. S., & Folkman, S. (1984). *Stress, appraisal, and coping*. New York, NY: Springer Publishing Company.

Lee, F. R. (2005, January 25). Driven by costs, fertility clients head overseas. *The New York Times*. Retrieved from http://www.nytimes.com/2005/01/25/national/25fertility.html

Lee, K. L., Couchman, G. M., & Walmer, D. K. (2005). Successful pregnancies with estrogenic annovulation after low-dose human chorionic gonadotropin therapy alone following hMG for controlled hyperstimulation. *Journal of Assisted Reproduction and Genetics, 22*, 37–40.

Leeb-Lundberg, S., Kjellberg, S., & Sydsjo, G. (2006). Helping parents to tell their children about the use of donor insemination (DI) and determining their opinions about open-identity sperm donors. *Acta Obstetrica et Gynecologica Scandinavica, 85*, 78–81.

Leiblum, S. R., Palmer, M. G., & Spector, I. P (1995). Non-traditional mother: Single heterosexual, lesbian women and lesbian couples electing motherhood via donor insemination. *Journal of Psychosomatic Obstetrics and Gynaecology, 4*, 321–328.

Leiblum, S. R., & Williams, E. (1993). Screening in or out of the new reproductive options: Who decides and why. *Journal of Psychosomatic Obstetrics and Gynaecology, 14*, 37–44.

Leith, K. P., & Baumeister, R. F. (1996). Why do bad moods increase self-defeating behavior? Emotion, risk taking, and self-regulation. *Journal of Personality and Social Psychology, 71*, 1250–1267.

Leondires, M. P., Ernst, S. D., Miller, B. T., & Scott, R. T., Jr. (2000). Triplets: Outcomes of expectant management versus multifetal reduction for 127 pregnancies. *American Journal of Obstetrics and Gynecology, 183*, 454–459.

Lessor, R., Reitz, K., Malmaceda, J., & Asch, R. (1990). A survey of public attitudes toward oocyte donation between sisters. *Human Reproduction, 5*, 889–892.

Levy, F., Hay, D., McLaughlin, M., Wood, C., & Waldman, I. (1996). Twin sibling differences in parental reports of ADHD, speech, reading and behaviour problems. *Journal of Child Psychology and Psychiatry, 37*, 569–578.

Lewis, S., & Roberts, A. R. (2001). Crisis assessment tools: The good, the bad, and the available. *Brief Treatment and Crisis Intervention, 1*, 17–28.

Lindblad, F., Gottlieb, C., & Lalos, O. (2000). To tell or not to tell—What parents think about telling their children that they were born following donor insemination. *Journal of Psychosomatic Obstetrics and Gynaecology, 21*, 193–203.

Lindemann, E. (1963). Symptomology and management of acute grief. *Pastoral Psychology, 14*, 8–18.

Lindheim, S. R., Chase, J., & Sauer, M. V. (2001). Assessing the influence of payment on motivations of women participating as oocyte donors. *Gynecology and Obstetric Investigation, 52*, 89–92.

Lipitz, S., Uval, J., Achiron, R., Schiff, E., Lusky, A., & Reichman, B. (1996). Outcome of twin pregnancies reduced from triplets compared with nonreduced twin gestations. *Obstetrics and Gynecology, 87*, 511–514.

Lo, B., Chou, V., Cedars, M. I., Gates, E., Taylor, R. N., Wagner, R. M., et al. (2004). Informed consent in human oocyte, embryo, and embryonic stem cell research. *Fertility and Sterility, 82*, 559–563.

Lopez Teijon, M., Serra, O., Olivares, R., Moragas, M., Castello, C., & Alvarez, J. G. (2006). Delivery of a healthy baby following the transfer of embryos cryopreserved for 13 years. *Reproductive Biomedicine Online, 13*, 821–822. Retrieved from http://www.rbmonline.com/4DCGI/Issue/Detail

Lornage, J., Chorier, H., Boulien, D., Mathieu, C., & Czyba, J. C. (1995). Six year follow-up of cryopreserved human embryos. *Human Reproduction, 10*, 2610–2616.

Ludwig, A. K., Sutcliffe, A. G., Diedrich, K., & Ludwig, M. (2006). Post-neonatal health and development of children born after assisted reproduction: A systematic review of controlled studies. *European Journal of Obstetrics and Gynaecology and Reproductive Biology, 127*, 3–25.

Lui, S. C., Weaver, S. C., Robinson, J., Debono, M., Neiland, M., Killick, S. R., & Hay, D. M. (1995). A survey of semen donors' attitudes. *Human Reproduction, 10*, 234–238.

Luk, J., & Petrozza, J. (2006). Evaluation of compliance and range of fees by ASRM listed egg donor and surrogacy agencies [Abstract]. *Fertility and Sterility, 86*(Suppl. 3), S190.

Lukassen, H. G., Braat, D. D., Wetzels, A. M., Zielhuis, G. A., Adang, E. M., Scheenjes, E., & Kremer, J. A. M. (2005). Two cycles with single embryo transfer versus one cycle with double embryo transfer: A randomized controlled trial. *Human Reproduction, 20*, 702–708.

Luke, B., & Brown, M. B. (2008). Maternal morbidity and infant death in twin vs. triplet and quadruplet pregnancies. *American Journal of Obstetrics and Gynecology, 198*, 401–411.

Luke, B., Brown, M. B., Grainger, D. A., Stern, J. E., Klein, N., & Cedars, M. I. (2009a). The effect of early fetal losses on singleton assisted-conception pregnancy outcomes. *Fertility and Sterility, 91*, 2578–2585.

Luke, B., Brown, M. B., Grainger, D. A., Stern, J. E., Klein, N., & Cedars, M. I. (2009b). The effect of early fetal losses on twin assisted-conception pregnancy outcomes. *Fertility and Sterility, 91*, 2586–2592.

Luke, B., Brown, M. B., Hediger, M. L., Misiunas, R. B., & Anderson, E. (2006). Perinatal and early childhood outcomes of twins versus triplets. *Twin Research and Human Genetics, 9*, 81–88.

Luke, B., Brown, M. B., Nugent, C., Gonzalez-Quintero, V. H., Witter, F. R., & Newman, R. B. (2004). Risk factors for adverse outcomes in spontaneous versus assisted conception twin pregnancies. *Fertility and Sterility, 81*, 315–319.

Luke, B., & Keith, L. G. (1992). The contribution of singletons, twins and triplets to low birth weight, infant mortality and handicap in the United States. *Journal of Reproductive Medicine, 37*, 661–666.

Lutchman Singh, K., Davies, M., & Cahtterjee, R. (2005). Fertility in female cancer survivors: Pathophysiology, preservation and the role of ovarian reserve testing. *Human Reproduction Update, 11*, 69–89.

Lutjen, P., Trouson, A., Leeton, J., Findlay, J., Wood, C., & Renou, P. (1984). The establishment and maintenance of pregnancy using in vitro fertilization and embryo donation in a patient with ovarian failure. *Nature, 207*, 174–176.

Lyall, E. G., Blott, M., de Ruiter, A., Hawkins, D., Mercy, D., Mitchla, Z., et al. (2001). Guidelines for the management of HIV infection in pregnant women and the prevention of mother-to-child transmission. *HIV Medicine, 2*, 314–333.

Lycett, E., Daniels, K., Curson, R., & Golombok, S. (2004). Offspring created as a result of donor insemination: A study of family relationships, child adjustment, and disclosure. *Fertility and Sterility, 82*, 172–179.

Lycett, E., Daniels, K., Curson, R., & Golombok, S. (2005). School-aged children of donor insemination: A study of parents' disclosure patterns. *Human Reproduction, 20*, 810–819.

Lyerly, A. D., Steinhauser, K., Namey, E., Tulsky, J. A., Cook-Deegan, R., Sugarman, J., et al. (2006). Factors that affect infertility patients' decisions about disposition of frozen embryos. *Fertility and Sterility, 85*, 1623–1630.

Lyerly, A. D., Steinhauser, K., Voils, C., Namey, E., Alexander, C., Bankowski, B., et al. (2008). Fertility patients' views about frozen embryo disposition: Results of a multi-institutional U.S. survey. *Fertility and Sterility.* Retrieved from http://www.fertstert.org/article/S0015-0282(08)04204-0/abstract

MacCallum, F. (2009). Embryo donation parents' attitudes towards donors: Comparison with adoption. *Human Reproduction, 24*, 517–523.

MacCallum, F., & Golombok, S. (2004). Children raised in fatherless families from infancy: A follow-up of children of lesbian and single heterosexual mothers at early adolescence. *Journal of Child Psychology and Psychiatry, 45*, 1407–1419.

MacCallum, F., Golombok, S., & Brinsden, P. (2007). Parenting and child development in families with a child conceived through embryo donation. *Journal of Family Psychology, 21*, 278–287.

MacCallum, F., Lycett, E., Murray, C., Jadva, V., & Golombok, S. (2003). Surrogacy: The experience of commissioning couples. *Human Reproduction, 18,* 1334–1342.

MacDougall, K., Becker, G., Scheib, J. E., & Nachtigall, R. D. (2007). Strategies for disclosure: How parents approach telling their children that they were conceived with donor gametes. *Fertility and Sterility, 87,* 524–533.

Machtinger, R., Dor, J., Levron, J., Mashiach, S., Levran, D., & Seidman, D. S. (2002). The effect of prolonged cryopreservation on embryo survival. *Gynecological Embryology, 16,* 293–298.

Mackay, A. P., Berg, C. J., King, J. C., Duran, C., & Chang, T. (2006). Pregnancy-related mortality among women with multifetal pregnancies. *Obstetrics and Gynecology, 107,* 563–568.

Macklin, R. (1996). What is wrong with commodification? In C. B. Cohen (Ed.), *New ways of making babies* (pp. 106–120). Bloomington: Indiana University Press.

Mady, T. M. (1981). Surrogate mothers: The legal issues. *American Journal of Law and Medicine, 7,* 323–352.

Magesterium of the Catholic Church. (1987, February 22). *Instruction on the respect for human life in its origin and on the dignity of procreation: Replies to certain questions of the day.* Retrieved from http://www.catholic.com/library/

Maheshwari, A., Porter, M., Shetty, A., & Bhattacharya, S. (2008). Women's awareness and perceptions of delay in childbearing. *Fertility and Sterility, 19,* 1036–1042.

Mahlstedt, P. P., LaBounty, K., & Kennedy, W. T. (2008, November). *The voices of adult offspring of sperm donation: Forces for change within assisted reproductive technology in the United States.* Poster session presented at the annual meeting of the American Society for Reproductive Medicine, San Francisco, CA.

Mahlstedt, P. P., & Probasco, K. A. (1991). Sperm donors: Their attitudes toward providing medical and psychosocial information for recipient couples and donor offspring. *Fertility and Sterility, 56,* 747–753.

Malinosky-Rummel, R., & Hansen, D. J. (1993). Long-term consequences of childhood physical abuse. *Psychological Bulletin, 114,* 68–79.

Mandelbrot, L., Heard, I., Henrion-Geant, E., & Henrion, R. (1997, May 10). Natural conception in HIV-negative women with HIV-infected partners. *The Lancet, 349,* 850–851.

Mansour, R. T., Kamal, A., Fahmy, I., Tawab, N., Serour, G. I., & Aboulghar, M. A. (1997). Intracytoplasmic sperm injection in obstructive and non-obstructive azoospermia. *Human Reproduction, 12,* 1974–1979.

Marshall, L. A. (2002). Ethical and legal issues in the use of related donors for therapeutic insemination. *Urologic Clinics of North America, 29,* 855–861.

Martin, J. A., & Park, M. M. (1999). Trends in twin and triplet births: 1980–1997. *National Vital Statistics Reports, 47,* 1–17. Retrieved from http://www.multiplebirth.com/nvs47_24.pdf

Martin, P. M., & Welch, H. G. (1998). Probabilities for singleton and multiple pregnancies after in vitro fertilization. *Fertility and Sterility, 70,* 478–481.

Martins, W. P., Ferriani, R. A., Nastri, C. O., dos Reis, R. M., & Filho, F. M. (2008). Measurement of endometrial volume increase during the first week after embryo transfer by three-dimensional ultrasound to detect pregnancy: A preliminary study. *Fertility and Sterility, 90,* 883–885.

Maun, A. R., Williams, R. S., Graber, B., & Myers, W. G. (1994). The passage of Florida's statute on assisted reproductive technology. *Obstetrics and Gynecology, 85,* 480–481.

Maxwell, K. N., Cholst, I. N., & Rosenwaks, Z. (2008). The incidence of both serious and minor complications in young women undergoing oocyte donation. *Fertility and Sterility, 90,* 2165–2171.

Mayhorn, C. B., Fisk, A. D., & Whittle, J. D. (2002). Decisions, decisions: Analysis of age, cohort, and time of testing on framing of risky decision options. *Human Factors, 44,* 515–521.

McCord, J. (1983). A forty year perspective on the effects of child abuse and neglect. *Child Abuse and Neglect, 7,* 265–270.

McElroy, S. L. (2004). Bipolar disorders: Special diagnostic and treatment considerations in women. *CNS Spectrum, 9,* 5–18.

McGee, G. (2000). *The perfect baby: Parenthood in the new world of cloning and genetics* (2nd ed.). Lanham, MD: Rowman & Littlefield.

McKinney, M., Downey, J., & Timor-Tritsch, I. (1995). The psychological effects of multifetal pregnancy reduction. *Fertility and Sterility, 64,* 51–61.

McKinney, M. K., Tuber, S. B., & Downey, J. I. (1996). Multifetal pregnancy reduction: Psychodynamic implications. *Psychiatry, 59,* 393–407.

McLachlan, H. V., & Swales, J. K. (2000). Babies, child bearers and commodification: Anderson, Bazier, et al., and the political economy of commercial surrogate motherhood. *Health Care Analysis, 8,* 1–18.

McMahon, C. A., Gibson, F., Cohen, J., Tennant, L. G., & Saunders, D. (2000). Mothers conceiving through in vitro fertilization: Siblings, setbacks, and embryo dilemmas. *Reproductive Technology, 10,* 131–135.

McMahon, C. A., Gibson, F. L., Leslie, G. I., Saunders, D. M., Porter, K. A., & Tennant, C. C. (2003). Embryo donation for medical research: Attitudes and concerns of potential donors. *Human Reproduction, 18,* 871–877.

McMahon, C. A., & Saunders, D. M. (2009). Attitudes of couples with stored frozen embryos toward conditional embryo donation. *Fertility and Sterility, 91,* 140–147.

McWhinnie, A. (1995). A study of parenting of IVF and DI children. *Medicine and Law, 14,* 501–508.

McWhinnie, A. (2001). Gamete donation and anonymity: Should offspring from donated gametes continue to be denied knowledge of their origins and antecedents? *Human Reproduction, 16,* 807–817.

McWhinnie, A. (2006). *Who am I? Experiences of donor conception.* London, England: Idreos Education Trust.

Meacham, R. B. (2005). Strategies for enhancing sperm survival in specimens obtained from patients with retrograde ejaculation. *Journal of Andrology, 26*, 174–175.

Meilaender, G. (1998). *The drive to have a child like me.* Retrieved from http://www.bioethix.net/resources/reproductive/meilaender_1998-10-09.htm

Melton, G. B., & Flood, M. F. (1994). Research policy and child maltreatment: Developing the scientific foundation for effective protection of children. *Child Abuse and Neglect, 18*, 1–28.

Mendes-Pereira, D. H., Cavalcante, E., Catafesta, L., Shimabukuro, L., Cury, M. C., & Cavagna, M. (2005). Oocyte donation does not influence adversely the outcome of assisted reproductive technologies [Abstract]. *Fertility and Sterility, 84*(Suppl. 1), S244.

Meniru, G. I., & Craft, I. L. (1997). Experience with gestational surrogacy as a treatment for sterility resulting from hysterectomy. *Human Reproduction, 12*, 51–54.

Meseguer, M., Molina, N., Garcia-Velasco, J. A., Remohi, J., Pellicer, A., & Garrido, N. (2006). Sperm cryopreservation in oncological patients: A 14-year follow-up study. *Fertility and Sterility, 85*, 640–645.

Meyer v. Nebraska, 262 U.S. 390 (U.S. 1923).

Miall, C. (1985). Perceptions of informal sanctioning and the stigma of involuntary childlessness. *Deviant Behavior, 6*, 383–403.

Miall, C. (1986). The stigma of involuntary childlessness. *Social Problems, 33*, 268–282.

Miall, C. (1989). Reproductive technology versus the stigma of involuntary childlessness. *Social Casework, 70*, 43–50.

Miall, C. (1994). Community constructs of involuntary childlessness: Sympathy, stigma, and social support. *Canadian Review of Sociology and Anthropology, 31*, 392–421.

Miller, K. (2005). *Communication theories.* New York, NY: McGraw Hill.

Miller, R. B., Anderson, S., & Keala, D. K. (2004). Is Bowen theory valid? A review of basic research. *Journal of Marital and Family Therapy, 30*, 453–466.

Minai, J., Suzuki, K., Takeda, Y., Hoshi, K., & Yamagata, Z. (2007). There are gender differences in attitudes toward surrogacy when information on this technique is provided. *European Journal of Obstetrics, Gynecology, & Reproductive Biology, 132*, 193–199. Abstract retrieved from http://www.ncbi.nlm.nih.gov/pubmed/17046144

Minkovitz, C. S., Strobino, D., Scharfstein, D., Hou, W., Miller, T., Mistry, K. B., & Swartz, K. (2005). Maternal depressive symptoms and children's receipt of healthcare in the first 3 years of life. *Pediatrics, 115*, 306–314.

Mlynarcikova, A., Fickova, M., & Scsukova, S. (2005). Ovarian intrafollicular processes as a target for cigarette smoke components and selected environmental reproductive disruptors. *Endocrine Regulations, 39*, 21–32.

Moore, J. (1984). The evolution of reciprocal sharing. *Ethnology and Sociobiology, 5*, 5–14.

Morley, W. E. (1965). Treatment of the patient in crisis. *Western Medicine: The Medical Journal of the West, 6*, 77–87.

Morrissette, M. (Ed.). (2006). *Voices of donor conception: Vol. 1. Behind closed doors: Moving beyond secrecy and shame*. Minneapolis, MN: Be-Mondo Publishing.

Morton, A. P. (2005). A case for altruistic surrogacy. *Medical Journal of Australia, 183*, 162–163.

Muasher, S. J., Abdallah, R. T., & Hubayter, Z. R. (2006). Optimal stimulation protocols for in vitro fertilization. *Fertility and Sterility, 86*, 267–273.

Mullick, M., Miller, L. J., & Jacobsen, T. (2001). Insight into mental illness and child maltreatment risk among mothers with major psychiatric disorders. *Psychiatric Services, 52*, 488–492.

Murray, C., & Golombok, S. (2005a). Going it alone: Solo mothers and their infants conceived by donor insemination. *American Journal of Orthopsychiatry, 75*, 242–253.

Murray, C., & Golombok, S. (2005b). Solo mothers and their donor insemination infants: Follow-up at age 2 years. *Human Reproduction, 20*, 1655–1660.

Murray, C., MacCallum, F., & Golombok, S. (2006). Egg donation parents and their children: Follow-up at age 12 years. *Fertility and Sterility, 85*, 610–618.

Nachtigall, R. D. (1993). Secrecy: An unresolved issue in the practice of donor insemination. *American Journal of Obstetrics and Gynecology, 168*, 1846–1851.

Nachtigall, R. D., Becker, G., Friese, C., Butler, A., & MacDougall, K. (2005). Parents' conceptualization of their frozen embryos complicates the disposition decision. *Fertility and Sterility, 84*(2), 431–434.

Nachtigall, R. D., Becker, G., & Wozny, M. (1992). The effects of gender specific diagnosis on men's and women's response to infertility. *Fertility and Sterility, 57*, 113–121.

Nachtigall, R. D., Tschann, J. M., Quiroga, S. S., Pitcher, L., & Becker, G. (1997). Stigma, disclosure, and family functioning among parents of children conceived through donor insemination. *Fertility and Sterility, 68*, 83–89.

National Academies, Institute of Medicine. (2007, February 6). *Assessing the medical risks of human oocyte donation for stem cell research*. Retrieved from http://www.iom.edu/cms/3740/36353.aspx

National Academy of Sciences, Committee on Guidelines for Human Embryonic Stem Cell Research, National Research Council. (2005). *Guidelines for human embryonic stem cell research* [Executive summary]. Retrieved from http://www.nap.edu/catalog.php?record_id=11278

National Advisory Board on Ethics in Reproduction. (1996). Ethical and policy issues related to oocyte donors in clinical settings. In C. B. Cohen (Ed.), *New ways of making babies* (pp. 270–292). Bloomington: Indiana University Press.

National Institute of Mental Health. (1998). *Genetics and mental disorders: Report of the National Institute of Mental Health's genetics workgroup*. (NIH Publication No. 98-4268). Rockville, MD: Author.

National Institutes of Health. (1994). *Report of the human embryo research panel.* Retrieved from http://www.nih.gov/science/library.html

National Research Council. (1993). *Understanding child abuse and neglect.* Washington, DC: National Academy Press.

Newton, C., Feyles, V., Tekpetey, F., & Power, S. (2007, July). The influence of mood, infertility stress and risk taking behavior on patient decisions about embryo transfer [O-163, Abstract]. *Abstracts of the Annual Meeting of the ESHRE,* Lyon, France. Abstract retrieved from http://humrep.oxfordjournals.org/cgi/reprint/22/suppl_1/i64

Newton, C. R., Fisher, J., Feyles, V., Tekpetey, F., Hughes, L., & Isacsson, D. (2007). Changes in patient preferences in the disposal of cryopreserved embryos. *Human Reproduction, 22,* 3124–3128.

Newton, C. R., McDermid, A., Tekpetey, F., & Tummon, I. S. (2003). Embryo donation: Attitudes toward donation procedures and factors predicting willingness to donate. *Human Reproduction, 18,* 878–884.

New York State Task Force on Life and the Law. (1998). *Questions and answers about infertility and its treatment* [Brochure]. Retrieved from http://www.health.state.ny.us

New York University Medical Center and School of Medicine. (2001, April, 16). Older fathers substantially raise the risk of having children with schizophrenia. *Science Daily.* Retrieved from http://www.sciencedaily.com/releases/2001/04/010413083401.htm

Nicholas, M. K., & Tyler, J. P. (1983). Characteristics, attitudes, and personalities of AI donors. *Clinical Reproduction and Fertility, 2,* 47–54.

Nichols, M. P., & Schwartz, R. C. (2001). Bowen family systems therapy. In M. P. Nichols & R. C. Schwartz (Eds.), *Family therapy: Concepts and methods* (pp. 137–171). Boston, MA: Allyn & Bacon.

Nielsen, A. F., Pedersen, B., & Lauritsen, J. G. (1995). Psychosocial aspects of donor insemination: Attitudes and opinions of Danish and Swedish donor insemination patients to psychosocial information being supplied to offspring and relatives. *Acta Obstetricia et Gynecologica Scandinavica, 74,* 45–50. Abstract retrieved from http://www.ncbi.nlm.nih.gov/pubmed/7856432

Nikolettos, N., Asimakopoulos, B., & Hatzissabas, I. (2003). Intrafamilial sperm donation: Ethical questions and concerns. *Human Reproduction, 18,* 933–936.

N.Y. CLS Dom. Rel. § 123 (2008).

Oehninger, S. (2005). Strategies for fertility preservation in female and male cancer survivors. *Journal of the Society for Gynecologic Investigation, 12,* 222–231.

Ohio Revised Code Ann. Sec. 3111.93 (2008).

Ohlschager, G. (2004). *American Association of Christian Counselors code of ethics.* Retrieved October from http://aacc.net/about-us/code-of-ethics

Okla. Stat. tit. 10, § 554 (2008).

Oktay, K., & Sonmezer, M. (2007). Fertility preservation in gynecologic cancers. *Current Opinions in Oncology, 19,* 506–511.

Olivennes, F., Golombok, S., Ramogida, C., Rust, J., & the Follow-up Team. (2005). Behavioral and cognitive development as well as family functioning of twins conceived by assisted reproduction: Findings from a large population study. *Fertility and Sterility, 84*, 725–733.

Olivennes, F., Schneider, Z., Remy, V., Blanchet, V., Kerbrat, V., Panchin, R., et al. (1996). Perinatal outcome and follow-up of 82 children aged 1–9 years old conceived from cryopreserved embryos. *Human Reproduction, 11*, 1565–1568.

Ombelet, W., & Campo, R. (2007). Affordable IVF for developing countries. *Reproductive Biomedicine Online, 15*, 257–265. Retrieved from http://www.rbmonline.com/4DCGI/Issue/Detail

Opsahl, M. S., Blauer, K. L., Black, S. H., Dorfmann, A., Sherins, R. J., & Schulman, J. D. (2001). Pregnancy rates in sequential in vitro fertilization cycles by oocyte donors. *Obstetrics and Gynecology, 97*, 201–204.

Orenstein, P. (1995, June 18). Looking for a donor to call dad. *The New York Times Magazine*. Retrieved from http://www.peggyorenstein.com/articles/1995_donor_dad.html

Osborne, T. (2006). Sperm retrieval in patients with Klinefelter's syndrome. *Nature Clinical Practice Urology, 3*, 121. Retrieved from http://nature.com/ncpuro/journal/v3/n3/index.html

Ostfeld, B. M., Smith, R. H., Hiatt, M., & Hegyi, T. (2000). Maternal behavior toward premature twins: Implications for development. *Twin Research, 3*, 234–241.

Packard, E. (2007, April). That teenage feeling. *Monitor on Psychology, 38*, 20–21.

Paling, J. (2003, September 27). Strategies to help patients understand risks. *BMJ, 327*, 745–748.

Pandian, Z., Templeton, A., Serour, G., & Bhattacharya, S. (2005). Number of embryos for transfer after IVF and ICSI: A Cochrane review. *Human Reproduction, 20*, 2681–2687.

Paoloni-Giacobino, A. (2007). Epigenetics in reproductive medicine. *Pediatric Research, 61*(5, Pt. 2), 51R–57R.

Papadimos, T. J., & Papadimos, A. T. (2004). The student and the ovum: The lack of autonomous informed consent in trading genes for tuition. *Reproductive Biology and Endocrinology, 2*, 56. Retrieved from http://www.rbej.com/content/2/1/56

Papageorghiou, A. T., Avgidou, K., Bakoulas, V., Sebire, N. J., & Nicolaides, K. H. (2006). Risks of miscarriage and early preterm birth in trichorionic triplet pregnancies with embryo reduction versus expectant management: New data and systematic review. *Human Reproduction, 21*, 1912–1917.

Papp, P. (1993). The worm in the bud: Secrets between parents and children. In E. Imber-Black (Ed.), *Secrets in families and family therapy* (pp. 66–85). New York, NY: Norton.

Parkes, C. M. (1972). *Bereavement: Studies of grief in adult life*. New York, NY: International Universities Press.

Parry, S. (2006). (Re)constructing embryos in stem cell research: Exploring the meaning of embryos for people involved in fertility treatments. *Social Science and Medicine, 62,* 2349–2359.

Partridge, A. H., Gelber, S., Peppercorn, J., Sampson, E., Knudsen, K., Laufer, M., et al. (2004). Web-based survey of fertility issues in young women with breast cancer. *Journal of Clinical Oncology, 22,* 4174–4183.

Patrick, M., Smith, A. L., Meyer, W. R., & Bashford, R. A. (2001). Anonymous oocyte donation: A follow-up questionnaire. *Fertility and Sterility, 75,* 1034–1036.

Patterson, C. J. (1992). Children of lesbian and gay parents. *Child Development, 63,* 1025–1039.

Paul, M. S., & Berger, R. (2007). Topic avoidance and family functioning in families conceived with donor insemination. *Human Reproduction, 22,* 2566–2571.

Paulson, R. J., Boostanfar, R., Saadat, P., Mor, E., Tourgeman, D. E., Slater, C. C., et al. (2002). Pregnancy in the sixth decade of life: Obstetric outcomes in women of advanced reproductive age. *Journal of the American Medical Association, 288,* 2320–2323.

Pearson, H. (2006). Special report: Health effects of egg donation may take decades to emerge. *Nature, 442,* 607–608. Retrieved from http://www.nature.com/nature/journal/v442/n7103/full/442607a.html

Peddle, N., & Wang, C. (2001). *Current trends in child abuse prevention, reporting and fatalities: The 1999 fifty state survey.* Chicago, IL: National Center on Child Abuse Prevention Research.

Pedersen, B., Nielsen, A. F., & Lauritsen, J. G. (1994). Psychosocial aspects of donor insemination. Sperm donors—Their motivations and attitudes to artificial insemination. *Acta Obstetricia et Gynecologica Scandinavica, 73,* 701–705. Abstract retrieved from http://www.ncbi.nlm.nig.gov/pubmed/7976245

Pennings, G. (1995). Should donors have the right to decide who receives their gametes? *Human Reproduction, 10,* 2736–2740.

Pennings, G. (1996a). The donor's right to retire. *Human Reproduction, 11,* 2569–2572.

Pennings, G. (1996b). Partner consent for sperm donation. *Human Reproduction, 11,* 1132–1137.

Pennings, G. (1997). The "double track" policy for donor anonymity. *Human Reproduction, 12,* 2839–2844.

Pennings, G. (2000a). Multiple pregnancies: A test case for the moral quality of medically assisted reproduction. *Human Reproduction, 15,* 2466–2469.

Pennings, G. (2000b). What are the ownership rights for gametes and embryos? Advance directives and the disposition of cryopreserved gametes and embryos. *Human Reproduction, 15,* 979–986.

Pennings, G. (2001). Distributive justice in the allocation of donor oocytes. *Journal of Assisted Reproduction and Genetics, 18,* 56–63.

Pennings, G. (2002). The validity of contracts to dispose of frozen embryos. *Journal of Medical Ethics, 28,* 295–298.

Pennings, G. (2005). Gamete donation in a system of need-adjusted reciprocity. *Human Reproduction, 20,* 2990–2993.

Perez-Albeniz, A., & de Paul, J. (2003). Dispositional empathy in high- and low-risk parents for child physical abuse. *Child Abuse and Neglect, 27,* 769–780.

Peterson, M. M. (2005). Assisted reproductive technologies and equity of access issues. *Journal of Medical Ethics, 31,* 280–285.

Petok, W. D. (2006). The psychology of gender-specific infertility diagnoses. In S. N. Covington & L. H. Burns (Eds.), *Infertility counseling: A comprehensive handbook for clinicians* (2nd ed., pp 37–60). New York, NY: Cambridge University Press.

Pettle, S. A. (2003). Psychological therapy and counseling with individuals and families after donor conception. In D. Singer & M. Hunter (Eds.), *Assisted human reproduction: Psychological and ethical dilemmas* (pp. 154–181). London, England: Whurr Publishers.

Pharoah, P. O., & Adi, Y. (2000, May 6). Consequences of in-utero death in a twin pregnancy. *The Lancet, 355,* 1597–1602.

Phelps, J. Y. (2007). Restricting access of human immunodeficiency virus (HIV)-seropositive patients to infertility services: A legal analysis of the right of reproductive endocrinologists and of HIV-seropositive patients. *Fertility and Sterility, 88,* 1483–1490.

Pinborg, A., Lidegaard, O., la Cour Freiesleben, N., & Andersen, A. N. (2005). Consequences of vanishing twins in IVF/ICSI pregnancies. *Human Reproduction, 20,* 2821–2829.

Pinborg, A., Lidegaard, O., la Cour Freiesleben, N., & Andersen, A. N. (2007). Vanishing twins: A predictor of small-for-gestational age in IVF singletons. *Human Reproduction, 22,* 2707–2714.

Pinborg, A., Loft, A., Rasmussen, S., Schmidt, L., Langhoff-Roos, J., Griesen, G., & Andersen, A. N. (2004). Neonatal outcome in a Danish national cohort of 3438 IVF/ICSI and 10, 362 non-IVF/ICSI twins born between 1995 and 2000. *Human Reproduction, 19,* 435–441.

Pinborg, A., Loft, A., Schmidt, L., Greisen, G., Rasmussen, S., & Nyboe Andersen, A. (2004, July 15). Neurological sequelae in twins born after assisted conception: Controlled national cohort study. *BMJ, 329,* 311–316.

Pinborg, A., Loft, A., Schmidt, L., Langhoff-Roos, J., & Andersen, A. N. (2004). Maternal risks and perinatal outcome in a Danish national cohort of 1005 twin pregnancies: The role of in vitro fertilization [Abstract]. *Acta Obstetricia et Gynecologica Scandinavica, 83,* 75–84. Retrieved from http://www.ingentaconnect.com/content/apl/aog/2004/00000083/00000001/art00013

Pinborg, A., Loft, A., Schmidt, L., & Nyboe Andersen, A. (2003). Morbidity in a Danish National cohort of 472 IVF/ICSI twins, 1132 non-IVF/ICSI twins and 634 IVF/ICSI singletons: Health-related and social implications for the children and their families. *Human Reproduction, 18,* 1234–1243.

Plotz, D. (2005). *The genius factory: The curious history of the Nobel Prize sperm bank.* New York, NY: Random House.

Politch, J. A., & Anderson, D. J. (2002). Preventing HIV-1 infection in women. *Infertility and Reproductive Medicine Clinics of North America, 13, 249–262.*

Porter, M., Peddie, V., & Bhattacharya, S. (2007). Do upper age limits need to be imposed on women receiving assisted reproduction treatment? *Human Fertility, 10, 87–92.*

Practice Committee of the American Society for Reproductive Medicine. (2006). Repetitive oocyte donation. *Fertility and Sterility, 86*(Suppl. 4), S216–S217.

Practice Committee of the American Society for Reproductive Medicine and the Practice Committee of the Society for Assisted Reproductive Technology. (2006). Elements to be considered in obtaining informed consent for ART. *Fertility and Sterility, 86*(Suppl. 4), S272–S273.

Practice Committee of the American Society for Reproductive Medicine and the Practice Committee of the Society for Assisted Reproductive Technology. (2008). 2008 guidelines for gamete and embryo donation. *Fertility and Sterility, 90*(Suppl. 3), S30–S44.

Practice Committee of the Society for Assisted Reproductive Technology and the Practice Committee of the American Society for Reproductive Medicine. (2008). Guidelines on number of embryos transferred. *Fertility and Sterility, 90*(Suppl. 3), S163–S164.

Prattke, T. W., & Gass-Sternas, K. A. (1993). Appraisal, coping, and emotional health of infertile couples undergoing artificial insemination. *Journal of Obstetrics, Gynecology, and Neonatal Nursing, 22, 516–527.*

Prescott, C. A., & Kendler, K. S. (1999). Genetic and environmental contributions to alcohol abuse and dependence in a population-based sample of male twins. *American Journal of Psychiatry, 156, 34–40.*

President's Council on Bioethics, Reproduction and Responsibility. (2004). *The regulation of new technologies.* Retrieved from http://www.bioethics.gov/reports/reproductionandresponsibility/index.html

Professional Counselor and Clinical Professional Counselor Licensing Act, 68 Ill. Admin. Code tit. 68, § 1375.225 (2008).

Provoost, V., Pennings, G., De Sutter, P., Gerris, J., Van de Velde, A., De Lissnyder, E., & Dhont, M. (2009). Infertility patients' beliefs about their embryos and their disposition preferences. *Human Reproduction, 1, 1–10.*

Purdie, A., Peek, J. C., Adair, V., Graham, F., & Fisher, R. (1994). Attitudes of parents of young children to sperm donation—Implications for donor recruitment. *Human Reproduction, 9, 1355–1358.*

Purdie, A., Peek, J. C., Irwin, R., Ellis, J., Graham, F. M., & Fisher, P. R. (1992). Identifiable semen donors—Attitudes of donors and recipient couples. *New Zealand Medical Journal, 105, 27–28.*

Putterman, S., Figueroa, R., Garry, D., & Maulik, D. (2003). Comparison of obstetric outcomes in twin pregnancies after in vitro fertilization, ovarian stimulation and spontaneous conception. *Journal of Maternal Fetal Neonatal Medicine, 14, 237–240.*

Quayle, D. (1992, May 19). *Poverty of values: The Murphy Brown speech* [Campaign speech presented to the Commonwealth Club, San Francisco, CA]. Retrieved from http://www.commonwealthclub.org/archive/20thcentury/92-05quayle-speech.html

Quill, T. E., & Cassell, C. K. (1995). Nonabandonment: A central obligation for physicians. *Annals of Internal Medicine, 122,* 368–374.

Ragone, H. (1994). *Surrogate motherhood: Conception in the heart.* Boulder, CO: Westview Press.

Raoul-Duval, H., Letur-Konirsch, H., & Frydman, R. (1992). Anonymous oocyte donation: A psychological study of recipients, donors, and children. *Human Reproduction, 7,* 51–54.

Rapport, F. (2003). Exploring the beliefs and experiences of potential egg share donors. *Journal of Advanced Nursing, 43,* 28–42.

Reading, A. E., Sledmere, C. M., & Cox, D. N. (1982). A survey of patient attitudes towards artificial insemination by donor. *Journal of Psychosomatic Research, 26,* 429–433.

Reefhuis, J., Honein, M.A., Schieve, L. A., Correa, A., Hobbs, C. A., Rasmussen, S. A., & the National Birth Defects Prevention Study. (2009). Assisted reproductive technology and major structural birth defects in the United States. *Human Reproduction, 24,* 360–366.

Rehabilitation Act of 1976, § 504, 29 U.S.C. § 794 (2008)

Reilly, D. R. (2007). Surrogate pregnancy: A guide for Canadian prenatal health care providers. *Canadian Medical Association Journal, 176,* 1–8. Retrieved from http://www.ncbi.nlm.nih.gov/pubmed/17296962

Remen, R. N. (1996). *Kitchen table wisdom.* New York, NY: Penguin Group.

Repetti, R. L., Taylor, S. E., & Seeman, T. E. (2002). Risky families: Family social environments and the mental and physical health of offspring. *Psychological Bulletin, 128,* 330–366.

Revel, A., Haimov-Kochman, R., Porat, A., Lewin, A., Simon, A., Laufer, N., et al. (2005). In vitro fertilization-intracytoplasmic sperm injection success rates with cryopreserved sperm from patients with malignant disease. *Fertility and Sterility, 84,* 118–122.

Revel, A., Safran, A., Laufer, N., Lewin, A., Reubinov, B. E., & Simon, A. (2004). Twin delivery following 12 years of human embryo cryopreservation: Case report. *Human Reproduction, 19,* 328–329.

Reynolds, M. A., Schieve, L. A., Jeng, G., & Peterson, H. B. (2003). Does insurance coverage decrease the risk for multiple births associated with assisted reproductive technology? *Fertility and Sterility, 80,* 16–23.

Robertson, J. A. (1994). *Children of choice: Freedom and the new reproductive technologies.* Princeton, NJ: Princeton University Press.

Robertson, J. A. (1995). Ethical and legal issues in human embryo donation. *Fertility and Sterility, 64,* 885–894.

Robertson, J. A. (2001). Recommitment strategies for disposition of frozen embryos. *Emory Law Journal, 50*, 989–1046.

Robertson, J. A. (2003). Extending preimplantation genetic diagnosis. The ethical debate: Ethical issues and new uses of preimplantation genetic diagnosis. *Human Reproduction, 18*, 465–471.

Robinson, B. E. (1997). Birds do it. Bees do it. So why not single women and lesbians? *Bioethics, 11*, 217–227.

Roe v. Wade, 410 U. S. 113 (1973).

Rohrbeck, C., & Twentyman, C. T. (1986). Multimodal assessment of impulsiveness in abusing, neglecting, and nonmaltreating mothers and their preschool children. *Journal of Consulting and Clinical Psychology, 54*, 231–236.

Romundstad, L. B., Romundstad, P. R., Sunde, A., von During, V., Skjaerven, R., Gunnell, D., & Vatten, L. J. (2008, August 30). Effects of technology or maternal factors on perinatal outcome after assisted fertilization: A population-based cohort study. *The Lancet, 372*, 694–695.

Rosenberg, H., & Epstein, Y. (1995). Follow up study of anonymous ovum donors. *Human Reproduction, 10*, 2741–2747.

Rosenblum, O., & Rampenaux, C. (2005). Psychological approach of young girls in situation of ovarian tissue cryopreservation treated by chemotherapy toxic for gonads [Article in French]. *Gynecology, Obstetrics, & Fertility, 33*, 809–812. Abstract retrieved from http://www.ncbi.nlm.nih.gov/pubmed/16139554

Rosso, I. M., Young, A. D., Femia, L. A., & Yurgelun-Todd, D. A. (2004). Cognitive and emotional components of frontal lobe functioning in childhood and adolescence. *Annals of the New York Academy of Sciences, 1021*, 355–362.

Rowland, R. (1985). The social and psychological consequences of secrecy in artificial insemination by donor (AID) programmes. *Social Sciences and Medicine, 21*, 391–396.

Rumball, A., & Adair, V. (1999). Telling the story: Parents' scripts for donor offspring. *Human Reproduction, 14*, 1392–1399.

Rutter, M., Thorpe, K., Greenwood, R., Northstone, K., & Golding, J. (2003). Twins as a natural experiment to study the causes of mild language delay. I: Design: Twin–singleton differences in language, and obstetric risks. *Journal of Child Psychology and Psychiatry, 44*, 326–341.

Ryan, G. L., Zhang, S. H., Dokras, A., Syrop, C. H., & Van Voorhis, B. (2004). The desire of infertility patients for multiple births. *Fertility and Sterility, 81*, 500–504.

Sadler, T. (1995). *Langman's medical embryology* (7th ed.). Baltimore, MD: Williams & Wilkins.

Santayana, G. (1905). *The life of reason*. New York, NY: Scribner.

Santema, J., Koppelaar, I., & Wallenburg, H. (1995). Hypertensive disorder in twin pregnancy. *European Journal of Obstetrics and Gynaecology and Reproductive Biology, 58*, 9–13.

Sathanandan, M., Macnamee, M. C., Rainsbury, P., Wick, K., Brinsden, P., & Edwards, R. G. (1991). Replacement of frozen-thawed embryos in artificial and natural cycles: A prospective semi-randomized study. *Human Reproduction, 6,* 685–687.

Sauer, M. V. (n.d.). Making babies. *PBS Frontline interview.* Retrieved from http://www.pbs.org/wgbh/pages/frontline/shows/fertility/interviews/sauer.html

Sauer, M. V. (1997, May 10). Exploitation or a woman's right? *BMJ, 314,* 1403.

Sauer, M. V. (2005). Sperm washing techniques address the reproductive needs of HIV-seropositve men: A clinical review. *Reproductive Biomedicine Online, 10,* 135–140. Retrieved from http://www.rbmonline.com/4DCGI/Issue/Detail

Sauer, M. V., Gorrill, M. J., Zeffer, K. B., & Bustillo, M. (1989). Attitudinal survey of sperm donors to an artificial insemination clinic. *Journal of Reproductive Medicine, 34,* 362–364.

Sauer, M. V., & Kavic, S. M. (2006). Oocyte and embryo donation in 2006: Reviewing two decades of innovation and controversy. *Reproductive Biomedicine Online, 12,* 153–162. Retrieved from http://www.rbmonline.com/4DCGI/Issue/List

Sauer, M. V., Paulson, R. J., & Lobo, R. A. (1992). Reversing the natural decline in human fertility: An extended clinical trial of oocyte donation to women of advanced reproductive age. *Journal of the American Medical Association, 268,* 1275–1279.

Sauer, M. V., Paulson, R. J., & Lobo, R. A. (1996). Oocyte donation to women of advanced reproductive age: Pregnancy results and obstetrical outcomes in patients 45 years and older. *Human Reproduction, 11,* 2540–2543.

Savulescu, J. (1999). Should doctors intentionally do less than the best? *Journal of Medical Ethics, 25,* 121–126.

Savulescu, J. (2001). Procreative beneficence: Why we should select the best children. *Bioethics, 15,* 413–426.

Scheib, J. E., Riordan, M., & Rubin, S. (2003). Choosing identity-release sperm donors: The parents' perspective 13–18 years later. *Human Reproduction, 18,* 1115–1127.

Scheib, J. E., Riordan, M., & Rubin, S. (2005). Adolescents with open-identity sperm donors: Reports from 12–17 year olds. *Human Reproduction, 20,* 239–252.

Scheib, J. E., Ruby, A., & Benward, J. (2008, November). *Who requests their sperm donor's identity? Analysis of donor-conceived adult requests at an open-identity program* [O-22, Abstract]. Abstract presented at the annual meeting of the American Society for Reproductive Medicine, San Francisco, CA.

Schenker, J. G. (1997). Infertility evaluation and treatment according to Jewish law. *European Journal of Obstetrics, Gynecology, and Reproductive Biology, 71,* 113–121.

Schieve, L. A., Meikle, S. F., Ferre, C., Peterson, H. B., Jeng, G., & Wilcox, L. S. (2002). Low and very low birth weight in infant's conceived with use of assisted reproductive technology. *New England Journal of Medicine, 346,* 731–737.

Schiff, H. S. (1977). *The bereaved parent.* New York, NY: Penguin Books.

Schloendorff v. Society of New York Hospitals, 105 N.E.2d 92 (N.Y. 1914), cited in Cruzan v. Director, Missouri Department of Heatlh, 497 U.S. 261 (1990).

Schneider, J., & Kramer, W. (2009, January 19). Egg donors need long-term follow-up: Recommendations from a retrospective study of oocyte donors in the US. *BioNews Online*. Retrieved from http://www.bionews.org.uk/page_38045.asp

Schover, L. R. (1999). Psychosocial aspects of infertility and decisions about reproduction in young cancer survivors: A review. *Medical Pediatrics and Oncology, 33*, 53–59.

Schover, L. R. (2005). Sexuality and fertility after cancer. *Hematology 2005*, 523–527.

Schover, L. R., Brey, K., Lichtin, A., Lipschultz, L. I., & Jeha, S. (2002). Oncologists' attitudes and practices regarding banking sperm before cancer treatment. *Journal of Clinical Oncology, 20*, 1890–1897.

Schover, L. R., Collins, R. L., Quigley, M. M., Blankstein, J., & Kanoti, G. (1991). Psychological follow-up of women evaluated as oocyte donors. *Human Reproduction, 6*, 1487–1491.

Schover, L. R., Rothman, S. A., & Collins, R. L. (1992). The personality and motivation of semen donors: A comparison with oocyte donors. *Human Reproduction, 7*, 572–579.

Schover, L. R., Thomas, A. J., Miller, K. F., Falcone, T., Attaran, M., & Goldberg, J. (1996). Preferences for intracytoplasmic sperm injection versus donor insemination in severe male infertility: A preliminary report. *Human Reproduction, 11*, 2461–2464.

Schreiner-Engel, P., Walther, V. N., Mindes, J., Lynch, L., & Berkowitz, R. L. (1995). First-trimester multifetal pregnancy reduction: Acute and persistent psychological reactions. *American Journal of Obstetrics and Gynecology, 172*, 541–547.

Schwartz, P. H., & Rae, S. B. (2006). An approach to the ethical donation of human embryos for harvest of stem cells. *Reproductive Biomedicine Online, 12*, 771–775. Retrieved from http://www.rbmonline.com/4DCGI/Issue/Detail

Scott, R. T., Jr. (2004). Diminished ovarian reserve and access to care. *Fertility and Sterility, 81*, 1489–1492.

S.D. Codified Laws § 34-14-17 (2008).

Seligman, M., & Darling, R. B. (2006). *Ordinary families, special children: A systems approach to childhood disability*. New York, NY: Guilford Press.

Semprini, A. E., Levi-Setti, P., Bozzo, M., Ravizza, M., Taglioretti, A., Sulpizio, P., et al. (1992, November 28). Insemination of HIV-negative women with processed semen of HIV-positive partners. *The Lancet, 340*, 1317–1319.

Senat, M. V., Ancel, P. Y., Bouvier-Colle, M. H., & Brerat, G. (1998). How does multiple pregnancy affect maternal mortality and morbidity. *Clinical Obstetrics and Gynecology, 41*, 79–83.

Serour, G. I. (2005). Religious perspectives of ethical issues in ART. Islamic perspectives of ethical issues in ART. *Middle East Fertility Society Journal, 10*, 185–190.

Shanley, M. L. (2002). Collaboration and commodification in assisted procreation: Reflection on an open market and anonymous donation in human sperm and eggs. *Law and Society Review, 36,* 257.

Shebl, O., Ebner, T., Sommergruber, M., Sir, A., & Tews, G. (2008). Birth weight is lower for survivors of the vanishing twin syndrome: A case-control study. *Fertility and Sterility, 90,* 310–314.

Shehab, D., Duff, J., Pasch, L. A., Mac Dougall, K., Scheib, J. E., & Nachtigall, R. D. (2008). How parents whose children have been conceived with donor gametes make their disclosure decision: Contexts, influences, and couple dynamics. *Fertility and Sterility, 89,* 179–187.

Sheldon, T. (2005, February 5). More counseling is needed for couples opting for donor insemination. *BMJ, 330,* 276.

Shenfield, F. (1998). Recruitment and counselling of sperm donors: Ethical problems. *Human Reproduction, 13*(Suppl. 2), 70–75.

Shenfield, F. (1999). Gamete donation: Ethical implications for donors. *Human Fertility, 2,* 98–101.

Shenfield, F., & Steele, S. J. (1997). What are the effects of anonymity and secrecy on the welfare of the child in gamete donation? *Human Reproduction, 12,* 392–395.

Sher, G., Davis, V. M., & Stoess, J. (2005). *In vitro fertilization: The A.R.T. of making babies* (3rd ed.). New York, NY: Checkmark Books.

Shuster, E. (1992). When genes determine motherhood: Problems in gestational surrogacy. *Human Reproduction, 7,* 1029–1033.

Sibai, B. M., Hauth, J., Caritis, S., Lindheimer, M. D., MacPherson, C., Klebanoff, M., et al. (2000). Hypertensive disorders in twin versus singleton gestations. National Institute of Child Health and Human Development Network of Maternal-Fetal Medicine Units. *American Journal of Obstetrics and Gynecology, 182,* 938–942.

Silber, S. J. (2005). *How to get pregnant.* New York, NY: Little, Brown.

Silber, S. J., Nagy, Z., Devroey, P., Camus, M., & Van Steirteghem, A. C. (1997). The effect of female age and ovarian reserve on pregnancy rate in male infertility: Treatment of azoospermia with sperm retrieval and intracytoplasmic sperm injection. *Human Reproduction, 12,* 2693–2700.

Silver, R. K., Helfand, B. T., Russell, T. L., Ragin, A., Sholl, J. S., & MacGregor, S. N. (1997). Multifetal reduction increases the risk of preterm delivery and fetal growth restriction in twins: A case-control study. *Fertility and Sterility, 67,* 30–33.

Simchen, M. J., Shulman, A., Wiser, A., Zilberberg, E., & Schiff, B. E. (2009). *The aged uterus: Multifetal pregnancy outcome after ovum donation in older women.* Abstract retrieved from http://humrep.oxfordjournals.org/cgi/content/abstract/dep238

Simoes, E., Kunz, S., Bosing-Schwenkglenks, M., & Schmahl, F. W. (2005). Association between method of delivery and puerperal infectious complications in the perinatal database in Baden-Wurttemberg, 1998–2001. *Gynecological and Obstetrical Investigation, 60,* 213–217.

Skinner v. Oklahoma ex rel. Williamson, 316 U.S. 535 (1942).

Smith, L. K., Roots, E. H., & Dorsett, M. J. (2005). Live birth of a normal healthy baby after a frozen embryo transfer with blastocysts that were frozen and thawed twice. *Fertility and Sterility, 83,* 198–200.

Snowden, C. (1994). What makes a mother? Interviews with women involved in egg donation and surrogacy. *Birth, 21,* 77–84.

Snowden, R., Mitchell, G. D., & Snowden, E. M. (1983). *Artificial reproduction: A social investigation.* London, England: George Allen & Unwin.

Söderström-Anttila, V., Blomqvist, T., Foudila, T., Hippelainen, M., Kurunmaki, H., Siegberg, R., et al. (2002). Experience of in-vitro fertilization in Finland. *Acta Obstetrica and Gynecologica Scandinavica, 81, 747–752.* Abstract retrieved from http://www.ncbi.nlm.nih.gov/pubmed/12174160

Söderström-Anttila, V., Foudila, T., Ripatti, U.-R., & Siegberg, R. (2001). Embryo donation: Outcomes and attitudes among embryo donors and recipients. *Human Reproduction, 16,* 1120–1128.

Spandorfer, S. D., Davis, O. K., & Rosenwaks, Z. (2007, October). *Deleterious consequences of vanishing twins (VT) in IVF/ICSI pregnancies: A large study from a single institution.* Paper presented at the annual meeting of the American Society for Reproductive Medicine, Washington, DC.

Sperm bank basics. (2009). Retrieved from http://www.fertilitycommunity.com/fertility/sperm-donor-basics.html

Sperm donor must pay maintenance. (2006). *Ananova.* Retrieved from http://www.ananova.com/news/story/sm_1571037.html?menu=news.quirkies.unlucky

State Children's Health Insurance Program, Eligibility for Prenatal Care and Other Health Services for Unborn Children, 67 Fed. Reg. 191, Oct. 2, 2002. Retrieved from http://www.cms.hhs.gov/quarterlyproviderupdates/downloads/CMS2127F.pdf

Steinbock, B. (1992). *Life before birth: The moral and legal status of embryos and fetuses.* Oxford, England: Oxford University Press.

Steinbock, B. (2004). Payment for egg donation and surrogacy. *Mt. Sinai Journal of Medicine, 71,* 255–265.

Steinbock, B. (2009, July 1). Paying egg donors for research: In defense of New York's landmark decision. *Bioethics Forum, 39.* Retrieved from http://www.thehastings center.org/Bioethicsforum/Post=aspx?id=3638

Stephen, E. H., & Chandra, A. (2000). Use of infertility services in the United States: 1995. *Family Planning Perspectives, 32,* 132–137.

Stern, J. E., Cedars, M. I., Jain, T., Klein, N. A., Beaird, C. M., Grainger, D. A., & Gibbons, W. E. (2007). Assisted reproductive technology practice patterns and the impact of embryo transfer guidelines in the United States. *Fertility and Sterility*, 88, 275–282.

Stern, J. E., Cramer, C. P., Garrod, A., & Green, R. M. (2001). Access to services at assisted reproductive technology clinics: A survey of policies and practices. *American Journal of Obstetrics and Gynecology, 184*, 591–597.

Stern, J. E., Cramer, C. P., Garrod, A., & Green, R. M. (2002). Attitudes on access to services at assisted reproductive technology clinics: Comparisons with clinic policy. *Fertility and Sterility, 77*, 537–541.

Stern, J. E., Cramer, C. P., Green, R. M., Garrod, A., & DeVries, K. O. (2003). Determining access to assisted reproductive technology: Reactions of clinic directors to ethically complex case scenarios. *Human Reproduction, 18*, 1343–1352.

Storrow, R. F. (2005). The bioethics of parenthood: In pursuit of the proper standard for gatekeeping in the clinical setting [Abstract]. *Fertility and Sterility, 84*(Suppl. 1), S20.

Storrow, R. F. (2006). Marginalizing adoption through the regulation of assisted reproduction. *Capital University Law Review, 2007*, 479–516.

Strachey, J. (Ed. & Trans.). (1974). *The complete psychological works of Sigmund Freud: Standard Edition* (Vol. 14, pp. 239–258). New York, NY: Norton.

Strandell, A., Bergh, C., & Lundin, K. (2000). Selection of patients suitable for one-embryo transfer may reduce the rate of multiple births by half without impairment of overall birth rates. *Human Reproduction, 15*, 2520–2525.

Stroebe, M., & Schut, H. (1999). The dual process model of coping with bereavement: Rationale and description. *Death Studies, 23*, 197–224.

Stromberg, B., Dahlquist, G., Ericson, A., Finnstrom, O., Koster, M., & Stjernqvist, K. (2002, February 9). Neurological sequelae in children born after in-vitro fertilisation: A population-based study. *The Lancet, 359*, 461–465.

Strong, C. (1996). Genetic screening in oocyte donation: Ethical and legal aspects. In C. B. Cohen (Ed.), *New ways of making babies* (pp. 122–137). Bloomington: Indiana University Press.

Strong, C. (2001). How should IVF programs handle initial disclosure of information to prospective ovum donors? *American Journal of Bioethics, 1*, 23–25.

Styer, A. K., Wright, D. L., Wolkovich, A. M., Veiga, C., & Toth, T. L. (2008). Single-blastocyst transfer decreases twin gestation without affecting pregnancy outcome. *Fertility and Sterility, 89*, 1702–1708.

Sutcliffe, A. G. (2000). Follow-up of children conceived from cryopreserved embryos. *Molecular and Cellular Endocrinology, 169*, 91–93.

Sutcliffe, A. G., DeSouza, S. W., Cadman, J., Richards, B., McKinlay, I. A., & Lieberman, B. (1995). Minor congenital anomalies, major congenital malformations, and development in children conceived from cryopreserved embryos. *Human Reproduction, 10*, 3332–3337.

Suzuki, K., Hoshi, K., Minai, J., Yanaihara, T., Takeda, Y., & Yamagata, Z. (2006). Analysis of national representative opinion surveys concerning gestational surrogacy in Japan. *European Journal of Obstetrics, Gynecology, & Reproductive Biology, 126*, 39–47. Retrieved from http://www/ncbi.nlm.nih.gov/pubmed/16171926

Swink, D., & Reich, B. (2007). Caveat vendor: Potential progeny, paternity and product liability online. *Brigham Young University Law Review, 2007*, 857–897.

Switzer, D. K. (1974). *The minister as crisis counselor*. Nashville, TN: Abingdon.

Sydsjo, G., Wadsby, M., Sydsjo, A., & Selling, K. E. (2008). Relationship and parenthood in IVF couples with twin and singleton pregnancies compared with spontaneous singleton primiparous couples—A prospective 5-year follow-up study. *Fertility and Sterility, 89*, 578–585.

Taanila, A., Syrjala, L., Kokkonen, J., & Jarvelin, M. R. (2002). Coping of parents with physically and/or intellectually disabled children. *Child: Care, Health, & Development, 28*, 73–86.

Takahashi, K., Mukaida, T., Goto, T., & Oka, C. (2005). Perinatal outcome of blastocyst transfer with vitrification using cryoloop: A 4-year follow-up study. *Fertility and Sterility, 84*, 88–92.

Tallo, C. P., Vehr, B., Oh, W., Rubin, L. P., Seifer, D. B., & Haning, R. V., Jr. (1995). Maternal and neonatal morbidity associated with in vitro fertilization. *Journal of Pediatrics, 127*, 794–800.

Tan, S. L., Doyle, P., Campbell, S., Beral, V., Rizk, B., Brinsden, P., et al. (1992). Obstetric outcome of in vitro fertilization pregnancies compared with normally conceived pregnancies. *American Journal of Obstetrics and Gynecology, 167*, 778–784.

Tang, N., & Zhu, Z. Q. (2003). Adverse reproductive effects in female workers of lead battery plants. *International Journal of Occupational Medicine and Environmental Health, 16*, 359–361.

Tang, Y., Ma, C., Ciu, W., Chang, V., Ariet, M., Morse, S., et al. (2006). The risk of birth defects in multiple births: A population-based study. *Maternal and Child Health Journal, 10*, 75–81.

Tangri, S. S., & Khan, J. R. (1993). Ethical issues in the new reproductive technologies: Perspectives from feminism and the psychology profession. *Professional Psychology: Research and Practice, 21*, 271–280.

Taus, L., & Gerzova, J. (1991). Personality of semen donors and their social behavior. *Czechoslovakian Medicine, 14*, 173–183. Abstract retrieved from http://www.ncbi.nlm.nih.gov/pubmed/2025897

Taylor, A. E. (2001). Systemic adversities of ovarian failure. *Journal of the Society for Gynecologic Investigation, 8*(Suppl. Proceedings 1), S7–S9.

Thorn, P. (2006). Recipient counseling for donor insemination. In S. N. Covington & L. H. Burns (Eds.), *Infertility counseling: A comprehensive handbook for clinicians* (2nd ed., pp. 305–318). New York, NY: Cambridge University Press.

Thorne, R., & Kischer, C. W. (2002). Embryos, preembryos and stem cells [Letter to the editor]. *Fertility and Sterility, 78,* 1355.

Thurin, A., Hausken, J., Hillensjo, T., Jablonowska, B., Pinborg, A., Strandell, A., & Bergh, C. (2004). Elective single-embryo transfer versus double-embryo transfer in in vitro fertilization. *New England Journal of Medicine, 351,* 2392–2402.

Tienari, P., Wynne, L. C., Moring, J., Lahti, I., Naarala, M., Sorri, A., et al. (1994). The Finnish adoptive family study of schizophrenia: Implications for family research. *British Journal of Psychiatry, 23,* 20–26.

Tiitinen, A., Unkila-Kallio, L., Halttunen, M., & Hyden-Granskog, C. (2003). Impact of elective single embryo transfer on the twin pregnancy rate. *Human Reproduction, 18,* 1449–1453.

Timor-Tritsch, I. E., Bashiri, A., Monteagudo, A., Rebarber, A., & Arslan, A. A. (2004). Two hundred ninety consecutive cases of multifetal pregnancy reduction: Comparison of the transabdominal versus the transvaginal approach. *American Journal of Obstetrics and Gynecology, 191,* 2085–2089.

Titelman, P. (1998). *Clinical applications of Bowen family systems theory.* Binghamton, NY: Haworth Press.

Trivers, R. L. (1971). The evolution of reciprocal altruism. *Quarterly Review of Biology, 46,* 35–57.

Trounson, A., Leeton, J., Besanko, M., Wood, C., & Conti, A. (1983, March 12). Pregnancy established in an infertile patient after transfer of a donated embryo fertilised in vitro. *BMJ, 286,* 835–888.

Troxel v. Granville, 530 U.S. 57 (2000).

Tschudin, S., & Bitzer, J. (2009). Psychological aspects of fertility preservation in men and women affected by cancer and other life-threatening diseases. *Human Reproduction Update, 15,* 587–597.

Tsuang, M. T., Bar, J. L., Stone, W. S., & Faraone, S. V. (2004). Gene-environment interactions in mental disorders. *World Psychiatry, 3,* 75–83.

Tully, L. A., Moffitt, T. B., & Caspi, A. (2003). Maternal adjustment, parenting and child behaviour in families of school-aged twins conceived after IVF and ovulation induction. *Journal of Child Psychology and Psychiatry, 44,* 316–325.

Turner, A. J., & Coyle, A. (2000). What does it mean to be a donor offspring? The identity experiences of adults conceived by donor insemination and the implications for counseling and therapy. *Human Reproduction, 15,* 2041–2051.

Tversky, A., & Kahneman, D. (1981, January 30). The framing of decisions and the psychology of choice. *Science, 211,* 453–458.

Tyler, J. P., Nicholas, M. K., Crockett, N. G., & Driscoll, G. L. (1983). Some attitudes to artificial insemination by donor. *Clinical Reproductive Fertility, 2,* 151–160.

Unborn Victims of Violence Act of 2004, 18 U.S.C. § 1841 (2009).

U.N. Convention on the Rights of the Child (1989). U.N. General Assembly Document A/RES/44/25. Retrieved from http://www.cirp.org/library/ethics/UN-convention/

U.S. Census Bureau News. (2008, February 20). *Majority of children live with two biological parents*. Retrieved from http://www.census.Gov/Press/Release/www/releases/archives/children/011507.html

U.S. Department of Health and Human Services. (2003). *Protecting the privacy of patients' health information* [Fact sheet]. Retrieved from http://www.hhs.gov/news/facts/privacy.html

U.S. Department of Health and Human Services, Centers for Disease Control and Prevention. (2006). *Assisted reproductive technology success rates: National summary and fertility clinic reports 2004*. Atlanta, GA: Author.

U.S. Department of Health and Human Services, Centers for Disease Control and Prevention; American Society for Reproductive Medicine; & Society for Assisted Reproductive Technology. (2007). *Assisted reproductive technology success rates: National summary and fertility clinic reports*. Atlanta, GA: U.S. Department of Health and Human Services, Centers for Disease Control and Prevention.

U.S. Department of Health and Human Services, Food and Drug Administration, Center for Biologics Evaluation and Research. (2009). *Guidance for industry: Eligibility determination for donor of human cells, tissues, and cellular and tissue-based products*. Retrieved from http://www.fda.gov/BiologicsBloodVaccines/Guidances/CellularandGeneTherapy/ucm072929.htm

Utian, W. H., Sheean, L., Goldfarb, J. M., & Kiwi, R. (1985). Successful pregnancy after in vitro fertilization and embryo transfer from an infertile woman to a surrogate. *New England Journal of Medicine, 313*, 1351–1352.

Va. Code Ann. § 20-160 (2008).

Va. H.B. 2123 (2007). (Bill failed)

Valentine, D. P. (1986). Psychological impact of infertility: Identifying issues and needs. *Social Work in Health Care, 11*, 61–69.

van den Akker, O. B. (2000). The importance of a genetic link in mothers commissioning a surrogate baby in the UK. *Human Reproduction, 15*, 1849–1855.

van den Akker, O. B. A. (2005). A longitudinal pre-pregnancy to post-delivery comparison of genetic and gestational surrogate and intended mothers: Confidence and genealogy. *Journal of Psychosomatics, Obstetrics, & Gynecology, 26*, 277–284.

van den Akker, O. B. A. (2007a). Psychological trait and state characteristics, social support and attitudes to the surrogate pregnancy and baby. *Human Reproduction, 22*, 2287–2295.

van den Akker, O. B. A. (2007b). Psychosocial aspects of surrogate motherhood. *Human Reproduction Update, 13*(1), 153–162.

Vanfraussen, K., Ponjaert-Kristoffersen, I., & Brewaeys, A. (2001). An attempt to reconstruct children's donor concept: A comparison between children's and lesbian parents' attitudes towards donor anonymity. *Human Reproduction, 16*, 2019–2025.

Vanfraussen, K., Ponjaert-Kristoffersen, I., & Brewaeys, A. (2003). Why do children want to know more about the donor? The experience of youngsters raised in lesbian families. *Journal of Psychosomatic Obstetrics and Gynaecology, 24*, 31–38.

Van Thiel, M., Mantadakis, E., Vekemans, M., & Gillot de Vries, F. (1990). A psychological study, using interviews and projective tests, of patients seeking anonymous donor artificial insemination. *Journal of Gynecological and Obstetrical Biological Reproduction, 19,* 823–828. Abstract retrieved from http://www.ncbi.nlm.nih.gov/pubmed/2277164

Viguera, A. C., Nonacs, R., Cohen, L. S., Tondo, L., Murray, A., & Baldessarini, R. J. (2000). Risk of recurrence of bipolar disorder in pregnant and nonpregnant women after discontinuing lithium maintenance. *American Journal of Psychiatry, 157,* 179–184.

Wada, I., Matsin, P. L., Troup, S. A., Hughes, S., Buck, P., & Lieberman, B. A. (1992). Outcome of treatment subsequent to the elective cryopreservation of all embryos from women at risk of the ovarian hyperstimulation syndrome. *Human Reproduction, 7,* 962–966.

Wade, N. (2009, April 14). New signs that mice make eggs after birth. *The New York Times,* p. D6.

Wahlberg, K.-E., Wynne, L. C., Oja, H., Keskitalo, P., Pykalainen, L., Lahti, I., et al. (1997). Gene-environment interaction in vulnerability to schizophrenia: Findings from the Finnish adoptive family study in schizophrenia. *American Journal of Psychiatry, 154,* 355–362.

Waldman, E. (2004). The parent trap: Uncovering the myth of 'coerced parenthood' in frozen embryo disputes. *American University Law Review, 53,* 1021–1062.

Walker, I., & Broderick, P. (1999). The psychology of assisted reproduction, or psychology assisting its reproduction. *Australian Psychologist, 34,* 38–44.

Waltzer, H. (1982). Psychological and legal aspects of artificial insemination (A.I.D.): An overview. *American Journal of Psychotherapy, 36,* 91–102.

Wang, C., Tsai, M.-Y., Lee, M.-H., Huang, S.-Y., Kao, C.-H., Ho, H.-N., & Hsiao, C. K. (2007). Maximum number of live births per donor in artificial insemination. *Human Reproduction, 22,* 1363–1372.

Wanjek, C. (2006). The good, the bad and the ugly sperm. *Health Science and Technology.* Retrieved from http://www.livescience.com/health

Warnock, J. K., Bundren, J. C., & Morris, D. W. (2000). Depressive mood symptoms associated with ovarian suppression. *Fertility and Sterility, 74,* 984–986.

Waterland, R. A., & Jirtle, R. L. (2003). Transposable elements: Targets for early nutritional effects on epigenetic gene regulation. *Molecular and Cellular Biology, 23,* 5293–5300.

Watson, M. A., & Money, J. (1975). Behavior cytogenetics and Turner's syndrome: A new principle in counseling and psychotherapy. *American Journal of Psychotherapy, 29,* 166–177.

Watt, H. (2004). Preimplantation genetic diagnosis: Choosing the "good enough" child. *Health Case Analysis, 12,* 51–60.

Weinstein, N. D. (1999). What does it mean to understand a risk? Evaluating risk comprehension. *Journal of the National Cancer Institute, Monographs, 25,* 15–20.

Weiss, M. G., & Ramakrishna, J. (2001). *Interventions: Research on reducing stigma.* Retrieved from http://www.stigmaconference.nih.gov/WeissPaper.htm

Weissenberg, R., Landau, R., & Madgar, I. (2007). Older single mothers assisted by sperm donation and their children. *Human Reproduction, 22,* 2784–2791.

Wen, S. W., Demissie, K., Yang, Q., & Walker, M. C. (2004). Maternal morbidity and obstetric complications in triplet pregnancies and quadruplet and higher-order multiple pregnancies. *American Journal of Obstetrics and Gynecology, 191,* 254–258.

Wennerholm, U. B. (2000). Cryopreservation of embryos and oocytes: Obstetric outcome and health in children. *Human Reproduction, 15*(Suppl. 5), 18–25.

Wennerholm, U. B., Albertsson-Wikland, K., Bergh, C., Hamberger, L., Niklasson, A., Nilsson, L., et al. (1998, April 11). Postnatal growth and health in children born after cryopreservation as embryos. *The Lancet, 351,* 1085–1090.

Wennerholm, U. B., Söderström-Anttila, V., Bergh, C., Aittomaki, K., Hazekamp, J., Nygren, K.-G., et al. (2009). Children born after cryopreservation of embryos or oocytes: A systematic review of outcome data. *Human Reproduction, 24,* 2158–2172.

White Stack, B. (2005, May 20). Sperm donor fights order to support 2 children. *Pittsburgh Post-Gazette.* Retrieved from http://www.forum.dadsontheair.com/viewtopic.php?t=3326

Whitney, E. (2005, February 24). *Assisted reproduction—A Christian clinician's view.* The American Surrogacy Center. Retrieved from http://www.surrogacy.com/Articles/news_view.asp?ID=83

Widdows, H., & MacCallum, F. (2002). Disparities in parenting criteria: An exploration of the issues, focusing on adoption and embryo donation. *Journal of Medical Ethics, 28,* 139–142.

Widom, C. S. (1989). Does violence beget violence? A critical examination of the literature. *Psychological Bulletin, 106,* 3–28.

Wiggins, D. A., & Main, E. (2005). Outcomes of pregnancies achieved by donor egg in vitro fertilization: A comparison with standard in vitro fertilization pregnancies. *American Journal of Obstetrics and Gynecology, 192,* 2002–2006.

Wilde, O. (1891). *The picture of Dorian Gray.* Philadelphia, PA: Lippincott.

Wilkinson, S. (2003). The exploitation argument against commercial surrogacy. *Bioethics, 17,* 169–187.

Wolfe, D. A. (1985). Child-abusive parents: An empirical review and analysis. *Psychological Bulletin, 97,* 462–482.

Worden, J. W. (1983). *Grief counseling and grief therapy* (1st ed.). London, England: Tavistock.

Worden, J. W. (1991). *Grief counseling and grief therapy: A handbook for the mental health practitioner* (2nd ed.). New York, NY: Springer Publishing Company.

Wright, J., Duchesne, C., Sabqurin, S., Bissonnette, F., Benoit, J., & Girard, Y. (1991). Psychosocial distress and infertility: Men and women respond differently. *Fertility and Sterility, 55,* 100–108.

Wright, V. C., Chang, J., Jeng, G., & Macaluso, M. (2008). Assisted reproductive technology surveillance—United States, 2005. *MMWR Surveillance Summaries, 57*, 1–23.

Yee, S., Hitkari, J. A., & Greenblatt, E. M. (2007). A follow-up study of women who donated oocytes to known recipient couples for altruistic reasons. *Human Reproduction, 22*, 2040–2050.

Yokoyama, Y., Shimizu, T., & Hayakawa, K. (1995). Prevalence of cerebral palsy in twins, triplets, and quadruplets. *International Journal of Epidemiology, 24*, 943–948.

Zepeda v. Zepeda, 41 Ill. App. 2d 240 (Ill. Ct. App. 1st Dist. 1963).

Zhu, J. L., Madsen, K. M., Vestergaard, M., Olesen, A. V., Basso, O., & Olsen, J. (2005). Paternal age and congenital malformations. *Human Reproduction, 20*, 3173–3177.

Ziadeh, S. M. (2000). The outcome of triplet versus twin pregnancies. *Gynecological and Obstetrical Investigations, 50*, 96–99.

Zinger, M., Liu, J. H., Husseinzadeh, N., & Thomas, M. A. (2004). Successful surrogate pregnancy after ovarian transposition, pelvic irradiation, and hysterectomy. *Journal of Reproductive Medicine, 49*, 573–574.

Zolbrod, A. P. (1993). *Men, women, and infertility: Intervention and treatment strategies.* Lexington, MA: Lexington Books.

Zweifel, J., Christianson, M., Jaeger, A. S., Olive, D., & Lindheim, S. (2007). Needs assessment for those donating to stem cell research. *Fertility and Sterility, 88*, 560–564.

Zweifel, J. E., Rathert, M. A., Klock, S. C., Walaski, H. P., Pritts, E. A., Olive, D. L., & Lindheim, S. R. (2006). Comparative assessment of pre- and post-donation attitudes towards potential oocyte and embryo disposition and management among ovum donors in an oocyte donation programme. *Human Reproduction, 21*, 1325–1327.

10 New York Codes, Rules and Regulations Sec. 52-8.9 (2009).

10 Okla. Stat. Sec. 554 (2008).

750 Ill. Comp. Stat. Ann. 47/10, *et seq.* (2008).

750 Ill. Comp. Stat. Ann. 47/20 (2008).

INDEX

ABOUT THE AUTHORS

Judith E. Horowitz, PhD, is a licensed psychologist in private practice in Broward County, Florida. After graduating Phi Beta Kappa from the University of Florida, Gainesville, she received her doctoral degree from the University of Florida as well. Dr. Horowitz is a member of the American Society for Reproductive Medicine and is a certified sexual therapist and diplomate of the American Association of Sex Educators, Counselors, and Therapists. She is also a diplomate of the American Board of Medical Psychotherapists and Psychodiagnosticians.

As an active member of the American Society for Reproductive Medicine (ASRM) since 1994, Dr. Horowitz was instrumental in establishing and developing the Mentoring Task Force of the Mental Health Professional Group (MHPG) and serves as its chair. She also served on the MHPG Membership Committee as well as on the ASRM Membership Committee and recently was appointed to the Steering Committee for Funding Development of the ASRM. In addition, she is chair of the Electronic (E)-Communications Committee of the MHPG. Dr. Horowitz is a member of the American Psychological Association, the Florida Psychological Association, and the Broward County Psychological Association. She is also a member of the American Fertility Association and Fertile Hope. Dr. Horowitz is a contributing author for the *Parklander Magazine* and writes a monthly column. She has published numerous articles on the psychological impact of infertility and has lectured nationally.

Joann Paley Galst, PhD, is a psychologist in private practice in New York City specializing in reproductive health issues. She is a past chair of the Mental Health Professional Group of the American Society for Reproductive Medicine. She was a founding member of the American Fertility Association (AFA) and received an AFA Family Building Award in 2002. She currently serves as the chair of the Mental Health Advisory Council and cochair of Support Services for the AFA. She is also a member of the Advisory Board of the Pregnancy Loss Support Program of the National Council of Jewish Women–New York Section. Her other professional affiliations include the American Psychological Association, the New York State Psychological Association, and the Association for Behavioral and Cognitive Therapies.

Dr. Galst graduated Phi Beta Kappa from the University of Wisconsin and received her doctoral degree from Columbia University, Teachers College, in New York City. She has written and spoken extensively on numerous topics regarding fertility, pregnancy loss, third-party reproduction, disclosure and parenting issues in third-party reproduction, and ethical issues in fertility counseling. She wrote an "Ask the Expert" mental health column for RESOLVE during 1997–1998 as well as a similar monthly column in the *AFA National Newsletter* during 2001–2003. She is coauthor of two chapters ("Women Treating Women: Behaviorists View the Case" and "Women Treating Men: Behaviorists View the Case" with E. T. Klass) in *Women as Therapists: A Multi-Theoretical Casebook.*

Nanette Elster, JD, MPH, is a visiting professor at DePaul University College of Law and the Health Law Institute at the College of Law in Chicago, where she teaches courses such as Genetics and the Law, Public Health Law, and Assisted Reproduction and the Law. She is also vice president of Spence & Elster, PA, a Chicago-area law firm working in the area of fertility law. She holds an adjunct faculty appointment at the University of Illinois at the Chicago School of Public Health. Ms. Elster is an affiliate scholar at the Institute for Biotechnology and the Human Future. She holds a bachelor of arts degree from the University of Illinois at Urbana–Champaign, a law degree from Loyola University School of Law in Chicago, and a master of public health degree from Boston University School of Public Health.

Ms. Elster currently serves on the Board of Directors of the Chicago Center for Jewish Genetic Disorders, as a member of the University of Illinois at Chicago Embryo Stem Cell Research Oversight Committee, and as a member of the American Bar Association Coordinating Group on Bioethics and the Law. She has spoken nationally and internationally and is the author of numerous articles on genetic and reproductive health with a particular focus on the legal and ethical implications.